BRITAIN'S JEWS IN THE FIRST WORLD WAR

BRITAIN'S JEWS IN THE FIRST WORLD WAR

Paula Kitching

AMBERLEY

First published 2019

Amberley Publishing
The Hill, Stroud
Gloucestershire, GL5 4EP

www.amberley-books.com

Copyright © Paula Kitching, 2019

ISBN 978 1 4456 6320 3 (paperback)
ISBN 978 1 4456 6321 0 (ebook)

British Library Cataloguing in Publication Data.
A catalogue record for this book is available
from the British Library.

Origination by Amberley Publishing
Printed in the UK.

CONTENTS

PREFACE

In this book the Anglo-Jewish contribution to the First World War is examined and explored predominantly through the actions and lives of individuals and the information recorded at the time. It cannot be a complete record of the whole community or a deep assessment of all those involved. Instead it draws upon existing research into the Jewish involvement and some of the new research carried out in the *We Were There Too* project on Jews and the First World War (for which I am the historian and project manager) and pulls all those different threads together, offering some context and interpretation. *We Were There Too* was a Heritage Lottery Fund-supported project and it is ongoing. It will continue to uncover the stories of those men and women, young and old, whose lives were caught up in one of the most important and transformative events of the modern period. The project website www.jewsfww.uk will be updated as more and more stories emerge. The website is a growing archive for the stories of the Jewish communities and individuals of that period.

When writing a book that covers the First World War there are so many factors to consider – the main issue being what to put in and what to leave out. There is then the question of how much detail to include, and for the subject of this book that means a consideration of how much to include about Judaism and being Jewish. After all, this is a book for the general reader as well as for those with a specific interest. I hope I have got the balance right as much as possible.

As with all social studies of this era, it is actually easier to find out about those who served and did not return than it is to find out about the roles and experiences of those on the home front or those who served and did return. Those who don't return are remembered on war memorials up and down the UK as well as in the many theatres of war. Those who returned from service or did not serve in the military do not have their names on memorials, and we are at the mercy of newspapers, family memories and genealogists for them. Nonetheless, the contribution of the Jewish community outside of military service is explored when it can be pieced together.

The stories of women were particularly difficult to research as these women rarely wrote down what they had done or experienced. For those who are on official documents for nursing and war work their story is often not recorded beyond that they were there, and furthermore they have the pesky habit of marrying and changing their name, making paper trails quite difficult to follow.

All in all, this book is about bringing to light the enormous contribution of a small community that 'did its bit' and then went back to the day job. A community about which there are many unfounded negative stereotypes that were even more prevalent then than they are today. The Jewish communities of Europe are more frequently discussed in association with the Second World War, and passed over for the first one, but often it is the dedication, participation and loyalty that Jews displayed to their nations in the First World War that made the anti-Semitism of the 1930s and 1940s come as such a surprise to them. They were not outsiders, but citizens and veterans.

This book should help audiences to understand the impact the First World War had on people and in particular on different aspects of British society. While there were universal experiences felt across all groups, such as fear and loss, there were also adjustments to be made in overcoming prejudice and adhering to religious practices at a time of conflict.

I am indebted to the research of the whole team of *We Were There Too*, in particular Alan Fell, Mandy King, Louise Scott, Rachel Fellman, Angeles Ruiz Monteagudo, and the incredible husband-and-wife team of Lola and Ronnie Fraser, as well as the regular contributors and volunteers. I would also like to thank my family for their remarkable patience throughout this process and for their continued patience when I move on to my next research project.

If I have one regret it is that I couldn't include more of the fascinating stories of the men and women of that time. I hope that because of this book some of the names of those from a hundred years ago will be read aloud for the first time in decades, and that through this act they will once again become real people with real experiences.

INTRODUCTION

The First World War was one of the most impactful events to take place in twentieth-century Europe. Empires and monarchies came to an end, independent countries arose and millions of people were killed or displaced. In the United Kingdom a new understanding of the realities of war emerged and left a legacy of remembrance that is still around us today; it was, for many, the Great War. Millions of people would be mobilised for the military and the workplace in ways unfamiliar to the people of Britain and its empire. Restrictions introduced on goods and activities alongside military attacks on the UK would all lead to changes in attitudes and security, as well as daily life and routine. The four years of warfare would ensure that men and women who had never dreamed of wearing uniform or working in a factory or the fields would do so. People from all walks of life would be asked to make their contribution to the war effort – and they would make it whether they agreed or not.

Over the course of the First World War, a minimum of 45,000 to 55,000 Jewish men would serve in the British Armed Forces. Approximately 50,000 names are recorded in the British Jewry Book of Honour, a remarkable physical record compiled in the days before computers and digital databases and published in 1922. There are duplications and mistakes in the British Jewry Book of Honour that reduce the total number of names included, but on the other hand there are known omissions from the books, both intentional and unintentional – this is all covered in greater detail in chapter 11. Nonetheless, the number is significant for a small community and means that approximately 13 to 14 per cent served in the military compared to the overall figure of 11 to 12 per cent for the general British population.

The Jewish Community in Britain up to 1914

Historically Britain has had a mixed history as regards the treatment and settlement of Jewish people. Jews are first recorded as arriving in the UK shortly after William the Conqueror. William used literate Jewish men during a time of general illiteracy to act as accountants and bookkeepers. Jewish communities then settled in what were the major cities and towns of England at the time, such as London, York, Lincoln and Winchester, with smaller communities elsewhere, such as at Norwich and Oxford. The Jewish settlers carried out a number of trades, but as Christians were not allowed to act as moneylenders or take employment in usury many Jews therefore took on these roles, especially as many of the official trades and guilds were closed to them.

During the aforementioned period Jews experienced a mixed reception and were subject to the usual prejudices, led by the Catholic Christian Church – not least the accusation of deicide (the killing of God – through the interpretation that it was a Jewish decision to crucify Christ rather than a Roman one). In the twelfth century, prejudice and scapegoating initiated by the English aristocracy and landowners and supported by the teachings of Church leaders led to growing hostility and violence against the Jewish population. In 1144, Jews in Norwich were accused of murdering a twelve-year-old boy to obtain his blood as part of a ritual murder for the religious celebration of Passover. Even at the time there was no case brought against anyone due to a lack of evidence, but the idea that Jews murdered Christian children as part of religious adherence nevertheless took root and rumours spread across England and Europe. The Blood Libel, as it became known, was still a popularly held accusation levied against the Jews until very recently – and indeed it is still used in extremist literature today.

As various rumours spread about the fictitious rules of Jewish life (and the stories were greatly embellished the more they were told), and with accusations and lies going unchallenged by the authorities, organised acts of violence spread across key cities in England, often leading to the deaths of Jewish individuals and even, sometimes, whole groups. The general hostility against Jewish communities was stoked and encouraged by many religious preachers, and in particular by those men who used the Jews as moneylenders. In York in 1190, amid rioting and looting against the Jews following a fire in the city, approximately 150 people belonging to between twenty and forty families were killed at the site of Clifford's Tower. Many believed that the attacks were initiated by men who wished to destroy the financial records of the major moneylenders in order to wipe clear their debts.

In 1290, King Edward I expelled all the remaining Jews of England in an act supported by the aristocracy and leaders of the Church. This act, along with many of the anti-Semitic accusations flying around at the time, set a tone and practice that was copied across Europe for centuries to come.

It was nearly four hundred years later that an official Jewish presence returned to Britain. In 1656, records show that a Jewish community was allowed once more to settle in England. This community had its roots mainly in the Sephardi tradition of Jews, which involves a community originating in Spain. Over time the community slowly grew, although overall it remained a small part of the total British population. The Jewish Naturalisation Act of 1753, although repealed the following year, paved the way for Jewish settlement across the UK. However, this four-century gap meant that Jews had become a people associated with myth and literature for many in Britain, and this affected attitudes and ideas about who they were in reality. It also meant that the new Jewish migrants to Britain were careful about their identity and how they would fit into British society.

By the nineteenth century, religious tolerance in the UK was considered quite progressive compared to that in many countries on mainland Europe. The result was that Britain became a place of settlement for Jews fleeing prejudice. The new Jewish arrivals were predominantly from the central and eastern European Jewish tradition known as Ashkenazi. The new and old communities began to look to each other to establish a British Jewish way of life.

Many of the Jewish families that settled took an active role in British life and were keen to engage with social work and philanthropy. Some of the wealthier members, such as the Rothschilds, helped to establish hospitals for the poor, Jews and non-Jews alike. Others became involved with politics and the arts. In 1850 there were approximately 50,000 Jewish people (using synagogue and community records) in a population of 18 million – 0.3 per cent of the population. The first Jewish MP, Baron Lionel de Rothschild, was elected in 1847 but he was unable to take his position in the house due to the oath to the Church. An Act of Parliament in 1858 changed the oath for Parliament and enabled Jews to take up their positions as MPs if they were elected, and opened up other elements of public life.

From 1880 the Jewish communities across the UK began to grow, with many arriving from eastern Europe and Russia. Russia under the Tsar had a strong policy of anti-Semitism, and the Jewish communities living in that country were frequently attacked and killed in events called pogroms that were organised and condoned by Russian state officials. Elsewhere, events such as the Dreyfus Affair,[1] growing political anti-Semitism and continued discrimination against Jews across Europe led to more Jews travelling to Britain and the New World countries to settle. The new Jewish arrivals to the UK settled all across the nation, usually in cities and larger towns. London aside, there were vibrant Jewish communities in most of the ports – Liverpool, Newcastle, Plymouth, Bristol, Glasgow, Grimsby and Hull. There were also smaller communities in places such as Birmingham, Blackpool, Bournemouth and Colchester. An estimated 150,000 arrived over a twenty-five-year period, bringing new foods and customs with them. The new arrivals that dispersed around the UK tended to concentrate in areas where there was work, or where there existed Jewish communal services (kosher butchers, bakers and synagogues). The largest community was in London, which had pockets of Jewish life all across the capital and a large community in the East End of the city. The 'Jewish East End' became a popular starting point for the new migrants, and this was where a large concentration of poor young Jews and Jewish families could be found, as well as large numbers of Jewish-funded community services to cater for them.

The British Parliament passed the 'Aliens Act' in 1905, which was introduced specifically to limit Jewish immigration, despite the fact that even with the new arrivals the Jewish population accounted for less than 1 per cent of the overall British population. The Alien Act was the culmination of a growing unhappiness with the perceived Jewish presence – one that seemed distinctly 'foreign'. Its introduction was the first British legislation on immigration and the first openly racist policy to limit those travelling and settling in the UK, irrespective of reason. The Act was met with vocal criticism from politicians as well as support.

By 1914 the Jewish community of the UK was really a mixture of a number of Jewish communities; some had integrated into British life at all levels, while others were still speaking Yiddish and finding their place in British society. The majority were working class, although there were quite a few who were middle class and had attended grammar schools and gone on to the professions, plus a small group of very established and wealthy families. The size of the Jewish community at this time was approximately 250,000–300,000, in a total British population of over 41 million. In 1914, many of those in the Jewish communities still spoke Yiddish as their main language and there were numerous Yiddish newspapers and entertainments available. Yiddish is a mixture of German dialects and Hebrew, often including Polish words or others bits of language from where the Jewish communities were settled. It was written down using Hebrew script.

Anti-Semitism before the War

In 1914, anti-Semitism was common across Europe, including in the UK. Newspapers and officials would frequently generalise and disparage Jewish groups and individuals. Stereotypes of Jews, especially in literature and newspaper cartoons, were a regular sight. Many of the ideas that ordinary people had of Jews came from the stories they had read and the stereotypical representations rather than from real encounters. Jews were considered as the 'foreigners' in most European societies – even if their presence did date back hundreds of years. Anti-Semitism in Britain was unsophisticated and often crude, invoking outdated biblical references whilst making sweeping stereotypes about Jews and Jewish people in a modern context, such as what their ambitions and their desires were. Those who experienced prejudice of that type had limited opportunity to appeal against it. The response from the new arrivals was often withdrawal, and the cultivation of a desire to remain within their own small, safe Jewish communities and neighbourhoods.

Compared to mainland Europe, however, the treatment of Jews in Britain seemed relatively good. While Britain was not free of civil unrest and Jews were on occasion subject to violent outbreaks against them,[2] this was certainly not considered the norm. Jews had freedom of worship; they were treated the same in the law as anyone else, with the same rights (and limitations) as any other British citizen or resident. It was more typical that the prejudice displayed against Jews reared its head in the choices made when people were hired for jobs or given access to elements of education or housing, and in the language used when describing Jewish people. There was no legal ban restricting Jews from any areas of employment or the professions. Jews went to university, became politicians and had access to all areas of society. Instead, the prejudices expressed and attempts to limit access to certain positions or professions manifested in a more insidious manner. Jews would be described as being 'not quite one of us'.

While Jews were often the group most likely to identified as being 'foreign' (whilst being resident and citizens of the UK), British society *circa* 1914 was prejudiced on many levels – sexism, class distinctions and racism were a commonplace and widely accepted part of daily life. It was not uncommon to see discrimination against many individuals and groups in the media, the courts and social interactions.

In the war years (1914–18), anti-German sentiment would often be directed against Jews whether they were of German descent or not. It would lead to many choosing to anglicise their surnames to deflect any hostility and to distance themselves from any German connections.

The Jewish Community – or Communities

The Jewish community of 1914 was really a mix of many different communities connected by their faith. Within the community there were prejudices and differences that formed a part of communal life. The old Sephardi community continued to keep separate synagogues from the Ashkenazi, with little intermarriage. Attitudes among the Ashkenazi were also often divided about the levels of religious life and orthodoxy that should be maintained. Although many of the new Jewish arrivals spoke Yiddish, there were still dialects that indicated where people had come from and who they would gravitate towards.

Many Jews who settled in the UK prior to the 1880s had been keen to assimilate into British life while keeping their Jewish faith. This community, encompassing Germans and central Europeans, was often keen to embrace a less regimented orthodox Jewish way of life and one that identified itself as a religious faith not a Jewish religious identity. The more established community was often concerned that the new immigrants, predominantly from eastern Europe, were not fully integrating or committing to an Anglo-Jewish life – many from this group wished to maintain their strict orthodoxy, or at least keep an identity distinct from the Christian society around them. They were unsure of their new 'home' and distrustful of some of those in authority, especially if they had been badly treated in the countries from which they had migrated. Schools and charitable organisations created by the Jewish community to help the new immigrants often stipulated the learning of English as a condition to accessing the services – all in an attempt to make the new arrivals 'fit in' and leave their old lives behind.

In the different communities within towns and cities across the UK, many different groupings for committees, charitable and religious practice were established. Different cities also established different community representation groups or governance structures. Many of the different sectors of the Jewish communities did come together regionally or nationally under the auspices of the Board of Deputies of British Jews,[3] which represented the interests of the community in secular matters to the British authorities. The Board (as is often known) was made up of elected or appointed members of the many communities around the UK. It would represent Jewish opinion both formally and informally – hoping to influence policy and opinion on matters such as the Anglo-Jewry's interests and loyalty. Alongside the Board was the United Synagogue (the US), founded in 1870 as the governing body for Orthodox Judaism (it based itself on the existing Church of England structures) in the UK, there were also community and religious leaders or representatives of the older Spanish and Portuguese Jewish (Sephardic) community. At the head of the US was the Chief Rabbi, who was acknowledged to be the leading rabbi of the UK and the British Empire. These groups, with the support of organisation such as the Anglo-Jewish Association (formed in 1871 for the 'promotion of social, moral, and intellectual progress among the Jews – and the obtaining of protection for those who may suffer in consequence of being Jews') and the Conjoint Foreign Committee (formed in 1871 to create and lead an Anglo-Jewish foreign policy), were key in the consolidation of the representation and leadership of the British Jewry prior to the First World War.

However, it would be unrealistic to assume that the Jewish communities operated with an agreed form of hegemony. In most communities there would be more than one synagogue, reflecting differing religious practices or different political concerns. While to the non-Jewish outsider the Jews may have seemed like one group, to those within the community it was a mixture of social classes, backgrounds, languages, ideas, politics and beliefs.

Zionism was a political idea being put forward at the start of the twentieth century that nurtured a form of Jewish nationalism, often in response to other forms of nationalism or as a result of anti-Semitism. It focused on the idea that there needed to be a Jewish homeland to ensure that Jews were no longer subject to discrimination and attack. In the UK of 1914, many of those in the Anglo-Jewish community, especially those who saw themselves as its leaders, felt that the best way to combat anti-Semitism was for Jews to assimilate into the countries in which they lived. This was not a religious assimilation but a cultural one. Lucien Wolf, a journalist, writer and President of the Conjoint Foreign Committee, campaigned and wrote tirelessly on the need to allow the Jews of Europe total emancipation in order to end anti-Semitism through full participation in society. In addition to being in charge of the Conjoint Foreign Committee, Wolf was editor of the popular newspaper *Jewish World*, through which he would promote the idea of the British Jew. Along with other Jewish establishment figures, Wolf was openly opposed to Zionism and viewed it as a movement that would increase anti-Semitism rather than end it.

The strength of British Zionism would grow during the First World War, with supporters inside and outside the Jewish communities as well as detractors from both those groups. This new political ideal would challenge some of the attitudes held by established Anglo-Jewry and help to pave a new direction for sections of British and worldwide Jewry. British non-Jewish political leaders would also see Zionism as a potentially useful political idea, especially in relation to British ambitions in the Middle East.

Jews and the British Armed Forces prior to 1914

Jewish men were able to join the British Army prior to the war and there is plenty of evidence that they did. They were also able to apply for commissions and become officers, something denied to some other ethnic minorities. The first Jewish recipient of the Victoria Cross (VC), the highest award for gallantry, was Lieutenant Frank de Pass. Pass was a commissioned officer in the British Army who took up his commission in 1906 and received his VC in October 1914. Other Jewish men had received awards and commendations for their military service during earlier campaigns, such as the Boer War.

Jews were serving in the Royal Navy from at least the time of Nelson and Trafalgar and undoubtedly earlier. However, all Jewish servicemen would have given up an element of religious life in order to fulfil their military duties – this is not particular to Judaism but simply reflected the fact that military practices are not always consistent with a strict religious adherence.

The Jews serving in the army and the navy prior to the First World War, like most volunteers who became professional soldiers at that time, usually joined a regiment that had a local or regional connection. This continued into the First World War, with those enlisting in 1914 and 1915 largely assigned to local regiments. In London, many joined the Royal Fusiliers – a London regiment. As the war progressed, Jews could be assigned to whichever regiment needed men, just like any other new recruit.

Undoubtedly, there was anti-Semitism or prejudice against Jews in some quarters of the army and navy, just as there was outside of the forces, but there was no orchestrated policy against Jews, no bar on promotion and no organised singling out. Commissions for the army were based largely on class and family connections; those prejudices often applied to Jews just as they would to anyone else. This meant that some regiments would have been very difficult for Jews to have joined prior to 1914, as some families had the old regiments practically 'sewn up', but that meant that would-be officers in the Jewish community saw themselves steered towards some of the newer regiments, especially the colonial ones. However, once the war started there were records of Jews being turned away from recruitment offices; it was at this point that Jews and non-Jews identified an issue they would have to rectify.

It is also worth noting that there were no legal rulings relating to racism at this time – those who were anti-Semitic would not be punished, and those who experienced anti-Semitism would not be protected. First World War volunteer Marcus Segal wrote about how many new friends he made among his fellow soldiers and did not talk about any prejudice directed against him; on the other hand, men such as the poet Isaac Rosenberg wrote to his friends about his experiences of being treated unfairly due to his being Jewish.

There is no evidence that Jews were targeted for any special treatment, negative or positive, once serving in the forces, although there may have been a few allowances to get them there. The melting pot of the British Army, especially after 1914, threw men (and eventually women) into contact with individuals they might otherwise never have encountered, and this would have both strengthened and challenged preconceived ideas and prejudices.

Throughout history, faith and religion have often been an important matter in military regiments, the guidance and support of a spiritual source being considered of particular importance during times of conflict. This understanding of religious support was first extended to the Jewish members of the armed forces with the appointment of a Jewish chaplain to the Territorial

Forces in 1909. Although it was only the Territorial Forces (and there was quite some lobbying to establish it), it was recognition that there were sufficient Jewish men in the armed forces to necessitate some form of religious representation. Once the war started, the number of Jewish chaplains would increase just as the numbers of serving Jews did. The need to support Jewish troops through special food and understanding during festival times would also be accepted.

By end of the First World War there would be Jews serving across the army, the Royal Navy and the newly formed Royal Air Force. There would be women in the nursing services and auxiliary units. At home Jewish families would be following the restrictions of the Defence of the Realm Act (DORA) and subject to the aerial bombing unleashed by the Zeppelins and Gotha bombers. Across all aspects of British society there would be a Jewish contribution. Across the battlefields of Europe, the Middle East and elsewhere, the Star of David would be present on headstones in the Commonwealth War Grave Commission cemeteries. Jewish names would be etched on war memorials on the battlefields and in the UK, in offices and town squares. Synagogues and community buildings would create rolls of honour. All of these public symbols would demonstrate that the Anglo-Jewish community was present and took part in the British contribution to the Great War.

THE JEWISH COMMUNITY RESPONDS TO THE ANNOUNCEMENT OF WAR

There has been a lot of discussion about the long-term causes of the First World War and which country was most to blame for starting it. It could be argued that it was just part of the long tradition of European wars but that new technology and the size of the global empires involved caused it to grow into the most devastating war that had yet occurred. Trying to unpick the different causes is problematic: the complex nature of the treaties and alliances that existed among the countries; the different rivalries and ambitions; historic tensions and state structures; new movements of nationalism and political ideals; empires expanding or crumbling; and industrialisation of people and society. All of these themes played a part, but ultimately one thing is for sure: when the nineteen-year-old Bosnian Serb nationalist Gavrilo Princip assassinated Archduke Franz Ferdinand and his wife Sophie in Sarajevo on 28 June 1914, European relations rapidly deteriorated.

This event in any area of the Balkans, famous for its wars, does not seem like something that would tip the world upside down; after all, the decision to go to war was not one to be taken lightly. Or was it? War then was not the terrible last resort we now consider it to be. Most countries, especially those in a dominant global position, felt that the use of force was an acceptable, even necessary way to assert authority and establish power. The previous centuries were a clear example of how often European nations would dive into war; in fact their regularity had helped to create a complex set of treaties that stretched across Europe, often creating unlikely bedfellows.

Germany and Austria-Hungary had an alliance (as well as a growing relationship with the Ottoman Empire), and Austria-Hungary controlled parts of the Balkans that sought independence. Russia also had influence in the Balkans, as well as growing hostility with Germany in mainland Europe and around the Black Sea. France feared the new Germany after its loss to Prussia in the Franco-Prussian war, while Germany was quite clear that it wanted an empire to match those of its neighbours – and possibly even include them. Britain had an alliance with France and Russia as well as a treaty to protect Belgium, throwing it into the mix of any European fallout. All of these countries had Jewish populations. Some had new-found emancipation; many were still persecuted and discriminated against; all were concerned about what a European war would mean for them.

During July 1914, as tensions mounted and war began to look like a possibility, many groups in the UK were concerned about committing to a war that included military support for Russia given its attitude to large swathes of its own population, including minorities and workers. The Jewish community was particularly concerned about Britain's alliance with Russia.

The reluctance in some quarters of Anglo-Jewry to commit to a war that supported Russia was expressed in the Jewish press in papers such as the *Jewish Chronicle* and *Jewish World* (sister papers but with different editors) and also in the Yiddish press, especially in *Die Zeit*. Criticism was primarily based on a dislike of Russia's continued persecution of Jews and a fear that a war would only escalate attacks on them. Russia was seen by most Jews living in Britain to be the main persecutor of European Jewry, and responsible for their poverty and alienation. The arrival of relatively large numbers of Jews from the 1880s to 1905 had largely been a result of anti-Semitism in central and eastern Europe, and in particular in those regions under the control of the Russian Tsar. *The Jewish Chronicle*, the leading newspaper for the Jewish community, stated on 31 July 1914 that it would be 'wicked' for Britain to fight alongside Russia.[1]

It was not just Jewish groups that expressed concerns in Britain; many people felt that Germany would be a more natural partner for Britain if it had not been for its recent threat to British naval supremacy. In fact, as the two sides of Germany and Austria-Hungary *versus* Russia and France edged closer and closer to a full conflict, many felt that Britain's best option was to stay out of the fight. This was not to be the case; having weighed up all of the options, Britain eventually declared war on Germany.

There was an immediate U-turn from the British Jewish media once war was declared. The voice of established Anglo-Jewry was one of full commitment to the war effort, with the mainstream Jewish press completely supportive of the UK government's efforts.

Patriotic Support

For many Jews living in the UK, and certainly for the leaders of the Jewish community, the war and military service offered an opportunity to prove loyalty to Britain and to demonstrate a commitment to its future. Many had come from countries where Jews were prevented from joining the armed forces (or at the very least the levels of anti-Semitism in the military made the choice to join impossible), or where they would be conscripted into an openly anti-Semitic environment. Therefore, to be able to join the military freely was something to be applauded and seized upon.

Newspapers and publications specifically for the Jewish communities encouraged support for the war effort and enlistment.

There were a number of Jewish newspapers and informal Yiddish newsheets, but the paper regarded as representing the leading Jewish voice was *The Jewish Chronicle*. Throughout the war it ran the banner: 'England has been all she could be to Jews, Jews will be all they can be to England.'[2] Its sister paper, *Jewish World*, did the same, with both publications covering the key news about the war and the involvement of Jewish men and women across the whole four years. Adverts for Jews to enlist and contribute to war work, as well as appeals for those affected by the war, were regular features. *Jewish World* dedicated nearly a quarter to a half of every publication to war news and images of those who had enlisted or been killed. Both papers are major sources for anybody trying to glean Jewish attitudes and opinions of the time.

To ensure that the Jewish community and the non-Jewish world knew the position of British Jews regarding the war, the 7 August 1914 editorial in *The Jewish Chronicle* made it clear:

We own but a single cause, a single dominate desire. Our cause is the cause of England our desire is the triumph of England with all that she stands for so that she may overcome her enemies and come forth, from the ... ordeal as free, great and mighty as ever. That in the terrible struggle Jews will be pitted against Jews, that brothers in faith will be mortal enemies is indeed a saddening thought. Push that thought aside ... In the struggle into which England has entered, the Jews of this country will know how to bear their share, nay will be willing, if need be to bear more than their share. They will stand shoulder to shoulder with their fellow citizens in the stern and unshakable belief that, come what may this land which has given them abundant cause for deep love and gratitude ... Every sacrifice that loyalty and affection demand will be made, and made readily. Let us, every one of us show ourselves strong and resolute.

We Jews, whether England is to us the beloved country of our birth, or equally beloved country of our adoption. Will go forward, our one inspiring motive our affection for England, our stern resolve that come what may her cause shall prevail.

It is clear from the editorial that for established Anglo-Jewry the commitment to the war was a demonstration that they were British and not foreigners. They were well aware that anti-Semitic slights against the Jews had often focused on a supposed 'international' character, with accusations that Jews were 'loyal to their race not their country'. Within the editorial there is an acknowledgement of that and a clear instruction to the Jewish community (who were of course the audience for the paper) that any question of loyalty to brethren overseas was to be forgotten about – loyalty to the British cause was more important than anything.

At the same time as announcements about enlistment went up in town halls and in local newspapers, announcements went up in Jewish areas and in Jewish organisations – usually created by the Jewish community. Jewish newspapers across Europe would be displaying similar messages. This conflict was a matter of nationhood; it was not to be another European war of religion where Jews would be the victims on all sides.

Recruitment posters were specifically created for Jewish organisations and areas (see overleaf). They first appeared as early as August 1914, and they continued to be created throughout the war years – they didn't come from the British government but from the Jewish community. The language was often very specific; in an early poster it stated that it was a young 'unmarried Jewish man's duty' to enlist. A married Jewish man's duty is to his family, but those without dependents were to 'do their bit' without question. Importantly, the message was often repeated in Yiddish underneath.

אויפרוף

פון ענגלישע ארבייטער פיהרער צו אידישע יונגע לייט.

דער ארבייטער מיניסטער מר. העגדערסאן, מר.
אפעלטאן, אגריידי און אנדרע אפעלירען צו אידי־
שע יונגע לייט צו געבוירען אין ענגלאנד. דאס זיי זאלען
טהון זייער פפליכט צום לאנד.

ענגלישע געבוירענע אידען און די סלחטה.

„ענגלאנד איז געווען אלין וואס זי האט
געקעגנס פאר אידען; די אידען וועלען זיין
אלין וואס זיי קעגען פאר ענגלאנד.״
(דזשואיש קראניקעל).

אין ענגלאנד זיגען דא סויזענדער אידען, וועלכע האבען צו פער־
דאנקען, אלץ וואס זיי ווינטשען פון פרייהעם און גערעכטינקייט, צו דיזען
לאנד וואס זיי בעשיטצט זיין. זיי זיגען אהער געקומען פון פיעלע לענדער, און
זיי זיגען דא, אין אלגעמיין גענומען, פריי פון ראסען פאראורטהייל און
ראסען האס. יעדער אפיעל צו אזעלכע ליידענשאפטען ווזט דערפאר
נ*ט אויסגעהארט ווערען; אבער אן אפיעל וועגען עהרע און דאנקבאר־
קייט וועט טאגע אנדערש אייסוזעהן.

אין יעצטיגען גרויסען קריזיס, האם דאס לאנד יאם גום די אידען
פלאץ צו וואהנען, און מעגליכקיט זיך צו ערהויבען, א רעכט צו פער־
דערען פון די אידען וייער הילף. פיעלע אידען האבען שון בעוויזען זייער
סומה און וייער פאטריאטיזם. אויסנעצבענדיג זייער לעבען פאר דעם
לאנד: עס זיגען אבער נאך ראם טייזענדער אידען וואם זיגען געבוירען
אין ריגען לאנד, וועלכע זיגען פאהיג צו טראגען וואפען, וועלכע האבען
זיך נאך נ*ט אנגעשלאסען אין דער ארמעע. עס ווערט בעהויפטעט, אז
פיעלע פון די אידען וועלען מיט צופרידעגהיים זיך אנשליסען אין די
רייהען פון די אידען זעלנער צו קעמפפען? פאר דער פערטהיידיגינג פון די
בירגער רעכטע, וואם זיי בעזיעגען איצם, אויב מען וועם זיי אנבערצוגען,
אז זייער דיענסט איז ווירקליך נוטינג און אז זיי וועלען זיין וויללקאמען
אין דער ארמעע.

מיר, וועלכע האבען פיעלע מאל ערהוזבען אונזע־
רע שטימען אין'ם אינטערעם פון די אידען, בעטען
זיי איצט. אז זיי זאלען בעוויזען. דאם מיר זיגען גע־
ווען בערעכטיגט אין דעם צוטרויען. וואם מיר האבען
געהאט צו זיי. עס איז קיין צווייפעל נ*ט, אז זיי וו*־
לען זיין ווילקאמען אויב זיי וועלען זיך אנשליסען אין
דער ארמעע. זיי האבען נאך א מעגליכקיים זיך אנ־
צושליסען אלם פרייוויליג; די רעקרוטינג אפיסעם
זיגען איצם אפען. און זיי וועלען פיעל העלפען די
מיליטערישע אויטאריטעטען אויב זיי וועלען זיך שוין
אנשליסען, אנשטאם צו ווארטמען ביז דער קאמפאל־
שאן געזעץ וועם ארין אין מאכם.

(אונטערצ*כענם:) העררי נאסלינג, ק. וו. באוערמאן דזשיימם
אגריירי, וו. א. אפעלטאן, דזשאן האדיש, ארטהור העגדערסאן.

PUBLISHED BY THE JOINT LABOUR RECRUITING OFFICE, 1 VICTORIA ST, LONDON, S.W.

PRINTED BY ROBERTS & LEETS LTD LONDON

Above and opposite: (Courtesy of the Library of Congress)

By 1914 many of the recent migrants had still not learnt English but they had reached enlisting age. The community leadership was keen to ensure that this group in particular demonstrated their loyalty to their new country of residence. Many more recruitment posters would be created over the years, many in Yiddish and all making it clear that it was a Jewish man's duty to show their support for the war effort, king and country.

The sustained campaign for Jews to support the war never faded across the war years – there was no wavering from those at the top in their desire to prove the loyalty of the community. As early as August 1914, the press began to report on the Jewish men already in the forces. In the 18 August edition of *The Jewish Chronicle* there were reports of two Jewish men of Liverpool returning to their regiments despite being on leave: 'Serjeant D Henry Jacobs and Private Maurice Goldstein of the King Edward's Horse – attached to fourth Cavalry division'. Over the coming weeks more lists of those serving would appear in prominent places in the paper alongside all news about the mobilisation for war.

Giving his blessing to Jewish enlistment and service was the Chief Rabbi. His support for the war effort was considered essential by the non-religious leadership, and they had no concerns in this as Chief Rabbi Joseph Hertz was extremely loyal to Britain. Born in Hungary but educated mainly in the United States, Hertz had nearly been expelled from South Africa as a young rabbi in 1899 for his pro-British sympathies. He was keen that his brethren knew who they should be supporting as Jews. He made it quite clear that it was a British Jew's duty to support his country at a time of war. He also believed that there was no religious reason that Jews could not go to fight for Britain and her empire, and published this conviction.

Leading from the Front

The Anglo-Jewish leadership threw its weight behind the war, with prominent Jewish men coming forward to step into uniform or government positions and their female counterparts taking on the charitable concerns. Those Jews in important positions were quick to volunteer for activities, using their positions in business, banking and industry or in social and political life to influence others and support the government.

One of the most prominent and important of the old Jewish families in Britain was the Rothschild banking dynasty. The Rothschild family were supporters of many British politicians, and Lionel Nathan Rothschild was the first Jewish MP able to take his seat as a practising Jew (he had been elected in 1847, but only Christians could take the oath for Parliament). A number of other Rothschild family members subsequently went on to be elected to Parliament. Through their philanthropy they had built and supported hospitals, health clinics for the poor, schools and other charitable concerns. Many of these places had been for non-Jews as well as Jews.

The Rothschild family was not only important in Britain; it was one of Europe's most influential banking families. Its influence in business and politics was immense, stretching across continents. The British branch were also famously patriotic; as such, the Rothschild family in England and the Rothschild banking house in France pulled together to do their duty for their countries. There were extended family members living and doing business in Germany and Austria, and they were to have limited contact with them during the war years. The war and political loyalty had separated them, and that was that.

One of the most important things for the government to do once war was declared was to ensure that Britain's financial position was secure so that it could expect good credit and a stable economy, albeit a war economy. That meant politicians needed to meet with the leading banks in the City of London, and top of the list were the Rothschild banking interests. The Lord Chancellor at the time of the outbreak of war was the Liberal politician David Lloyd George. He did not always get on with the Rothschild family; in particular, he famously clashed with Lord Rothschild in 1909 over the proposed Liberal budget, which Lord Rothschild had recommended be rejected by the House of Lords. Other members of the family had also in recent years tended to align themselves with the Conservative Party rather than their previous bedfellows in the Liberal Party. Nonetheless, according to the Rothschild archives there was a meeting between Lloyd George and the senior partner of N. M. Rothschild & Sons, 'Natty', 1st Lord Rothschild (1840–1915), as soon as war broke out. At the meeting it is recorded:

'Lord Rothschild,' said Lloyd George as he shook hands, 'we have had some political unpleasantness ...' Natty brushed the attempted apology aside with his famous curtness. 'No time to bring up such things. What can I do to help?' 'I told him,' wrote Lloyd George. 'He undertook to do it at once. It was done.'

For Lloyd George, Natty was someone who 'had a high sense of duty to the State ... and was prepared to make sacrifices for what he genuinely believed in'.[3]

Natty was too old to serve in uniform and was happy to set about helping the government through his bank and other connections in stabilising and assisting the British economy. He reached out to all his important contacts and used all his influence to ensure Britain could afford to go to war. Accompanying Lord Rothschild in his task were his two brothers Leopold and Alfred, along with many in the younger generations – some of whom did take on military roles.

Leopold's son Lionel Nathan de Rothschild, born in 1882, was an officer in the Royal Buckinghamshire Regiment when war was declared, and in addition to his senior role as a partner at the bank he was also the MP for Aylesbury. It is said that he was stopped from going off to war by King George V, who believed it was important that he stay behind to help with the family banking business. Disappointed at not being able to serve abroad, Major Lionel de Rothschild threw his energies into supporting the war in any way he could. The family opened a recruitment centre at the company offices in New Court, St Swithin's Lane, London, in autumn 1915 after reports of Jews not being able to enlist at the regular recruitment centres. He put his name to endless recruitment campaigns and helped to establish the Jewish Recruitment Committee in 1915. His loyalty to his local area in Buckinghamshire meant that he was also an active recruiter and supporter of all the Buckinghamshire regiments. Jewish men from all parts of East London presenting themselves at his office would often find themselves not in a London regiment but a Buckinghamshire one – where they would be allowed to serve together. In 1917, Lionel was awarded the Order of the British Empire (OBE) for his recruitment activities.

Lionel's two brothers also became officers in the army as well as working in the family business, but unlike him they were allowed to go on active service abroad. Evelyn, born in 1886, and Anthony, born in 1887, both served with the Buckinghamshire Yeomanry (Royal Bucks Hussars). Anthony, known as 'Tony', went with his unit to Gallipoli in 1915. While there he was wounded and returned home; however, he continued his military service, eventually rising to the position of major with the General Staff.

Typical of the time, the Rothschild family paid the price for service. Evelyn, the middle brother, was mobilised in 1914 and was also sent to Gallipoli, where he was wounded. After a quick recovery he was posted to the Middle East and was mentioned in despatches. On 13 November 1917, at the Battle of El Mughar, he was part of a cavalry charge. Despite being an excellent horseman, he was severely injured in the fighting. He died on 17 November 1917 in a hospital in Cairo. One of his closest friends, his cousin Neil Primrose, fell on the same day.

The records in the Rothschild Archive contain the letter sent by the Officer Commanding of the Bucks Yeomanry:

> The Regiment was taking part in a mounted charge on the Turkish infantry, who were very strongly posted on some high ground, El Mughair. I attacked with the Regiment in a column of squadrons, and Evelyn was with the 2nd Squadron and was to take command of the two leading Squadrons on reaching the objective. We had some two miles of open country to cross, which was fairly swept by machine-gun and rifle fire. It was about half-way across this plain that Evelyn was struck down by a bullet. After all his death was a glorious one, killed when charging at the head of his men of Bucks.

Writing to his father, Leopold, Evelyn's commanding officer said:

> And then Evelyn has gone – a friend of fifteen years. Evelyn was a 'very perfect gentle knight; and as Second-in-Command of the Regiment almost more royalist than the king'.

Evelyn's mother, Marie, was deeply affected by her son's death; she never fully recovered.

Alfred Rothschild followed the trend of many wealthy landowners and donated land in the UK for military use. The grounds and large estate of Halton House near Wendover, Buckinghamshire, were given to the army for billeting and training facilities. Towards the end of the war the RAF moved into the training facilities at Halton, formally buying the land later. RAF Halton still remains on the site today. Also located on the site are a series of original First World War training trenches – a lasting legacy of that time.

Of course, the Rothschilds were not the only leading members of the Jewish community involved with the war. There were Jewish MPs on both sides of the Houses of Parliament in 1914, some as ministers, such as Edwin Montagu (who was a very outspoken opponent of Zionism) and Sir Rufus Isaac (who was the first Jewish head of the judiciary as the Lord Chief Justice; he also later became Viceroy and Governor-General of India). They both served in the war government, with Isaac working strongly to support British and American relations.

Sir Herbert Samuel was a senior Liberal politician who was also a practising Jew. He served as a Home Secretary during the war years, and he would later go on to be the first British High Commissioner of Palestine. He said at the end of 1914 that he had thirteen nephews and cousins serving with the colours.[4]

Other prominent Jewish families also gave up their sons for the war. Commissioned officers were one of the groups hit hardest by casualties, as they led their men from the front. According to the historian Harold Pollins, 'There were ten Sassoons [serving], there were forty-one members of the family of Sir Isidore Spielmann and his relatives; three were killed. The Beddington family contributed thirty-seven, all five sons of Mrs Arthur Sebag Montefiore served, one being killed at Gallipoli. One of the two officer sons of Sir Marcus Samuel, Bart., was killed.'[5]

Captain Robert Sebag Montefiore, one of the five sons of Mrs Arthur Sebag Montefiore, of Ramsgate, was educated at Clifton College (a well-established public school that had a Jewish boarding house which catered for many young Jewish boys of the most established and wealthy families) and then Oxford University. After university he became a barrister, and like all young men from a wealthy, established background he also took a commission in a local regiment. He joined the East Kent Yeomanry in 1904 as a lieutenant.

He married in 1910 and lived in Battersea, becoming a London county councillor in 1913. He was sent with his regiment to fight at Gallipoli, where he was badly wounded by a shell. He was transferred to Alexandria Military Hospital. Unusually, his wife Ada bravely travelled out to visit him; there were enemy ships in the Mediterranean ready to attack British shipping at this time. According to records, Robert was suffering from septic poisoning and fever as a result of injuries to his shoulder and leg. He died on 19 November 1915, aged thirty-three. His funeral was in Alexandria, and he is buried at the Alexandria Jewish Cemetery. Deal Street Elementary School, on the corner of Hanbury Street in Whitechapel, was renamed after him; he had been vice chair of the London County Council Education Committee. Now used for other educational and community purposes, the building is known as the Montefiore Centre. In Ramsgate Synagogue there is a brass memorial plaque near the entrance to Captain Robert Sebag Montefiore. The inscription reads:

> This tablet is erected by the Ramsgate congregation to the memory of Captain Robert Montefiore Sebag Montefiore, Royal East Kent Mounted Rifles, eldest son of Arthur and Harriette Sebag Montefiore, who died at Alexandria November 17th 1915, 12th Kislev 5676, in the thirty fourth year of his age [*sic*] from wounds received at Gallipoli in the service of his King and Country.

There were four other brothers who served. One was 2nd Lieutenant John (Jack) Sebag-Montefiore of the Royal Field Artillery. The youngest of the brothers, Lieutenant Charles Edward

Sebag-Montefiore, received his commission in 1918 for the Royal Horse Artillery; interestingly, his son Hugh went on to become Bishop of Birmingham. Captain William Sebag-Montefiore served in the 5th Royal Irish Lancers and was awarded the Military Cross (MC) in 1918. The other brother, Thomas Sebag-Montefiore, went to the Royal Military Academy in Woolwich after attending Clifton to become a professional soldier. He had received his commission in 1906 in the Royal Artillery. In 1914 he became a captain and fought in France, Belgium, Italy and Germany, gaining the rank of major in 1917. He was awarded the Distinguished Service Order (DSO) and the Military Cross (MC). He continued his military career after the war and gained the rank of lieutenant colonel in 1934. He was commander of the 1st Regiment, Royal Horse Artillery. During the Second World War he continued to be on active service with the Royal Artillery. He died in 1954.

If age or gender prevented a military contribution there remained nevertheless a requirement to serve, as demonstrated by industrialists and scientists such as Dr Chaim (Charles) Weizmann and philanthropists and believers in social care such as Dame Beatrice Lever. Mrs Arthur Sebag-Montefiore held regular sales in her garden to raise funds for young women left destitute through no fault of their own – something she put even more effort into during the war years.

Early Recruits

With the recruitment posters across the country and the daily newspaper articles it was almost impossible to ignore the patriotic calls to enlist. The pressures on the Jewish community from its leadership may have been considerable, but many young Jewish men joined up in 1914 for the same reasons that thousands of young men were flocking to the recruitment centres across the UK – the excitement of war!

As the British Expeditionary Force and the Territorial Forces were getting ready for dispatch, the young men accepted at the recruitment centres were being sent to training camps to spend the next few months training for what they thought would be their new adventures – if it wasn't all over by Christmas, that is. By 1915 those men would replace the thousands of professionals and semi-professionals already killed or injured on the Western Front.

Maurice Marcus Van Thal was born in Catford in 1897, the only child of parents Marcus and Marie. He was a bright, educated young man, but with the calls to enlist everywhere he gave up his plans and joined the Rifles Brigade on 11 September 1914. As a language scholar he acted as an interpreter to his commanding officer when his regiment was posted to France in March 1915. Tragically, he was killed in action on 9 May 1915 at Fromelles in northern France. His section commander wrote that 'he was a good soldier, and when we charged he went forward very gallantly. He was killed by a German shell.'

Of course, one of the issues that would affect recruitment in the Jewish community was eligibility. Many in the community were not naturalised citizens – even some who had lived in Britain for most of their lives. Some of those who had arrived as immigrants had not officially become citizens of the UK; they had never bothered to start the process of getting the right British papers. Their children, if born in the UK, would be British citizens, while they themselves were often wary of the authorities.

The war gave an opportunity and an impetus to some of the young men to apply for naturalisation and step out of their immigrant background. One, Albert Roth, was born Avram Rothenberg on 4 April 1888 in Romania. His father, Karl, a shopkeeper, travelled to the UK in 1892 with his younger brother. Albert's mother, Seama, brought the children – Albert, his two sisters and a younger brother – to London in 1894 or 1896. They settled in Parfitt Street, Stepney, London, while Karl Roth worked as a peddler or travelling salesman. At school Albert joined the Officer Training Corps and the Jewish Lads' Brigade. After leaving school he became a crockery salesman, but when war broke out in 1914 all he wanted to do was to join up. It was then that he realised that he had never been naturalised. He quickly set about changing that.

According to the family story, the day Albert got his naturalisation papers in 1914 he ran from the Home Office straight along Whitehall to the War Office to enlist. It was also as he naturalised that he chose to anglicise his name from Avram Rothenberg to Albert Roth. He joined the Royal Army Ordinance Corps and received a commission to lieutenant, and was later posted to France. During his time on the Western Front he was gassed but was fortunate enough to recover. He continued his military career and by the end of the war he had reached the rank of major and had been made an Order of the British Empire.

He left the army in 1919 and married in 1927. In 1937, when war began to seem a possibility again, he rejoined the army, this time with the 54th Highland Division. He was posted to the Continent once the war started. Along with thousands of others he was captured and made a prisoner of war during the Allied withdrawal from France in 1940. Despite being captive as a Jewish man under Nazi control, there is nothing to suggest that he was treated any differently to the other British POWs. He returned home to his wife and family in 1945 but remained in the army until 1947 before setting up in business. He died in 1971 in Teesside. For Avram Rothenberg, the desire to enlist triggered so many other decisions that helped him to become Albert Roth. Enlistment provided him with a strong and recognised military career, and helped him to become the proud British citizen that he became.

The Jews' Free School

The men who had been in the Officer Training Corps at school or in similar organisations were often the first to enlist in those early days of the war. These men were hopeful of attaining a commission, or at the very least of getting into the regiment that they wanted. School experiences had provided these young men from across Britain with a sense that they knew what was to come, and just as the big organisations such as the Board of Deputies sent out messages of encouragement so did the local communal institutions, including schools.

Jewish schools ensured that that their pupils were taught that it was their duty to support the war and, where possible, to participate. The Jews' Free School was a school that had 4,000 pupils in 1900 and educated approximately 1 in 3 Jewish children in London; understandably it wielded a very important influence across the different Jewish communities. It had a very clear line on supporting the war. Articles in the school magazine immediately listed those old boys who were in the forces, and as the war progressed it would celebrate those old boys who had joined up, with their names printed with pride and collected for their roll of honour. All the old boys who joined up were requested to visit the school while on leave to ensure that their names would be kept and correctly recorded. They were also encouraged to talk to the children still attending school.

In the 21 April 1916 edition of *The Jewish Chronicle*, the Jews' Free School headmaster, Laurence G. Bowman, had a large article starting with an early quote from Browning: 'Here and here, has England helped me, how can I help England say?' to encourage patriotism and loyalty. Midway through the article he boasted that the school had '580 Old Boys in khaki' and he went on to say that 'there must be some hundreds more, whose names for several reasons have not reached me. Some are shy of publicity, a few I am sorry to say, wish to hide their origin and others simply forgot to notify me.'

Alternatively, they may not have notified him due to the school's decision during the war to only record in the magazine the names of those old boys who had enlisted. The edition of March 1916 states, 'It should, however, be noted that in the case of unmarried men who joined the Army after March 1st, it would not be appropriate to include their names in our Roll of Honour, as such men are serving under the Compulsion Act.'[6] Men who were conscripted were not considered to have behaved in the honourable way to their country, even if their commitment once at the front was just as strong as that of any of the enlisted men. By the end of the war 1,129 old boys of the Jews' Free School are recorded as having served, but the real number is likely to be far higher. Many of them were injured or killed.

A lasting legacy in the school of the war was a School Peace Prize that was created in the name of Claude Bowman, the son of headmaster Laurence and his wife, Fanny. Claude Bowman was born in 1897. He was sent to the more illustrious St Paul's School rather than the Jews' Free School. He went on to Exeter College, Oxford. He joined the Officer Training Corps of the 2nd Artist Rifles in 1915 and in 1916 enlisted. He was quickly gazetted as 2nd Lieutenant to the Oxford and Bucks Light Infantry. He was in Flanders during the summer of 1917 and took part in the Third Battle of Ypres (often known as Passchendaele) and was killed there on 16 August 1917.

His obituary in *The Jewish Chronicle* was written by the Jewish reverend Walter Levin, who referred to a recent conversation between them:

He went from all the delights of ordered life and intellectual growth – from school hall and college cloisters – to take his part in the most awful warfare in the world's history – not for glory but for the sake of the land he held so dear and his community he loved so well ... As he wished me Goodbye, his last words to me were 'I am only going to do my duty as a man is bound to do and if I die it will be but the resignation to God's will, as in no other way can I to-day better uphold the name of English Jewry.'

Also in *The Jewish Chronicle* was a letter from his commanding officer who described Bowman:

A nicer and a firmer friend I have never had; so staunch, so brave, when in the midst of real danger, without any thought or fear whatever. He was so cheerful and bright wherever he was situated which caused his men to adore him. They would have followed him anywhere. He was extremely popular with everyone in the Battalion both the officers and men. He died a hero's death at the head of his men.

It seems that Laurence Bowman had instilled in his son a real sense of duty and loyalty. His effect was probably similar on many of the pupils at the school.

It is clear from the Jews' Free School magazine that the institution was an active supporter of Britain's role in the war in many ways. It supported and raised funds for a number of war-related charities – the War Relief Funds, the National Union of Teachers War Aid Fund, the Blinded Soldiers Fund and the Comfort Soldiers Fund are all mentioned. It provided a regular update on the actions of some of the old boys.

In addition to the old boys and the pupils at the school, teachers of service age were also encouraged to enlist. In the summer 1917 issue of the school magazine, a number of sports events were reported to have been cancelled due to lack of staff as they had gone off to war.

Youth Groups

Towards the end of the nineteenth century the arrival of the new immigrants led some people in the community to find ways to help the new arrivals to 'fit in' and to become British. Of particular concern to some were the children; it was felt that they really needed to be taught a strong and morally positive message of British life.

Across the Jewish communities of the UK, youth clubs and sports groups began to be established. The poorer areas in particular were targeted for recreational activities to ensure 'excess energy was well spent'. Just as sports clubs were set up for the Christian poor in the streets and neighbourhoods of East and South London, they were also set up for Jewish youth. East London with its tightly packed streets and tenement buildings had a number of clubs that each catered for hundreds of members.

The Brady Club was founded in 1896 as the first Jewish boys' club in Britain, in a building in Durward Street, off Brady Street, Whitechapel, East London. It was founded and funded by Lady Charlotte Rothschild, Mrs Arthur Franklin and Mrs N. S. Joseph, to provide underprivileged boys from the East End with recreational and educational opportunities, and frequently a hot meal. As the years went on it also gave them a chance to attend a summer camp, outside of London to get some fresh air. The Girls' Club was founded in 1921. Many former Brady Club attendees would enlist and find that the skills and comradeship they had developed at the club would be very useful once they were in khaki uniform.

One such Brady Club graduate was Samuel Jacobs, known as Jake. He was born in Russia in March 1896 and was brought to Britain aged two in 1898. His father was a rabbi and spent most of his time in the study house discussing the Talmud. While his father never learnt English, Samuel attended the Foundation School in Whitechapel and was desperate for a new life.

According to his family, Sam loved sport and would play football and cricket after school. On one occasion he had to go to his friend's house rather than return home for the Shabbat meal as he had lost his cap while playing a game after school. He attended the Brady Club, which allowed him to develop his own interests and widen his experiences. He became a leader at the club, helping other poor young Jewish boys. In 1913 he decided to emigrate to Canada so that he could develop his new life away from the restrictive religious gaze of his parents – he was seventeen years old.

When the war started in 1914, Jake, as Sam was often known, wanted to enlist in the Canadian Army, but under Canadian rules he needed the permission of his father or guardian to enlist as he was younger than nineteen years of age. To get around this he added two years to his age, declaring himself to be twenty years old, and enlisted in the Canadian Expeditionary Force.

He served with the Ambulance Corps, in which role he regularly rescued the wounded from the battlefield. He told a story to his daughter about a photo of a dead horse lying in a field that he had kept: 'They [the Ambulance Corps Men] would tie a wire round its leg and unreel the wire back to a position of safety; in this way they were able to orientate themselves at night or under fire' while they risked their own lives to recover the injured. Jacobs also kept a letter from 1915 from an old friend he met in the Brady Club:

My Dear Jacob

I have received your address from Sam Simons, and, am writing you these few lines just before I leave here for the Front, in order to say how very glad I was to hear that you were doing such excellent work with the Ambulance Section. I wonder if you found your work in the Brady and the JLB of any value.

I have heard very little of Brady since the war broke out, but, as far as I can gather, it is going strong. May it go 'from strength to strength' as the good old saying is.

I have had an interesting and trying time – the first six months of the war I was in England, then we were at Malta for another six months, and now, after a stay of about a fortnight here, we are off in a couple of days' time to where the actual business is taking place.

I often think of you and of the dear old days at Brady. I wonder if they will ever come back again.

I hope that you, too, sometimes give a thought to the Club, and that your recollection is of pleasant memories. The very best of good luck to you, wherever you may be and whatever you may do!

Yours sincerely

H.L. Hatham

As the war developed Jake served as a signaller, delivering messages, and as a gunner. Interestingly, he always had his pay sent home to his father who now lived in Notting Hill, London. He spent the whole war with the Canadian Forces, but returned to London following his demobilisation in 1919, and stayed, eventually becoming a furrier. The beret from his army days was something he always kept, wearing it when he gardened.

Being part of a club in his youth had left a keen sense of duty and belonging in Jake. He was an early member of the Association of Jewish Ex-Servicemen and Women (AJEX), and always marched with them at their remembrance parade while he was alive.

Like many of those who were fortunate to survive the war, Jake did not come out unscathed. A gas attack had left him without his sense of smell, and it was lung cancer that killed him in 1953.

Over twenty years before the First World War, in April 1891, *The Jewish Chronicle* had published a letter from Revd Francis Lyon Cohen headed 'But what about the boys?' in which he called for the creation of a Jewish youth group, modelled on the Boys' Brigade. He believed it would channel and control the working-class youth in the East End of London at a crucial period of their development; otherwise, he feared, they were at risk of negative or even criminal behaviour. He was particularly concerned with those young men at the age of 'leaving school and their attainment of manhood'. A British Jewish army officer, Colonel Albert Goldsmid, then stepped in, making the idea a reality and creating the Jewish Lads' Brigade. Goldsmid had served in the British Army around the world; indeed, he would leave the Jewish Lads' Brigade for a time to serve in the Boer War.

Following a lecture from Colonel Goldsmid before the Order of Ancient Maccabeans at a meeting held at the Jews' Free School in the East End of London on 16 February 1895, the brigade was formally created. Six weeks later the first company of boys started the first weekly drill. Emphasising that the Jewish Lads' Brigade was to have an anglicising and conforming influence that sought 'to instil in the rising generation, from earliest youth, habits of orderliness, cleanliness, and honour, so that in learning to respect, so they will do credit to their community', the first young men were recruited at the Jews' Free School, the Norwood Orphanage and other local schools. In 1896, the first summer camp, with nineteen boys, was held at Sandhills, Deal (near Kent), and social and athletic clubs were also organised. It was at this point that the group began to be treated as a real organisation with a proper purpose and structure.

The Brigade's primary objective, however, was to organise the boys and drill them as a military body. Clubs for athletic, social and intellectual purposes were formed among the members. Over the next few years, more and more companies of the Jewish Lads' Brigade would be created across the East End of London and then in the provincial towns and cities of Liverpool, Newcastle, Manchester, Birmingham and Cardiff – and even further afield across the British Empire, with Jewish Lads' Brigade branches in Montreal and Johannesburg.

In 1904, Colonel Goldsmid died and was succeeded by another career soldier, Colonel Emanuel Montefiore, as commandant. Montefiore had been a professional soldier in the Indian Army, spending twenty-one years there as well as serving in Nova Scotia and the West Indies. His ambition for the Jewish Lads' Brigade was just as strong; he hoped to create a military atmosphere among the boys that would promote loyalty to king and country.

The Brigade initially shared headquarters with the Russo-Jewish Committee and the Jewish Athletics Association – both indicating the backgrounds of the boys it was hoping to attract. In 1913 the

Refugee children at an American Red Cross Centre in the East End, 1919. (Courtesy of the National Archives and Records Administration)

Brigade was large enough and supported enough by donors to move into a purpose-built centre named Camperdown House.

In September 1914, a recruiting meeting at Camperdown House, attended by a representative of the War Office, the Mayor of Stepney and Stuart Samuel MP, led to 150 Jewish volunteers for the British Army. The Brigade was represented, through its chairman Max Bonn, on the Juvenile Organisations Committee, set up by the Home Office to encourage voluntary war work among young people. Ernest Woolf, who joined the Hackney Company of the Brigade in 1914, remembered 'marching round the streets of Hackney with the band playing, finishing up on the steps of the Town Hall. I was a bugler at the time and we were all blowing away like mad to attract the people to come and listen to an Army Officer making his speech calling for recruits.'

Earlier, in 1907, Secretary of State for War Richard B. Haldane, who believed that another European war was likely, wanted all youth organisations to affiliate to the Cadet Forces to create a direct link to army recruitment. The Jewish Lads' Brigade, Boys' Brigade, Church Brigade and Scouts all rejected this suggestion; while all promoted military behaviour, they did not want to be seen as actual military organisations. They believed that they were building young men who would go into many areas of life with a strong sense of duty and order. The arrival of war changed this attitude, and in March 1915, six months into the war, the Brigade applied for recognition by the Territorial Forces Association. For the remainder of the war, the London battalion styled itself as the 1st London Cadet Battalion, Jewish Lads' Brigade, and the Manchester one as the 1st Manchester Cadet Battalion JLB. All Brigade companies, except Dublin, transformed themselves into cadet units and adopted a uniform of regulation 'service pattern'.

During the war, day-to-day Brigade activities were inevitably reduced. Many companies collapsed, and the 1914 summer camps were hastily curtailed on the outbreak of hostilities. The Sandhills site at Deal was appropriated by the War Office. Nevertheless, small camps were held in August 1917 for about sixty lads at Goring and 150 lads from Manchester at Kettleshulme in Derbyshire. The Manchester Jewish Lads' Brigade Scout Company also held weekend camps at Marple during the war, and the Glasgow Company held two camps of its own. It was due to the dedication of older officers and some of the men who were ineligible for army service (largely due to health reasons), especially Joseph and Ernest Hallenstein and the acting paymaster, Max Bonn, that the organisation kept going. They were determined that young Jewish men would continue to be ready to do their duty – and be prepared for service, regardless of the circumstances.

The Jewish Lads' Brigade ethos of duty and loyalty meant that when war was declared its former members were some of the first to enlist. Many already belonged to the Territorial Forces and were recalled anyway. According to the official Jewish Lads' Brigade records, 535 former Brigade men made the ultimate sacrifice during the war. Their names appear on the Jewish Lads' Brigade roll of honour. The British Jewry Book of Honour notes that eighty out of a total of ninety Brigade officers became officers in the war, and that thirty-nine of them never returned. The Victoria Cross awardee Issy Smith was a former Jewish Lads' Brigade boy, along with many others who received awards.

Another East End Club that provided young men with additional support and stability was the Stepney Jewish Lads' Club, founded in Stepney in the East End of London in 1901. George Joseph Forstein was born in 1895 in Stepney and attended the Stepney Jewish School and the Stepney Jewish Lads' Club. He joined the army before the war, anglicising his name to George Foster at the same time. For the first time in his life he left behind his small community of Stepney for a big adventure. He became a soldier in the Norfolk Regiment and was deployed to the Western Front early in the war, fighting at the disastrous August battle at Mons. The British Army had come up against a huge German force determined to push through Belgium to reach northern France. The professional forces of the British Expeditionary Forces had done their best to hold their ground but had eventually been forced to retreat at the cost of many of its best men.

George was killed on 24 August 1914, one of the first Jewish casualties. He has no known grave and instead is remembered on the La Ferte-sous-Jouarre Memorial to the Missing, a British war memorial to the 3,740 officers and men who fell in the early battles. The memorial is approximately 66 kilometres east of Paris. The announcement in *The Jewish Chronicle* in September 1914 under 'Jewish casualties' has in brackets that he is an old Stepney Club boy, and just beneath him is listed Private J. W. Jacobs of the

George Joseph Forstein.

1st East Surrey Regiment, another professional soldier. Jacobs was wounded and moved to a Glasgow hospital; he is also listed as an old Stepney Club boy. It appears that Jacobs went on to recover from his wounds and survive the war.

The British Jewry Book of Honour lists twenty Jewish schools, school groupings and clubs and their old boys' contributions:

	On Active Service			Died		
	Officers		Men	Officers		Men
Bayswater Jewish School, W London	?	141	?	?	9	?
Borough Jewish Schools, SE London	3		160	?		
Grove House Club, Manchester	?	274	?	?	13	?
Hayes Industrial School for Boys	1		139	–		14
Hutchinson House Club, E London	19		328	2		18
Hebrew Schools, Liverpool	12		250	1		31
Hebrew Schools, Birmingham	6		258	1		23
Jewish House, Cheltenham	40		–	8		–
Jewish House, Clifton	132		6	24		–
Jewish Lads' Brigade		?		39		525
Jews' Hospital & Orphan Asylum, Norwood	4		135	1		14
Jewish Working Men's Club, Manchester	11		210	–		5
Jews' School, Manchester	?	464	?	?	21	?
Jewish Lads' Club, Notting Hill, W London	24		159	6		14
Jews' Free School, E London	19		1210	1		78
Stepney Jewish Lads' Club, E London	16		417	6		35
The Maccabeans	74		6	10		3
The Old Boys' Club, E London	10		115	?	11	?
Victoria Working Boys' Club, E London	?	435	?	13		18
Westminster Jews' Free School, W London	7		290	?	16	?

2

GOING OFF TO WAR

One of the Team?

The initial excitement of the war carried through August 1914 and into September despite the failings at the Battle of Mons and elsewhere. From August 1914, casualty reports of Jews began to appear in the Jewish press. *The Jewish Chronicle* announced on 18 September that it was creating a list of all those from the Jewish community that were serving, just as the young men from the community were heading to the recruitment offices. However, it wasn't all plain sailing. Many Jews were still concerned that they would be met with prejudice and they were not always wrong.

There were mutterings reported in local newspapers that the Jews of Leeds were not enlisting – despite statements in *The Jewish Chronicle* that fifty Jews of Leeds had enlisted in the first few weeks. In autumn 1914 there were stories in London of Jews being turned away from recruitment offices and told they were not wanted. *The Jewish Chronicle* first reported the incidents on 9 October. The response from the military authorities was quick and clear – Jews were not to be turned away.

On 1 January 1915 there was a letter in *The Jewish Chronicle* from Dr Henry Dutch NDTF, Surgeon Major RAMC, that said:

Sir I regret that you should draw attention in your column to an incident in which a Jewish would-be recruit was informed at the Mansion House that 'no Jews would be enlisted in the Reserve Battalions of the 4th City of London Regiment TF'. It was explained that such a remark was made by an irresponsible person who was duly dealt with.

I can assure you that no one in authority connected with this battalion has ever shown the slightest anti-Semitic feeling. As medical officer for over twenty years I have passed scores of Jewish recruits wherein if eligible we gladly welcome and I believe forty Jewish men of the newly formed reserves attended divine service held recently by our chaplain the Rev M. Adler (Jewish). We are now raising a second reserve battalion.

This letter raises a number of things: firstly, Jews were being turned away by some soldiers at recruitment centres because they were Jews; secondly, in times of need, high-level figures were prepared to publicly rebuke anti-Semitism. Whether they would have challenged that prejudice in peacetime we cannot tell, but it is exactly these small challenges to otherwise acceptable levels of prejudice that begin to change wider practices and attitudes across British society.

These small challenges were embraced by the Anglo-Jewish elite and presented in the Jewish press to reassure Britain's Jews that this war was exactly the time that Jewish loyalty could be used to counter the anti-Semitism that may influence some people's behaviour. Stories were found that proved that anti-Semitism did not lie under every stone and that the Jewish contribution would be embraced. As early as September 1914 there had been attempts to assure young Jewish men (and their families) that they would be well respected. The following article was published in *The Jewish Chronicle* on 11 September of that year:

Jews in the Black Watch – 'Bonnier Lads and Braver I don't wish to see'
Somebody asked a question about the Jews – what were they doing?
A Highlander broke in sharply 'Doing? Well, their duty. We had three with us, and bonnier lads and braver I don't wish to see. They

fought just splendid.' There was a Private of the Berkshire Regiment with the Highlanders and he also had a good word to say of the Jews at the Front. 'We had ten in our company,' he remarked, 'all good fighters and six won't be seen again. So don't say a word against the Jews.'

Although there is no reason to assume that there is anything false in this report, it does remind us that attitudes of anti-Semitism we would consider unacceptable today were quite common a hundred years ago and that many ordinary people would have thought of them as 'normal'. Here the paper is keen to demonstrate that not everyone would perpetuate the stereotypes and be disparaging of the efforts of Jews as soldiers. The reality was that many Jews joined up in the early months despite anti-Semitism, while others didn't notice it or never experienced it.

Prejudice or not, the pressure from the Anglo-Jewish leadership to enlist did not abate. If anti-Semitism did exist, then men such as Lucien Wolf, a leader in Anglo-Jewry and editor of *Jewish World*, believed that continued duty and a mainstream presence in British life would be the way to stop it. Through his publication there was a constant stream of positive representations of Jews and of positive non-Jewish opinion towards them.

The Jewish Recruitment Committee

Anti-German sentiment did not help some Jews feel comfortable. Partially stoked by government restrictions (see chapter 7), German residents of the UK – of which there were approximately 53,000 in 1914 – began to be singled out as a threat to Britain. Their names, whether German or simply 'foreign sounding', could lead to verbal and sometimes physical attacks as the swell in patriotism showed its darker side. Following the sinking of the British ship *Lusitania* in May 1915 by a German U-boat, the mainstream British press made a direct connection to the German enemy and Germans in the UK: 1,950 German (or German-sounding) properties in London came under attack.[1]

To ensure that this latest wave of violence did not put off potential Jewish volunteers or see them turned away from recruitment offices, the Anglo-Jewish leadership stepped up its efforts. More men were steered towards the Rothschild premises. Lionel de Rothschild in his capacity as a major of the Oxford and Bucks Light Infantry recruited men to his regiment, even if they were from London. This helps to explain why in the British Jewry Book of Honour there are 273 Jewish men and twelve Jewish officers listed as serving in the Oxford and Bucks Light Infantry, with many of their home addresses indicating a London residence. One such man was Private Jack Jacobs, who is buried at Tyne Cot Commonwealth War Graves Commission Cemetery in Belgium; he was killed in the Third Battle of Ypres. His home address is that of his parents, Harry and Esther Jacobs, of 58 British Street, Bow, London, but he served with the 2nd/4th Battalion of the Oxford and Bucks Light Infantry. His headstone is inscribed 'Gone from our sight but ever in our hearts, father, mother & brothers'.

Others, such as Private Richard Da Costa of East London, who was twenty years of age when war broke out, served with the 6th Battalion of the Oxford and Bucks Light Infantry and survived the war. Despite being gassed, Da Costa was able to return home to marry his wartime girlfriend, Rebecca, at Bevis Marks Synagogue in 1919. He lived until 1963.

Further posters went up, and the press reported more stories of how happy Jewish servicemen were. In autumn 1915 the Jewish Recruitment Committee was established, with Mr Edmund Sebag-Montiefiore as the chairman and Major Lionel de Rothschild

MP as vice chairman. The offices were at New Court, St Swithin's Lane, London. The committee's role was to coordinate Jewish enlistment as well as to encourage it. Events overseas in the Middle East as well as incidents in the UK had convinced the British authorities that they did not want to lose Jewish support and the valuable pool of young men it provided. If that meant cutting the Jewish leaders a few breaks, then that was fine; if it meant condemning anti-Semitism, then that was fine too. In December 1915, the Jewish Recruitment Committee was formally recognised by the War Office.

In a circular of 18 December, the following instructions were sent to all recruitment offices:

Although many Jews are already serving in the Army, it is known that there are still a large number in the country who are eligible but have not yet enlisted, especially in such centres as London, Leeds, Manchester, Hull, Liverpool, Glasgow, Birmingham and other large cities, and it is hoped that it be found possible with the assistance of the committee to induce many of these to come forward for enlistment.

In this connection recruiting officers should be informed that a man born in this country is a British Subject although he be of alien parentage, and consequently, if otherwise suitable and acceptable, is eligible for enlistment in the Army.

An English-speaking British-born subject of friendly alien parentage who presents himself for enlistment may therefore, if otherwise considered suitable, be accepted by the recruiting officer, and in the case of a Jew, if there is any reason to doubt the bona fides of such a candidate, or if he bears a German or Austrian name, a preference should be made to the Secretary of the Jewish Recruitment Committee be for he is finally accepted.

A British-born Jew of enemy parents will only be accepted if he is able to speak English, has lived continuously in this country since his birth, is otherwise suitable, and is vouched for by the Jewish Recruiting Committee.

Recruiting Officers in the whose areas there are considerable numbers of eligible Jews should arrange with commanding officers of units so that Jews who enlist may be enabled as far as possible to serve with their friends.

It could not be clearer – Jews were to be recruited.

The year 1915 had been a difficult one for the Allies. The British has suffered high casualties at the Second Battle of Ypres, the Battle of Loos and in the Dardanelles Campaign. The professional forces of 1914 had nearly all gone, and new recruits were now more crucial than ever. The introduction of gas as a weapon by the Germans had increased the brutality of the conflict. At the same time, Jewish bravery had been recognised with a second Victoria Cross, and the Zion Mule Corps had demonstrated the commitment of overseas Jewish nationals to the British cause. As the year drew to a close, the British authorities wanted to ensure their volunteers kept coming, especially after they introduced conscription.

In June 1916 the decision was made that the Jewish Recruitment Committee, the Jewish military chaplains and others would all come under one committee or group of organisers. It was led by the same men who had been leading the war work from the start of the war.

Further Afield and Close to Home

When we talk of the British involvement of the war and of British troops during the First World War it is not uncommon for us to immediately think of the men and women of Great Britain. However, the Great Britain of 1914 was an empire, holding power over approximately a quarter of the world's population and nearly a fifth of its geography. As such, when references are made to British troops during the war this could as much refer to those from parts of the empire and the British dominions as it could to those from the United Kingdom.

When Britain declared war on Germany in August 1914, the dominions were asked if they would also commit to the war – they all did. In the countries that were colonies, volunteers were sought and many enlisted. Why so many men decided to enlist, in some cases for a country thousands of miles away, is not always clear to us today. Some did it out of a sense of duty, others for adventure and excitement. For the Jewish populations across the British Empire, it was often a mixture of the two. Whatever their perception of anti-Semitism in their own countries and in Britain, many Jewish communities still thought of the British Empire as being better for them than Germany or Austria-Hungary; after all, discounting Russia, those were the countries that many of the immigrants had left behind.

The Canadian Jews

Canada had a Jewish population of approximately 100,000 when war was declared. A large proportion of these were first- and second-generation immigrants from central and eastern Europe, although some had also made a stop in Britain before carrying on to Canada. According to records in the British Jewry Book of Honour, around 2,700 Canadian Jews served in the Canadian Expeditionary Force. As is the case for the British Jews, the actual number is likely to be far higher, as to avoid anti-Semitism many did not register as Jewish when they enlisted. Others, such as Samuel Warshawsky from Winnipeg, changed their name to avoid standing out. Waskey, as he renamed himself, was born in London, England to Polish parents and was aged around nine when the family moved to Canada. He joined the 44th Battalion of the 4th Canadian Division early and arrived in Britain in 1915. He was killed during the Battle of the Somme in October 1916. For him, his British connection was very obvious.

Edward Joseph Seidelman, twenty, of Vancouver (his father was Hungarian and emigrated to the United States before settling in Canada), was born in 1898. He was a student at the University of British Columbia when he enlisted in 1916 in the 196th Battalion (Western Universities). He arrived in England in November 1916 then went to France in early 1917. He took part in the Battle of Vimy Ridge in April 1917, one of the most important Canadian-led British victories for the Allies. Furthermore, that April battle also saw snowstorms, making the achievement of taking a ridge that the Germans had held for three years all the more impressive. After recovering from a wound to the leg, Seidelman was returned to the front, this time in Belgium. He took part in the start of the Canadian engagement at the Third Battle of Ypres and was killed on 26 October 1917; he is buried there.[2]

Not all the Canadian volunteers went into the army; some joined other branches of the forces. Harry Walter Jassby was born in Montreal, Canada in 1896. According to his family he had wanted to fly from a young age, so in 1917 he gave up his studies at McGill University and enlisted. He added two years to his age so that he could be posted abroad to join the Royal Flying Corps. He trained in Toronto before being posted to the RFC in Fairlop, East London, and subsequently the RAF when it was formed in 1918.

In letters home he talks about wanting to go and fight; he is 'keen to get into a scrap with the Hun'. Initially he wants to go to France, but he then decides on Egypt as he believes the weather is better. However, he remains at Fairlop. He hopes that in the future he will be able to transfer to the newly created Canadian Flying Corps.

Harry Walter Jassby.

By early November 1918, when there are signs of the Allied victory, Jassby is selected to be one of the pilots to fly their aircraft in a V shape as part of any victory celebration. It was while he was rehearsing this move on 6 November 1918 with other pilots that one of the engines in another aircraft failed, crashing into Jassby and causing him to crash. He was killed instantly and, as is the practice for pilots, was buried in the nearest churchyard – St Peter's in Essex.

The reverend of the church allowed the headstone to include the Star of David, which was pretty unusual for that time (and probably still today). Over the years, Jassby has created a strong interfaith relationship in the area. In recent years the reverend of the church invited the local rabbi of South-West Essex Reform Synagogue to attend and say prayers over the grave. Now a service is held every year jointly between the two congregations. Jassby's grave is still maintained and visited by members of the local community and great pride is taken in making sure that their Canadian airman is not forgotten so far from home.

Not Canadian then, but Canadian now is the area of Newfoundland on the eastern coast of Canada. Population-wise it was a small dominion, but with a large land area – its main output was from the coast (fishing and similar) or timber and farming. Maurice Comor was born in Blackpool in 1894. As a young man he left his family to travel to Newfoundland to make his fortune. However, as soon the war started he enlisted in St John's, Newfoundland, at the Church Lads' Brigade Armoury. He attested on 15 December 1914 and departed Newfoundland for overseas service on 5 February 1915, travelling first to Malta, then he served at Gallipoli and then he went to the Western Front. He was promoted to lance-corporal and was fighting with his regiment at the Battle of Gueudecourt (part of the Battle of the Somme) when he was seriously wounded by mortar fire on 12 October 1916.

He was evacuated to England and spent some months in a hospital in Folkestone before being transferred to one in Stockport closer to his family. On 5 December 1917 he died as a result of his injuries. He was buried in Blackpool Jewish Cemetery; on his headstone is the Newfoundland cap badge, the caribou, a rare sight in Blackpool.

The Jews of Canada as troops under British command are listed in the British Jewry Book of Honour, and many of their activities were reported in the British Jewish press.

Anzac Forces

Australia was also a dominion of Britain in 1914, and was keen to join the fight. In order to do their part, the Australians had to quickly develop their forces for overseas conflict. It was in the Australian forces that the most senior Jewish officer during the First World War can be found – General Sir John Monash.

His parents were German (Prussian) Jews who had settled in Australia before he was born in Melbourne in 1865. He began his service career in 1887 when he joined his university militia. He remained as a Territorial officer while pursuing his civilian career. In 1912 he became a colonel. When the war started, he decided to commit to the military full time.

In September 1914 he was given command of the 4th Infantry Brigade. According to Daniel Mendoza-Jones, a former director of the New South Wales Association of Jewish Ex-servicemen and Women,[3] Monash's appointment was met by some resistance in Australia due to his Jewish and German background. The language of his childhood was German and so there were those who questioned his loyalty. Fortunately, he was liked and admired by the senior British general Sir Ian Hamilton, who was in charge of the Egyptian Expeditionary Force during the Gallipoli campaign, and this ensured that any resistance was ignored and his appointment went through.

Monash bravely led his men in the difficult Gallipoli campaign, resulting in his promotion to brigadier-general in the summer of 1915. After the evacuation of troops away from the Dardanelles, Monash travelled with his men to the UK where he trained with them before being posted to the Western Front, arriving in 1916. He played an important role in the planning and execution of the Battle of Messines in June 1917, where Anzac forces played a key role in the taking of the ridge.

Their success led to their involvement in the less successful and bloody Third Battle of Ypres, starting in July 1917. Although Monash had some successes in the battle, he also experienced heavy casualties, providing him with a strong lesson in the impact of ground conditions on the outcome of a battle.

Wounded being transported on the light railway at Messines. (Courtesy of the National Archives and Records Administration)

Despite the limited success of the Third Battle of Ypres, Monash and his men fought bravely and his reputation continued to grow. The following year, in May 1918, he was promoted to lieutenant general and was engaged in the planning for some of the most important battles of 1918. Back in Australia, a number of other Australian military officers and politicians were trying to convince the Prime Minister, Billy Hughes, to replace him, based on their own anti-Semitic prejudices. Their plot failed when Hughes visited the Western Front and saw how affective Monash's planning was and how admired he was by those around him. The British officers in particular liked and respected him – not always an easy thing to achieve when tensions could be strained between the British and the increasingly confident Australians.

As a trained engineer, Monash was interested in the new technology developed during the war and he was eager and able to embrace it in his planning. His battle plans combined the use of infantry with artillery, air power and tanks as well as new thinking around strategy and how to use the skills of the men he commanded.

The regard and admiration that Monash garnered was most clearly illustrated when he was knighted on 12 August 1918 on the battlefield by King George V – the first time in 200 years that a monarch had done such a thing. He is perhaps the most famous Australian military commander and the most famous Jewish military commander outside of the Israeli forces. It has been suggested that in the years following the First World War anti-Semitism in Australia was greatly reduced as no one would engage in an activity that might result in a criticism or attack on Sir General John Monash, their greatest military hero.

Another senior Jewish Australian military man was Lieutenant Colonel Eliazar Margolin. He was born in Russia in 1878 before he left with his family and settled in Palestine when he was seventeen. The family ran a vineyard. Following the death of both his parents he sold it and in 1902 decided to move to Australia, where he was naturalised in 1904. He settled in Western Australia and helped to form the Collie Company of the 1st Battalion Western Australian Infantry Regiment in 1911. He was commissioned as a second lieutenant. Once the First World War started he was mobilised and was promoted to captain of the 16th Battalion Australian Imperial Force in December 1914. This was just in time for him to be a part of the Gallipoli landings in April 1915. While there he was awarded the Distinguished Service Order and appointed temporary lieutenant colonel. For a while he was appointed to the Zion Mule Corps, a British labour corps created from Palestinian and Russian Jews who volunteered to fight or work for the British forces against the Turks and served in Gallipoli. Following that he returned to regular duties with the Australian Infantry, but was now excited about the idea of a Jewish military force. In

March 1918 he resigned from the Australian forces to take up a commission as lieutenant colonel in charge of the 39th Battalion Royal Fusiliers, one of the newly created Jewish regiments, known as the Judeans. It was with the Judeans that he fought in Palestine as part of the Middle East campaign.

Following the end of the war, Margolin stayed in Palestine and in 1919 helped to form the First Jewish Battalion of Judea, paid for and supported by the British Army as part of its duties in governing Palestine.

During Arab–Jewish riots in Tel Aviv in 1920, Margolin and his 300 soldiers intervened, preventing deaths on both sides. This made him a hero of the Palestinian Jews and a heroic figure for Zionists around the world. Not surprisingly, he was then appointed as Governor of Jerusalem. In 1921 he returned to Australia but he continued to be involved with veterans' groups and Jewish issues. When he died in 1949 he was cremated in Australia and his ashes were scattered on his parents' grave in what had recently become Israel.

According to Mark Dapin, an Australian author on Jewish Anzac troops, Jewish engagement with the First World War is connected 'with the relatively low incidence of anti-Semitism in Australia, Australian Jews' British allegiance and desire to "prove themselves worthy of the empire that had granted them equal rights wherever English was spoken". Australia at the time was a progressive and optimistic culture that afforded Jews all the rights of full citizenship denied to them almost everywhere else.'[4] He also records that, 'like other Anzacs, the Jews came from all strata of society. The pre-war occupations of some of those who died in France included jockey, sign writer, cigar-maker, ship's steward.'[5] That statement is easily borne out simply by looking at the British Jewry Book of Honour; there are 252 Jewish officers listed and 1,750 Jews who were 'NCOs and men'.

Some of those men had remarkable stories that demonstrate the *Australian* British Jewish journey. Adolf Saarijarvi was born in Orivesi, Finland in 1877. He travelled to Australia via Norway, arriving in 1902, and settled in Chinchilla, Queensland. According to his records he was a farmer in Australia. He enlisted in March 1916 and was with the 4th Australian Pioneer Battalion, having previously served with the military in Finland. His battalion was sent to the Western Front. In April 1918 Saarijarvi's battalion was required to take up arms, and as the result of a subsequent engagement he was recommended for the Military Medal:

Private Saarijarvi was one of the Pioneer working party under Lieut. Reid on 5 April 1918. In the severe enemy attack on that date, Pte Saarijarvi displayed great courage and presence of mind, he continuously placed himself in position from which effective fire could be made from his rifle and passed messages to Lieut Reid and those about him so that men in the vicinity could be used to the best advantage during the attack. He was on post all the time and proved of valuable assistance to both Lieut. Reid and the party.[6]

He was awarded the Military Medal on 16 July (although he did not receive it on that date). On 10 August he received a gunshot wound in the arm and was evacuated to the 3rd Australian Military Hospital in Dartford, Kent, England. He died from flu on 28 October; he had married one month earlier, on 28 September. As he died in England he is buried at Brookwood Military Cemetery, now part of the Commonwealth War Graves Commission (Pirbright, Surrey). He is the only Jewish First World War burial there.

New Zealand, even with its small Jewish community, provided fifteen Jewish officers and 144 NCOs and men. One of these was

Albert Anker, who was born in London in 1891 but moved to Auckland, New Zealand, to work as a tailor. In 1914 he enlisted in the New Zealand Expeditionary Force and was sent to the 3rd Auckland Infantry. It was with them that he was despatched to Gallipoli in 1915. He was part of the landing force there and was injured in early June, dying on 9 June 1915. He is remembered on the Lone Pine Memorial in Turkey – he was a British New Zealand Jew who became one of the Anzac heroes of Gallipoli.

Another important Anzac connection came in 1918 when the Jewish Legion came under the command of Major-General Edward Chaytor, who commanded the Anzac mounted division in Palestine.

South Africa, India and the Caribbean

A small but strong Jewish community existed in the key cities of South Africa. It was made up of German, eastern European and British Jews who had either fled persecution of wanted to try their hand in a new and exciting area of the world. On the whole the Jewish community there was very patriotic towards Britain, although Jews fought on both sides during the Boer War. There was already legislation in South Africa for young men to do a form of military service even before the First World War started; however, South African agreement to willingly participate on behalf of the British was not assured. Many, including the Germans, gambled on the South Africans wanting to stay out of the conflict; however, they did join the Allied cause. According to the British Jewry Book of Honour there were seventy-six Jewish officers in the South African Forces in addition to 1,227 NCOs and men. They fought in East Africa and in the European theatres. There are many Jewish names on the South African war memorial at Delville Wood on the Somme.

It was mainly Jewish merchants who chose to settle in the British West Indies and create a small Jewish community there. Once war was declared the islands were asked to do their bit. Consequently, there are thirty-seven Jewish officers listed as being in the British West Indies Regiment, and ten in the ranks.

In all, 109 Jews from Bombay served in the Indian Defence Corps throughout the war, ensuring that India remained peaceful. Looking at the British Jewry Book of Honour there are also names listed as volunteers in the Gibraltar Volunteer Force. It is clear that the Jewish men and women of Great Britain and across the British Empire stood up and were prepared to do their bit.

3

WE WERE THERE TOO

Britain has a long military tradition, with wars and conflicts a regular occurrence. Through a combination of trade and power the British had built an empire that reached around the globe. Britain had been at the forefront of the Industrial Revolution that had ushered in much of the modern era, and that was reflected in sections of its military. However, nothing could prepare the British people for what was about to be unleashed during four years of war.

In 1914, before the war started Britain had the largest and most effective navy in the world – it is still referred to as the Senior Service. It was needed to support and control the British Empire and its trade. The Royal Navy was admired and feared in equal measure throughout the world. On the other hand, the British Army was relatively small, comprising no more than 300,000–400,000 professional soldiers, compared to the armies of numerous European countries with over a million men each. Britain therefore looked potentially weak on land. As for the air – aircraft were in their infancy, and the Royal Air Force had yet to be created.

Over the four years of war, all of these services and their distinct identities would be developed, transformed, challenged and reorganised to create a more modern military. This was only possible because of the incredible men and women who served in these organisations at the time.

The Royal Navy

Following the creation of Germany in 1871, the German Kaiser began to develop his new country in the centre of Europe. When the Kaiser Wilhelm II took over in 1888, he wanted to expand Germany's influence and its control. One of the things he sought to do was to expand the German navy. Under the naval leadership of Alfred von Tirpitz, the Germans began to challenge the British in a naval arms race, especially from 1906 with the introduction of the modern battleship, the dreadnought. Britain claimed that it would make two dreadnoughts to each one that Germany built, and so the naval race began.

When war was declared, the Royal Navy had hundreds of ships and nearly double the dreadnoughts that Germany had. With over 200,000 sailors, Britain had the largest and most modern fleet. It did not need to undergo the massive recruitment drive that the army did, but it would still require extra volunteers and lots of support.

Jewish sailors had long been present in the Royal Navy; there was no bar on entry or rank, and they had served as officers and seamen. Many were already on ships when war was declared.

As soon as war was declared, the fleet was put into defensive and offensive positions; it blockaded the seaways of the enemy, laid mines, destroyed underwater communication cables and prepared to support British trade routes. The blockade made it problematic for the fleets of the Central Powers (Austria-Hungary, Germany, Bulgaria and the Ottoman Empire) to operate and for supplies to reach those countries. Germany, in turn, used its U-boats to attack British shipping and prevent supplies reaching the UK and the Western Front.

The U-boats quickly became Germany's strongest weapon at sea. One of the first recorded Jewish casualties of the war was a sailor, Stoker William Stern,[1] who was killed when his ship

HMS *Pathfinder* was sunk after being hit by a torpedo fired from a submarine on 5 September 1914. Stern was from Bishopsgate, London, and his name is on the Chatham Naval Memorial in Kent.

When a U-boat sunk the civilian ship *Lusitania* in May 1915, leading to the deaths of 1,198 people including 128 Americans, there was an international outcry. The Germans were forced to stop unrestricted U-boat activity following pressure from the Americans, although that agreement did not last beyond early 1917.

One of the youngest Jewish casualties of the First World War was also from the navy; Vivian George Edward Spencer Schreiber was born in February 1899. His father had been a major in the Suffolk Regiment, so military service was in the family. Having attended Bognor Naval Preparatory School, he joined the Royal Navy as a midshipman and was posted to HMS *Monmouth* on 4 August 1914. Schreiber was part of the British West Indies Squadron commanded by Rear Admiral Sir Christopher that took

Vivian George Edward Spencer Schreiber.

part in the Battle of Coronel on 1 November 1914 against the Germans off the coast of Chile. The British defeat in the battle and the sinking of the British cruisers *Good Hope* and *Monmouth* led to the deaths of 1,570 men including Schreiber. The British were appalled and angry at the loss and sent further ships to the area, defeating the German forces on 8 December 1914 at the Battle of the Falklands. Schreiber is remembered on the Plymouth Naval Memorial. He was only fifteen years of age (an acceptable age to have joined the Royal Navy) when he was killed.

Another Jewish sailor already part of the Royal Navy when the war started was Morris Moss Bright. Bright was born in 1890; both of his parents were UK citizens and had also been born in the UK. They were not a wealthy family, especially after Morris's father died when he was thirteen years old. He was the eldest of the five children and was keen to go out and make a living. In 1905 he told his mother that he needed her signature on a document to

Morris Moss Bright.

join the General Post Office as a telegram boy and she did (she was illiterate, and able to write only her name); instead he had enrolled as a boy entrant into the Royal Navy.

From an early age Morris had visited the docks and always wanted to go to sea, so becoming a sailor in the Royal Navy was something he was prepared to work hard for. Over the following years he rose up through the ranks to the position of warrant officer. In 1911, Winston Churchill, then First Lord of the Admiralty, introduced a regulation that 'men of the "Lower Deck" who are outstanding could apply for a commission'. In 1913, at the age of twenty-three, Morris was awarded his commission – the first Jewish man to go from the 'Lower' to the 'Upper Deck'. When the war started he was posted to the Minerva, a light cruiser, and dispatched to Africa where he fought in sea attacks on coastal forts in the area. That included the bombardment of Akaba. On 27 November 1914 he had a letter published in *The Jewish Chronicle* in which, with his captain's permission, he described the bombardment.

Now Officer Bright, he was involved in the landings and evacuation at Gallipoli. He went on to serve in the High Fleet and finished the war a full lieutenant. After the war he continued his studies at the Royal College, Greenwich. In 1920, although Bright retired from the navy to be with his wife and young family, he was given the post of lieutenant commander (retired) on the active list. In 1939, when the Second World War began, he returned to the navy, saw action and was awarded the DSC (Distinguished Service Cross). He was once again fortunate to survive the war and after its end returned to civilian life. A long-term supporter of the Association of Jewish Ex-Servicemen and Women, Bright became its national vice president. He died in 1965, proud of his contribution to the Royal Navy, the Jewish community and his country.

Approximately 354 Jewish men served in the Royal Navy during the war, and they fought in many key battles. A Jewish warrant officer was yeoman of the signals on board the admiral's ship at the momentous Battle of Jutland, while Lieutenant Commander R. Saunders received the DSO as part of his role in blocking Ostend and Zeebrugge in 1918.

At the start of the war, the Royal Naval Division was formed from the Royal Navy and the Royal Marine reservists and volunteers not needed at sea. This was to be an infantry division that would fight on land, first at Antwerp and then at Gallipoli. As the war went on, men of the Royal Naval Division would fight alongside the army across the Western Front. A total of 143 Jewish men served in the Royal Naval Division according to the British Jewry Book of Honour, from the lowest rank up to captain.

In 1917, it was apparent to all sections of the military that more men were needed to fight in front-line roles. Therefore, in 1917, the navy and the army created women's auxiliary units. The Women's Royal Naval Service (the WRENS) worked in admin, supplies, logistics, etc. They were very strictly prohibited from serving aboard ships – that would not change until 1990.

When peace was declared in 1918 the Royal Navy appeared to have had a relatively quiet war, but the reality was that serving on a ship always had its dangers. Many lives were lost at sea. Without the vigilance of the navy and the security it provided for Britain's shores and shipping, an Allied victory may not have been possible.

The British Army

The opening battles of 1914 proved immediately that thousands more men would be needed for the army, and recruitment quickly got underway. Men who had retired from the armed forces (while still young), those in the reserves and anyone who had been in a cadet force or Officer Training Corps) were the first to join up. Anglo-Jewry followed this pattern, although with the occasional hiccup. Undoubtedly the overwhelming majority of the 45,000–55,000 Jewish men who served did so in the army. When you look through the list in the British Jewry Book of Honour there are endless regiments represented. In *The Jewish Chronicle* and the *Jewish World* there were weekly reports and pictures of those who had joined up as well as the casualty lists and battle reports. Jews served in all the key battles – Mons, first, second and third Ypres, Loos, Gallipoli, Jutland, the Somme, Gaza, Arras, Messines, and so on. A week never went by without a report about a Jewish serviceman or women in the paper, and usually there was an addition to the casualties list as well. Some of the stories were straightforward battle reports or tales about families, while others could be quite light-hearted.

In September 1914 a Captain Vivian Lee wrote to *Jewish World* apologising that he couldn't attend a board of deputies meeting as the representative for North Shields as he was in Flanders with the Royal Army Service Corps. Letters were written to the newspapers from those who had enlisted encouraging others to join and to state that there were no problems for Jews in the services.

On 14 October 1914, a young private wrote to the paper about life at his training camp. It was published with the heading 'A Jew Boy in Kitchener's Army'. It goes on to report:

Pte S. Palmer No 2 Company, 7th Service Batt, Royal Berks Regiment form Sherrington Camp, Wilts 'I think,' he says, 'it is very lively and healthy here. For instance, we get plenty of food and hard training. It's absolutely jolly from morn till night. I am called Jew Boy Sam, and I might say that every soldier in the camp treats me as an old friend. I hope to have a smack at the Germans very shortly and sooner the better. My intended brother-in-law, H Rosen, has been good enough to send me a Jewish flag worked in silk, so I have combined it with the Union Jack and placed it outside of my tent, so that everyone who passes knows that Jew Boy Sam may be found here, a good sign of Jewish faith. My chums including another Yiddisher boy whose name is S. Lubeck, send the best respects and success to your paper.'

Examining the records, it looks as though the cheerful and committed S. Palmer survives the war, finishing as a corporal. 'Lubeck' goes on to be mentioned in despatches but is not as lucky as Palmer – Sidney Lubick of the Royal Berkshire Regiment is listed as killed in action on 25 September 1918 aged twenty-five. He is remembered on the Doiran Memorial in Greece, close to the border with Macedonia, one of the forgotten battlefronts, where the Allies were involved with heavy fighting from 1917 to 1918. His next of kin were his parents Mark and Sarah Lubick of London.

The *Jewish World* regularly included a double-page spread of images in its weekly edition during the war to show all those who had joined up, and it was particularly keen to showcase those families where numerous family members were serving. In the February 1916 issue of *Jewish World* there are pictures of the Woolf family. Mr and Mrs Woolf of Hove tell of their six sons and a grandson who are serving: Pte M. Woolf RAMC, Pte A. Woolf RAMC, 2nd Lieut J. Woolf 4th Battalion Australian Light Infantry, Pte Michael Woolf 1st East Sussex, Pte Samuel Woolf 17 KRR, Cpl E. Woolf RFA (in hospital) and Rifleman Michael Jay 17th KRR. There were regularly lists of three brothers, including the Haagmans and the Adlers both in the March 1916 edition of the *Jewish World*.

At various points during the war there were accusations that the Jewish community in Leeds was not doing enough – the pictures of the five brothers from the Leeds area in *Jewish World* in March 1916 helped to counter this. Four of the Harris brothers were serving with the West Yorks, while one was with the Middlesex regiment.

On 1 March 1916, *The Jewish Chronicle* reported on 'thirteen members of one family in the Colours' who between them covered all the services – Guards, Middlesex regiment, Royal Flying Corps, Royal Naval Air Service and the Royal Navy. Mrs Sanders, who was mother to seven of the family, had received a letter of thanks from His Majesty King George V.

Often letters of condolences were published in the Jewish press following the death of a serviceman, especially in the early days when encouragement about the nobility of sacrifice was still being promoted in all countries desperate for more volunteers. The following letter appeared in the 12 November 1915 edition of *The Jewish Chronicle*:

News has just reached Mr. Reuben Jacobs that his son Pte. Arthur Jacobs, 2/7 Batt London Regt., has been killed at the front. We now publish a letter addressed to the parents before the lad's departure for the fighting line. He wrote: 'Just a few lines telling you I am going abroad on Sunday, 15th inst. Dear Mother, do not worry about me because if I know that you are doing so you will put bad heart into me, so don't fret as I will be alright. Bear in mind there are thousands of others besides me. What I am doing is that I am protecting you and our family and home. I have not the slightest idea where we are going. It might be India, the Dardanelles or Malta. If anything happens to me it will be a deed of honour to our religion. If I come home safe and sound, you will be proud of me and we will be happy for ever.'

The letters and obituaries are reminders of how people viewed service and the war at the time. They are also a reminder that war made no discrimination between religion, rank and social status.

Arthur Charles Lionel Abrahams was born in London in January 1898. The family address was 18 Porchester Terrace, Hyde Park, which was just as exclusive and wealthy an address then as it is now. Arthur was the son of Sir Lionel, Financial Secretary to the Council of India. After attending Westminster School he went to Oxford in 1915, but he left the same year with a commission to the Coldstream Guards. His obituary was published in *The Jewish Chronicle* in April 1918, shortly after his death:

He had been an attractive child and had grown into a most lovable man, robust in intellect, affectionate in disposition, modest in his successes, imbued with a deep Jewish feeling and looking forward to being of use to his people. He gave early evidence of inheritance of intellect above the average from his gifted parents. In 1911 he was elected to a King's Scholarship at Westminster School where he instantly became, and always maintained, immense popularity with his master and his fellow pupils.

In 1915 he obtained a Scholarship at Christ Church Oxford but immediately joined the Army in accordance with his ardent longing to be of service to his country. He had already reached the rank of sergeant in the school O.T.C. and was gazetted to the Coldstream Guards. In the Army, as in school, his unassuming ability won him the confidence of his superiors, and the affection of his comrades.

The commanding officer with whom he served during the greater part of his service abroad has written to Sir Lionel Abrahams, 'I knew your boy well and was commanding the battalion when he joined. He was most popular with all ranks, and he was particularly fearless ... Arthur was a Coldstream Guarder through and through. He fought like one and he died like one.' The colonel commanding the Guards wrote: 'The regiment can ill afford to lose men like him', and from the ranks there has reached his family the equally prized message: 'The boys would follow him wherever he wanted them to.'

His father died the following year, and in his obituary it was said that he never got over the blow of his son's death.

Diaries and Letters

One of the advantages of researching events which took place a century ago is that men and women were far more likely to write letters or keep a diary than they are today. Louis Harris was born in 1890. He trained as a master tailor before joining the North Staffordshire Regiment in 1916. Throughout the war he kept a diary in which he recorded some of his experiences: 'Hours further agony, falling in shell holes and slipping about carrying heavy loads we go into the trenches.'

Louis Harris.

He also records, 'Somehow I was left alone with the dead mules etc., I felt real panicky. I remember the New Zealander who took my place in the trench asking me what it was like and I told him it was not too bad as I did not want to make it sound as it was actually fearful!!' At one point in his diary he apologises for going two weeks without writing, stating that he simply felt 'too miserable'.[2] Louis survived the war and returned to be a tailor once more. He did not pass away until 1984.

Lewis Henry Phillips went to Haberdashers' Aske's Hampstead School, serving in the school cadet corps before leaving in June 1913. He joined the army in October 1915 and received a commission in January 1916 in the Royal Field Artillery. He kept a diary, some of which has survived. In it he reveals his boredom, his fears and how awful the weather often was. After a quite serious injury to his back and hip from a horse falling on him, Phillips returned to his unit and finished the war. He survived the conflict and went on to study chemistry, as he had originally planned to do if the war hadn't come along.

Marcus Segal was born on 5 December 1896 in Newcastle-Upon-Tyne, later moving to Kilburn in London with his family. After school he went straight into the London Regiment. He was then commissioned (made into an officer) as a temporary second lieutenant in the 16th Battalion King's Liverpool Regiment on 29 October 1915. In September 1916, Segal was part of the British forces serving in France where he wrote regularly to his family.

He was very proud of his Jewish identity and religion, and through his letters we know that he asked his parents to 'let Grandma know I have been carrying on my work as a Good Jew'. He also tried to arrange Jewish services in the trenches with chaplains Revd Jacob Phillips and Revd Adler and to participate in Jewish festivals such as Succot:

I had my last dug-out full of leaves on top in honour of Succot but I dare not put any fruit hanging as fruit would not hang long here ... life out here makes one very religious and it makes one think what the Almighty can do ... we get issued with biscuits just like Matza.

His letters reveal some of the tedium of warfare as well as the fear, as in this missive from 23 April 1917:

I am writing this letter at 11.40 pm and am very very tired as we have done a lot of heavy fighting today and have been very successful as no doubt you will read about. It was not my turn for over the top today and have been in Reserve all day and have had the benefit of Fritz bombardment all day but the Battery T.G. has suffered no casualties. It has been a gorgeous day and such an Artillery barrage from our guns has never been witnessed in this War and never likely to be. My servant has just come up from Arras and tells me there is a parcel of magazines awaiting me. He has brought me this book and the enclosed was inside and when I shewed it to the Captain it was the first hearty laugh he has had today. There is practically nothing to write you and so writing this in a very cold dug-out by means of candle-light. I have just collared this German ink so excuse the colour. I am hearing quite well and all I want is to get home and see your dear faces once again. I must now conclude.

Heaps of love, God bless you,

Your loving son, Marcus

Marcus had always been keen on sport and was the head of the sports committee for his regiment. He played football and rugby: 'Yesterday we had a quick game of rugby against the Brigade staff and had a fine game. I came back full of bruises just as in olden times.' In letters back home to his sisters he talks about reading a lot but also finding time to play sports and poker, listen to music and write home. He frequently requested that his gramophone be sent to him so that he could play music.

It is through his letters that we also know that Marcus was a very popular officer with his fellow officers and men and made many friends: 'I have met men galore I know out here and it makes matters very much jollier ... naturally I am somewhat popular as I am jack of all trades.'

For many soldiers at the front, letters from home were an essential part of keeping up morale. Marcus wrote, 'I had no letters from home yesterday and felt very disappointed as that's all we look forward to and keep awake to absurd hours to see if there are any letters for us, so you can imagine how we appreciate any correspondence and especially from our dear ones.'

Marcus Segal was killed by a shell at Arras on 19 June 1917. He is buried in Faubourg D'Amiens Cemetery, Arras. He was only twenty when he died. The Jewish Military Museum has 150 letters written by him.

Ernest Michael Green, another prolific letter writer, was born in London and went to St Paul's School. In addition to being a member of the OTC, he was interested in youth work and volunteered with a number of East End clubs that supported the Jewish poor, such as the JLB and the Brady Street Club. He left his accountancy practice at the start of the war and joined the Inns of Court Officer Training Corps. He was later commissioned into the Hampshire Regiment.

Green wrote sixty-seven letters during his time in the army. In a letter from 1916 he writes that 'since my last letter we have been shifting about the place doing nothing in particular, in consequence

Ernest Michael Green.

I have nothing to write about'. In another letter he asks his mother to send a cookery book as they have been using a primus stove to do some cooking on. In 1916 he is moved with his regiment to the Somme ready for the battle there. He was killed on 3 September 1916 and his parents were sent his final letter, which according to the notation on the top was in his uniform pocket with instructions to send it if he has been killed. In it he writes, 'I am not going to write a long letter but I want to thank you both for bringing me into this world and for bringing me up in it ... I only pray that I may meet my end as an Englishman and a Jew should. I have always been proud to have been both.' He is buried at Serre Road Cemetery, Somme, France.

Key Battles

Unsurprisingly, it has been much easier to find the records of those killed than to provide a list of all the men who served in the key battles, which is almost impossible. However, using the British

Jewry Book of Honour it is possible to isolate some of those killed at specific times, and using battle diaries and other records we can explore in more detail some of the men who were there.

The Battle of the Somme is probably the most famous battle of the First World War, unfortunately not for the successes of the battle but because of the terrible death toll on the first day. After weeks of planning and a week-long bombardment of 1.6 million shells fired at the German lines, the British attacked on a 15-mile front in the Somme region of northern France on 1 July 1916. It was supposed to be the day that broke the deadlock. Instead, strong German defensive positions and poor communications resulted in the largest casualty numbers the British had ever experienced in a single day. There were 58,000 British troop casualties, over 19,000 of them fatal; over the coming months, many more would succumb to their wounds. The lists of the casualties appeared in all the newspapers; *The Jewish Chronicle* and *Jewish World* were no different.

From the lists provided and the records subsequently proffered we can prove that there were thirty-two reported Jewish deaths on that first day:

Captain C. L. Hart, West Riding Regiment, London
Second Lieutenant J. Josephs, London Regiment, London
Second Lieutenant M. G. Klean, Northumberland Fusiliers, London
Second Lieutenant W. A. Kohn, East Lancashire Regt, London
Captain R. Litten, Royal Berks. Regt, London
Rfm S. Abrahams, London Regt, London
Pte P. Braham, King's Liverpool Regt, Liverpool
Pte B. Cohen, Manchester Regt, Manchester
Pte J. Cohen, King's Liverpool Regt, Liverpool
Rfm J. Cohen, Rifle Brigade, London

Rfm J. David, London Regt, London

CSM H. S. Davis MC, East Yorks. Regt, London

L/Cpl E. Gerber, Lancashire Fusiliers, Manchester

L/Cpl S. Gilbert, London Regt, London

Rfm M. Gordon, London Regt, London

Rfm B. Griew, London Regt, London

Pte A. Hansell, Manchester Regt, Manchester

Rfm S. Hart, London Regt, London

Pte A. Isaacs, London Regt, London

Pte A Lappin, R.W. Surrey Regt, London

L/Cpl H. Levy, Devon Regt, London

Pte L. Levy, Hants. Regt, London

Rfm D. H. Marcus, London Regt, London

Pte H. Pitt, R. Warwick Regt, Birmingham

Rfm J. Polakoff, K.R.R.C., London

Cpl E. J. Ramus, London Regt, Harrogate

Pte H. Rosenberg (Ross), West Riding Regt, Leeds

Pte M. Rosenthal, Lancashire Fusiliers, Manchester

L/Cpl W. Shenow, R. Berks. Regt, London

Rfm J. Tobias, London Regt, London

Rfm J. D. Weiner, London Regt, London

Pnr H. L. Woolf, 1st Bn. Special Bde. R. E. London (also listed elsewhere as being killed on 29 June 1916)

While any number of these men are worthy of investigation, it is L/Cpl H. Levy, Devon Regt., London, who has always caught my attention. L/Cpl H. Levy's headstone with its lone Star of David sits in the Devonshire Trench Cemetery on the Somme. The Devonshire Trench contains 163 graves, only two of which are not from the Devonshire Regiment. While the Jewish community in Devon was far more widespread in 1914 than it is today, with the exception of Plymouth and Exeter, the county has never been famous for its large Jewish community. Is H. Levy from one of those cities? After some research, it appears he is not. Harold Levy was from Whetstone, Middlesex. His registered next of kin is his mother, Elsie Levy, of 1 Guy Cliff Cottage, Oakley Road, Whetstone, London.

In the 1901 census, the Levy family is listed as being at the Whetstone address. Harold is listed as being three years of age with a slightly older brother, Herbert, and a sister, Miriam. His father is listed as Joseph. On the documents for his death in 1916 only his mother Elsie is mentioned and she is listed as receiving his final probate of £1 9s 2d. Aside from that, nothing else has come to light thus far about Harold or his family, but he is significant, not just because of his sacrifice but because of where he lays. At the entrance to the Devonshire Trench Cemetery is the statement 'The Devonshires held this trench, the Devonshires hold it still'. Harold may not have been born in Devon but through his service

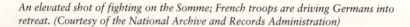

An elevated shot of fighting on the Somme; French troops are driving Germans into retreat. (Courtesy of the National Archive and Records Administration)

and his death he will now always be a 'Devonshire', his story entwined with those of the other 162 men in that cemetery and with those of all the men of Britain who served. Anglo-Jewish history is British history.

The lists of Jewish casualties continued to be published throughout the Battle of the Somme, which did not end until 8 November 1916, with approximately 420,000 British casualties, 195,000 French casualties and around 650,000 German casualties.

Another of the famous battles, the Third Battle of Ypres, more popularly known as Passchendaele, also saw heavy Jewish casualties. Over 350 Jews are known to have been killed under British command during the period of intense fighting between 31 July and 10 November 1917 in the Ypres area of Flanders. One of those is Alfred Abraham Pampel, from London, another former pupil of Stepney Jewish School. He fought in the battle with the King's Royal Rifle Corps. He was killed on 8 August 1917 and

The notorious mud of Passchendaele. (Courtesy of the National Archives and Records Administration)

like so many in that battle he has no known grave, and is instead remembered on the Menin Gate. Shortly after his death, his mother was sent a letter from a fellow soldier:

Dear Mrs Pampel,

I have just had my last letter to Alfred returned marked 'Killed in Action' and am hoping that some mistake has been made as in your letter you said he was still in hospital.

If however the worst has happened, allow me to express, as one of his chums, my sympathy and sorrow with you in your loss. We did nearly all our soldiering together, doing our training together and going out in the same draft and I have lost a good lad and one who was so well liked by all the boys in the platoon.

If you have not heard very much from the regiment, I will write to one of the men from his platoon and find out all I can for you.

I shall be in London very soon on sick leave and shall be very pleased to call on you.

Yours sincerely,

A Johnes[3]

The letter shows the bonds that were formed between many men as a result of the conflict. Men who may never have met during peacetime found friendship when it was needed.

Across the UK and Home to Blighty

They came from all across the UK. While the majority came from the cities of London and Manchester, there were soldiers from many locations, such as Lewis Moses from Birmingham. He was one of thirteen children who enlisted and became a gunner in the Royal Garrison Artillery; he was killed on 22 July 1917 and is buried at Hedge Row Trench Cemetery, Belgium.

There were two very different men from South Wales. Andrew (Albert) Moss Belman, who was born in South Wales in 1888, was one of seven children from a very ordinary background. He became a signaller with the Lancashire Fusiliers and was killed during the Battle of Arras on 22 April 1917. He is buried at Gorre British and Indian Cemetery, France. Nathan Leonard Harris, on the other hand, was born in 1894 in Wales, and the family home was in Newport. He went to a good school before going to University College Cardiff. He was commissioned to the Royal Welsh Fusiliers and served at the Battle of the Somme. He was awarded the Military Cross. Below is his citation:

For conspicuous gallantry and devotion to duty as acting adjutant in an attack. When the enemy forced the front line back from some high ground he went forward and led his men in the face of the enemy's fire and recaptured the position. It was greatly due to his gallant conduct in moving along the line to reorganise regardless of the enemy's fire that the battalion was ready to meet an attack which was delivered shortly afterwards.

Andrew Moss Belman.

He was killed on 28 August 1918 and is buried at Chocques Military Cemetery, France.

Louis Blint was born in Dublin in 1897 but brought up in Glasgow. He enlisted in 1915, joining up with the Highland Light Infantry. He survived the war, with some lung damage due to gas, finishing as a lance-corporal. He returned to Glasgow after the war, dying there in 1972.

There was also Harry Racionzer, who seemed to get around a bit as a result of the war. He was born in 1896 in Barony, Glasgow, and when he enlisted he was assigned to the Northumberland Fusiliers. After he was seriously injured in spring 1917 he was returned to Britain. He died in a hospital in Liverpool and is buried at Liverpool (Broad Green) Jewish Cemetery, Lancashire.

Arthur Teacher was born in Cornwall in 1898 but enlisted in 1914, meaning that he must have lied about his age. He joined the King's Royal Rifle Corps. While at school in Essex he took an interest in religion, according to family legend:

> His parents were fairly strict at keeping to the rules of Judaism. At school during R.E. the Jewish boys were sent to the back of the room and told to read the Old Testament. Arthur was interested in what the teacher was saying and learnt about Jesus. During the exam, the boys were told to just answer the Old Testament questions but he also answered the questions on Jesus. He won the prize, which was a Bible, and had to smuggle it home so his mother didn't see.[4]

Arthur survived the war, dying in 1956. He had two brothers who also served: Albert, who was a drummer, and Nathan, who was in the RAF. All of them survived the war.

The stories of some men indicate not only how far some people travelled prior to the First World War seeking work and

Arthur Teacher.

opportunities but also how far people were prepared to travel in order to serve in the war.

Emanuel Bigofski was born in Stepney in 1897. In 1901, his father, Barnett, is listed as a bootmaker, working from home. By 1911, Barnett had become a butcher, living in Tottenham with his wife, Sarah, and daughters Celia, twenty, and Pauline, sixteen, in five rooms above the shop. Most of the rest of the family lived in another house around the corner – Becky, twenty-three, a dressmaker; Saul (Solomon) and Emanuel, fourteen; and Louis, ten, are all listed as students. In early 1915, Emanuel and Solomon travelled to the USA on the SS *St Louis*, giving their occupations as butchers. Emanuel returned some months later and enlisted on 2 November 1915. He served with the Labour Corps, was injured during the Third Battle of Ypres and died on 9 October 1917. He is buried at Lijssenthoeck Military Cemetery, Belgium.

On 5 January 1916, *Jewish World* ran a story from the *Yorkshire Observer* entitled 'Two Thousand Miles to Serve' about one Henry Grews:

> At a time when, rightly or wrongly, the Jews of Leeds are being submitted to rather severe censure owing to an alleged disinclination on their part to heed the call to arms, the story of this stirring action of one of their compatriots who formerly lived in the city comes to force. Henry Grews was born in Leeds 22 years earlier but moved to America with his parents (Russian born Jews). In Boston he was a 'British Jew'. He sailed for Glasgow and immediately joined the 5th Scottish Rifles after a 2000-mile journey.

The *Jewish World* reporter added: 'Bravo Henry Grews. He is lucky too not to have fallen in with a recruiting officer who would have rejected him.'

Recruits' names and regions of origin do not always correspond with the regiments in which they serve, and this can sometimes be confusing. As early as September 1914 *The Jewish Chronicle* reported on one Private Isaac Levy from Leeds, who was serving with the Royal Munster Fusiliers (an Irish regiment). In a story that follows on from a report about Levy being in a military hospital in the UK suffering from 'poisoning/gastritis', the background to his being in an Irish regiment is told:

> Private Levy ... is not the only Jew in the Munsters, the Irish lads have two other Hebrew comrades who bear, however, the unlikely

Isaac Levy.

names of Sergeant Jacks and Private Callagher. Strange but true. Private Levy left them at the Front 'hearty and well'. Indeed it was Sergeant Jacks an old chum who got Levy to enlist 10 and a half years ago. Levy was in Ireland and three years in the army seemed like a holiday – he joined the Irish men. He has been to Gibraltar and India. Six and a half years ago he returned to tailoring in Leeds. Then as a reservist he was called back to the Colours, was taken to Le Havre and then to Mons where he was soon in action.

Of course, as the war progressed many Jews changed or anglicised their names, and just like any other soldier they could find themselves serving with pretty much any regiment if they were required.

Some of those killed are buried or commemorated on memorials far around the world in battle zones more familiar to us today than in the First World War. Joseph Herberts, who was born in Birmingham in 1886 and later moved to Blackburn, is on the Basra Memorial in Iraq. His obituary in the local paper reads:

Joseph Herberts, of the Machine Gun Corps, has been killed in action in Mesopotamia. Joining the East Lancs in

September 1914, he was transferred to the machine Gun Corps and took part in the capture of Kut and Bagdad. Sergt. Herberts, who rendered much valuable assistance in the British Forces as a Scout during the Boer War, is the third Jewish soldier from Blackburn to have fallen. An upholsterer by trade, he was well respected by Jews and Christians alike. He leaves a widow and three children. It may be added that 99 per cent of the Jewish boys in Blackburn who were born in this country are in khaki, a record for any town in the United Kingdom.[5]

Underage

In the early stages of the war, before the many wounded began to return, the conflict held an element of excitement. It was every young man's duty to serve according to the posters, the newspaper reporters and public speakers in schools and clubs, and of the 6 million men who served in the British Army, an estimated 250,000 of them joined up when they were underage. The Jewish community was no exception; boys as young as fourteen would borrow their brother's, uncle's or father's documents or simply lie to the recruitment officer. The boys had to be eighteen years of age to join and nineteen years of age to be deployed overseas, but many recruitment officers (who were paid 2s 6d for each recruit) were willing to overlook details like official documentation.

For some boys it wasn't just the sense of adventure; the army provided pay, regular food and a uniform, things that might not have been so readily available at home. Furthermore, many of these young men were already working, having left school at fourteen – they didn't see why joining the army would be any different to any other rotten form of employment.

Morris Wein was born in 1899 in Stepney, East London. According to records he enlisted in 1914 when he was only fifteen years old.

As a former member of the Jewish Lads' Brigade, he will have been able to fit into training quite quickly when he joined the Queen's Own (Royal West Kent) Regiment. Evidently his family either didn't know that he had enlisted or they didn't mind; with six other children, it is possible that they simply saw this as one less mouth to feed. Wein served for four years before being killed in action on 27 September 1918. He is buried at Gouzeaucourt New British Cemetery, France.

In another case, so desperate to enlist was Jack Mendelovitch that he made three attempts. Jack was born in St George in the East, London, in November 1898. Jack joined the British Army in 1914, when he was only sixteen years of age. When his mother, Fay, found out, she revealed his true age and had him withdrawn. Jack then enlisted again at the age of seventeen, and once again his mother had him removed. In 1916, when Jack had turned eighteen, he was called up to serve his country.

Jack carried a cigarette case in his breast pocket, and one time he opened it and inside found not only his cigarettes but also a

Jack Mendelovitch.

German bullet it had stopped. Fortunately, Jack himself survived the war completely unscathed. He went on to marry, and ran a successful business. He died in 1958.

Abraham Bevistein was not so fortunate. Bevistein's family were from Warsaw in Poland and travelled to the UK when he was three years old. He was very much an East End British Jewish boy. Inspired by the call to arms, Bevistein enlisted in September 1914 when he was only fifteen years of age. He joined the 11th Battalion of the Middlesex Regiment, enlisting under the name of Harris, and his family only knew what he had done when he returned home in uniform. After basic training he spent most of 1915 on the Western Front, where he was wounded in December. His injuries were not considered serious, and he was returned to duties.

On 12 or 13 February 1916, Bevistein was deafened by a grenade and probably shell-shocked. He asked for medical help but was sent back to his trench. Instead of doing as the medical officer told him, he went off to the rear. In a letter he wrote to his mother he said: 'We were in the trenches and I was ill so I went out ... They've taken me to prison and I'm in a bit of trouble now.' He was court-martialled for desertion and executed on 20 March 1920. He was still only seventeen years of age – underage for service and for execution. He was buried in Labourse Cemetery, France. He has a standard Commonwealth War Graves Commission headstone; there is no mention of how he died.

A total of 305 British and Commonwealth soldiers were executed under the laws governing military punishments during the First World War. They have all now been posthumously pardoned.

The Royal Flying Corps (RFC), the Royal Naval Air Service (RNAS) and the Royal Air Force (RAF)

In 1914, air power and aircraft were very much in their infancy. The Royal Flying Corps was formed in 1912 and the Royal Naval

Air Service just before the outbreak of war. Between them they had fewer than 200 planes. Aircraft were very basic, made from stretched canvas, wood and wires. Their initial role was in reconnaissance, which was essential once the trench lines of the Western Front became static. Pilots flew over enemy lines and beyond to report on what they had seen. The first cameras used on planes were heavy and difficult to operate, and it took some time for specially crafted cameras and radios to be designed and installed. Initially a pilot had to fly low enough to commit to memory what he could see and then repeat that information once he had landed.

One of the first 100 English officers to qualify as a pilot was Jewish – Cecil Hoffnung Marks. He was born in December 1887 and grew up in a privileged family, attending Eton College before going on to become a career soldier by commissioning in 1906. He qualified as a pilot on 9 May 1911 and transferred to the Royal Flying Corps. In October 1915 he was on a reconnaissance mission over Saint Quentin, France, when it was reported that he was attacked and fatally shot down by a German aircraft. His observer, Lieutenant Will Lawrence, brother of Lawrence of Arabia, was also killed. They were both buried at the German Soldiers' Cemetery and then moved to St Souplet British Cemetery after the war. In 1919 there was a report through a German source that the two men had in fact landed and been murdered, but this has never been proven.

Being a pilot could be extremely dangerous, and in 1915 the life expectancy of an Allied pilot was approximately seventeen hours of flying time, or just eleven days. This was due to a combination of factors: fragile aircraft, low flying, enemy attack and unpredictable weather conditions. Although pilots on both sides experienced similar problems, the German planes were more advanced, and this meant they suffered fewer losses.

Light railways in the trench system at Arras. (Courtesy of the National Archives and Records Administration)

It wasn't always fighting the enemy that made flying risky – training was dangerous too because of the unsophisticated aircraft. Myer Joseph Levine was born in Norwich on 10 September 1899, attending grammar school there. He first enlisted as a private in the Northumberland Fusiliers but was transferred to the Royal Flying Corps. Part of the newly formed RAF, Levine was killed in an aerial collision near Stamford, Lincolnshire, on 8 May 1918. He is buried in the Jewish Cemetery in Norwich. Tragically, in the same cemetery is his brother, Pvt Cyril Isaac Levine, who served in the 112th Coy Machine Gun Corps. Cyril was seriously wounded at the Battle of Arras in 1917 and died in the UK of his wounds aged twenty.

Another was Leonard Judah Fleet, from Manchester, who was killed on 27 October 1917 and is listed as having been 'accidently [*sic*] killed whilst flying'. He is buried at Manchester (Phillips Park) Cemetery, and was only twenty-two when he died.

Others were killed in accidents a long way from home, such as Solomon Fine, known as Solly. Solly was born in Monmouthshire, South Wales, in 1899 but he grew up in Southend, attending school there, and joined Southend Technical School Cadet Corp. Solly was in the Essex Motor Volunteer Corps (EMVC) based in Hamlet Court Road for some months, his squadron commander describing him as 'smart, capable and most intelligent' when recommending his application for the Inns of Court Training Corps. However, Solomon enlisted as a private with the Machine Transport section of the Army Service Corps (ASC) in February 1917, serving as a driver.

He had been a driver for five months when he was recommended for a transfer to the Royal Flying Corps (RFC). He qualified as a pilot and was in France when he and his observer were caught up in a thunderstorm that put his aircraft out of control. He died on 18 May 1918. A letter from his flight commander read:

I am writing on behalf of the officers of A Flight to express our heartfelt sympathy at the loss you have sustained through the death of our gallant comrade. Although he had not been with us long he was very popular and showed signs of being one of our most useful pilots. His work was the preliminary of, alas! what might have been. As I was his Flight Commander for some time I knew him very intimately and have never met such an enthusiastic pilot before. As long as there is a squadron in France, his name will always be remembered. In another packet I am sending you photographs of his resting place. The memorial at the head was made by his own mechanics and daily the French children come and place flowers there. It will be a comfort to you that he died as he lived, a very gallant gentleman. When his country called he answered freely and his death has made a milestone on our road to victory.[6]

As the war progressed, the aircraft were improved, and their uses became more sophisticated. They were flown not only for reconnaissance but also to communicate what was happening during a battle, initially through dropping pre-agreed colour-coded streamers and eventually by radio. Guns were fixed on to the planes so that they could become armed instruments of war, leading to some dramatic dogfights and aerial displays. In the latter stages of the war, the aircraft were used for dropping propaganda and small bombs.

The expanding role and importance of air power in the conflict led to many recognising the importance of a co-ordinated air fleet, and on 29 November 1917 an Act of Parliament created the new Royal Air Force (RAF), which formally came into being on 1 April 1918. The new RAF was an amalgamation of the RFC and the RNAS, and it was the first, separate air force in the world. It was also the first British military service to have a women's wing from the very start – the WRAF was formed from some of those serving with the WAAC and the WRNS.

One Jewish man who joined the RNAS and finished with the RAF was Isaak Henry Woolf Barnato. He was keen to serve and he applied immediately when war was declared, but he was initially rejected, with no reason given. It may, however, have been due to him listing himself as head of household with the care of his widowed mother. Undaunted, he tried again on 15 September 1914 and this time was accepted. He earned his Aviator's Certificate at RNAS Eastbourne on 20 August 1915. He was involved in one of the earliest examples of aircraft attacking using bombs when he was involved with the bombardment of Constantinople. He was a captain when he died from influenza in October 1918.

Another victim of illness rather than accident or fighting was Michael Crook of Sunderland. He was serving as a carpenter, repairing wooden airframes in Kantara East, Egypt. He contracted pneumonia and died on 5 February 1919 at twenty-nine years of age. He is buried at Kantara War Memorial Cemetery, Egypt.

According to the British Jewry Book of Honour, approximately 260 Jewish men served in the RAF as officers and approximately 2,073 Jewish men were listed as NCOs and other ranks. Some of the officers were awarded the Distinguished Flying Cross. It was also observed that a number of Jewish tailors were recruited to work on the fabric used to cover the aircraft and make them safe and secure. One of these was Joseph Conn, born 1896 in East London. He is listed as being an 'Air Mechanic 2/Sailmaker' and had a relatively safe war on the ground in the UK. Similarly, Frederick Michael Green, or Fred, from Paddington in London, completed his training to become a civil engineer and became an engineer in the RAF. Frederick was awarded the Commendation for Home War Service for efforts contributing to war work in England.

For some the RAF offered an opportunity for excitement even as the war finished. Henry Bader was born on January 1900 in London. He enlisted in 1914 at only fourteen years of age, giving his age as nineteen. According to his family he was inspired to join up through a mixture of patriotism and a desire to avoid working in the family business, his father Jacob's chain of ladies' hairdressing establishments in London.

According to the story given by Henry's son Lawrence for We Were There Too,

In order to delay his return, he joined the French Fire Brigade in Calais, France. He rose to the rank of Pompier Premier Classe but in 1921, there was a very rainy summer and fires were few and far between. He was made redundant.

'Good,' his father Jacob said. 'Now Henry will come home.' But Henry was still reluctant to turn his hand to ladies' hairdressing and in 1921 he joined the Royal Air Force. He was trained as a bomb-aimer and navigator and was sent to Baghdad where the UK had responsibilities.

He flew every day from Baghdad to Basra and returned to deliver forces' mail. He sat in the rear seat of an open two-seater bi-plane. The pilot for his eighteen-month service was T. E. Lawrence, known as Lawrence of Arabia ... In 1931, I arrived and I was named Lawrence to commemorate my father's brush with fame.[7]

Henry Bader later went into the family business of hairdressing, and died in 1969.

The range of Jewish contribution is broad. All areas of the services appear to have some form of Jewish representation, in all the different theatres of war around the globe and in the many military occupations. Jewish servicemen are some of the earliest casualties, and also some of the very last; Philip Marcus Levy, born in Sunderland and serving with the 9th Battalion of the Yorkshire Regiment, was killed aged twenty-one on 6 November 1918. He is buried in France with the inscription 'Always in our thoughts'.

Henry Bader.

4

NURSES, DOCTORS AND HOSPITALS AT HOME AND ABROAD

There was no National Health Service in 1914 but most towns and all cities had hospitals with trained medical staff paid for by individual donations and rich sponsors. Many of those hospitals offered professional training for women to become nurses. Some of the courses were relatively short while others would take three years; it depended on the patients they were to attend to and the level of medical care they were expected to give. Organisations such as the Union of Jewish Women, which was created in 1902 to help promote training and education to Jewish women, in particular to be nurses or governesses, offered one way for women to afford their training. Initially the Union of Jewish Women was an organisation of wealthy women trying to assist the Jewish lower classes in the cities, but in the years just before the war its work began to expand and it also encouraged and supported the education and training of some middle-class women.

Military Nurses

The British military decided in 1866 that nurses should be formally appointed to military general hospitals. This was followed by the creation of the Army Nursing Service in 1881. Women recruited to the service served in military hospitals in the UK but were also dispatched to the Boer War in South Africa, Sudan, Egypt and anywhere that a British medical hospital was established.

There was no doubting the impact that professionally trained medical teams of doctors and nurses could have on survival and recovery rates for injured and sick servicemen. Having men recover and return to service was an asset in a professional army such as Britain's, where an endless pool of conscripted recruits did not exist. The Royal Army Medical Corps was formed by royal warrant on 23 June 1898 and the Director General of the Army Medical Services, Alfred Keogh, placed army nursing sisters of the Army Nursing Services into the war establishment of the Medical Services in 1901. In 1902, the War Office officially formed the Queen Alexandra's Imperial Military Nursing Service (QAIMNS) under a royal warrant to replace the Army Nursing Service and the Indian Nursing Service.

QAIMNS

The QAIMNS nursing service was the first official female unit formally attached to the British military at the start of the First World War. All women in the QAIMNS had to be qualified nurses with three years' training in a civilian hospital, aged between twenty-five and thirty-five, educated, single and from 'good families' with a 'good reputation' before they could join. The QAIMNS nurses were stationed all over the UK and frequently very close to the front lines wherever the British troops were fighting. These nurses often risked their own safety and health to carry out their duties. A number were injured while close to the front line and in some instances they were killed if the location they were working in came under attack. Some of the strict recruitment conditions were relaxed once war broke out and the need for nurses increased, but certainly not the rules about training and good character.

There was a particularly large increase in the QAIMNS reserves once the war started; this was due to there being fewer than

200 members of the reserve available for mobilisation in August 2014. The women were initially to serve at military hospitals in the UK, but this quickly changed as the severity of the fighting was realised and instead they were sent to all the theatres of fighting.

One woman keen to join the QAIMNS was Florence Oppenheimer, born on 13 April 1882 in Islington, North London, into a large middle-class Sephardi family. Oppenheimer's parents had no expectation that she should work. However, she wanted to become a nurse and engaged her brother to lobby her father on her behalf. Her brother was able to convince their father that she should be allowed to train as a nurse at a good hospital and she went to the Royal Sussex Hospital in Brighton in 1911. She passed her three years of training and was ready for a professional posting when the war started.

As a professionally trained nurse she was able to join the QAIMNS and she did so after seeing their recruitment campaigns. On 19 July 1915 she travelled with them into the warzone of the Middle East. She noted in her diary: 'There are 80 sisters on board (the greatest number that has ever gone out together), 400 officers (169 of which are RAMC) and I think about 11,000 men. Nobody knows where they are going to, but there are rumours that we going to a small island much nearer the Dardanelles than Alexandria.'

Her journey was risky, as enemy ships and U-boats were around to prevent support reaching Allied locations in their attacks against Turkey; her ship was accompanied by a torpedo destroyer. The nurses mixed with the doctors and the officers, having to act as their own chaperones as there were none officially appointed – quite an unusual thing for many of the young men and women who were now together.

Much to Florence's surprise, she even received a proposal of marriage on her journey, which she found quite funny:

> The very atmosphere makes people very sentimental. After chatting for a couple of days to an apparently quite serious doctor he was foolish enough to propose to me this afternoon. I wanted to laugh at him, however, he really seemed in earnest so I thought the best way out was to tell him my religion, in any case that hurt his feelings least. I cannot think what made him do it. I certainly had not encouraged him at all. He is a Roman Catholic ... Ah me: it is a funny world.

For much of the journey she was bored – there was indecision about where the medical staff should be based, and they were provided with very little information about where they were travelling to and how long it would take. She wrote in her diary on 4 August 1915: 'Where are they going to take us? Do they think we all want a holiday at the government's expense? We are all thoroughly sick of it all.'

Within days the situation had changed, however, and on 6 August another major assault on the Dardanelles resulted in lots of casualties. Florence was transferred to the hospital ship *Alounia*, near the Turkish island of Imbros, to take care of the injured. On 8 August she recorded:

> I got landed right in the depths of the boat, a dreadful hole with nearly hardly any air. This was supposed to be for minor cases but of course lots of serious ones got sent down as well ... when I got my 200 men fairly well settled in bed I wandered upstairs ... but stretcher bearers were simply piling in so I stayed in another ward and got them fairly comfortable. Then I heard that stretcher

cases were going down to my ward – down I flew … Leaving a Doctor in charge of my men I went for a lie down for 2 hours. Then up again to hear that we were going to take on another 800 stretcher cases and by breakfast time we had 1,980 cases on board. At last I realised what war really meant. All these cases straight from the battlefield and other ships all around us also taking the poor fellows on as fast as ever they could. All the deck, every hole and corner of the place was utilised.

Half the Sisters went off onto another ship during the morning leaving us with our proper number – 12 – two of these were ill so we had 10 to look after nearly 2000 patients.

There is no doubt that the QAIMNS saw the real force of warfare and felt its dangers. After the Gallipoli withdrawal Florence was based in Egypt for a time at one of the military hospitals. She found Egypt quite lonely at times and started to attend one of the local synagogues, where she then met up with other British Jews who were serving out there as well as some local Egyptian Jewish families. While there she recorded in her diary a meeting with Norman Bentwich and his wife. Bentwich was serving as a Captain in the Camel Transport Corps.[1]

In 1917 she returned to England and spent some time at a Canterbury Military Hospital, taking charge of the Jewish patients and attending a special service at the synagogue at Canterbury. From there she went to a London hospital but she became bored with the simple routine and applied for a transfer back to Egypt. There were plenty of battles in the Middle East during 1918 and wounded men were regularly sent to Alexandria for treatment. She was there when the Armistice was announced and within a few months Florence was offered a chance to leave the QAIMNS and return home. She declined the offer and instead signed on for a further six months; however, by autumn 1919 she felt too tired to extend her contract again and returned home to England in December 1919.

Florence Oppenheimer had served four years in a distant theatre of war doing a dangerous job and yet her military contribution is largely unknown. Interestingly enough, thousands of Jewish families (and quite a few non-Jewish ones) do have a book she wrote on their shelves – but not one of her wartime experiences. After returning to England, she met and married Leopold J. Greenberg, editor of *The Jewish Chronicle*, in May 1920. He suggested that she write a weekly cookery column for the paper. She went on to write a Jewish cookery book and appeared on the BBC, being known to many as Florence Greenberg, cookery writer. She also carried out work with charity organisations until her death. Florence Greenberg died aged ninety-eight at Hammerson House in London on 4 December 1980, and was survived by her daughter and two grandchildren. Her diary is now with the Jewish Museum.

At the end of the war, over 2,200 QAIMNS were serving full time with 12,000 serving as part of the reserve. Most of them were on yearly contracts due to a stipulation by the War Office to ensure that they could dismiss the women easily if the war ended. Women were essential to the war effort as nurses from the start. Over 100,000 would serve in nursing roles.

VADs

It was not just in the QAIMNS that Jewish women served as nurses – many were also VADs. The Scheme for the Organisation of Voluntary Aid in England and Wales was set up in 1909 by the War Office to create male and female Voluntary Aid Detachments to support Territorial medical services. The VADs were organised and trained by the Red Cross and St John's Ambulance Association. Even before war broke out the units had become popular, with 1,823 female detachments and 551 male ones. Once war broke out the VADs were formally put under the Joint War Committee of the British Red Cross and St John of Jerusalem. Over 90,000 women served as VADs over the course of the war.

The women volunteers came with a variety of skills and ages, although most would be described as being from the middle classes, with some upper-class volunteers. The majority had never been in paid employment yet despite this they went on to staff hospitals and other auxiliary units. The thousands of women in the military hospitals at home and overseas provided the face of home and peacetime to many of those injured. They carried out basic nursing support and in some cases they were trusted with advanced surgical support and care, but they also spent time with patients, writing letters for those unable to and providing comfort to those who needed to share the horror of what they had seen and been part of. VADs were also often given administration work in hospitals, plus cleaning duties and laundry work.

For many women becoming a VAD meant being able to 'do their bit' just as their brothers, fathers, uncles, sweethearts and sons were. In whatever capacity they served they were often required to face the reality of the conflict, stripped of romance and idealism in a way that they had not been expecting. They were at the front line both physically and emotionally. Probably the most famous VAD of the First World War was Vera Brittain, who went on to write about her experiences in *A Testament of Youth*. Many women from the Jewish community stepped up to volunteer as VADs.

Being a VAD could also be dangerous, even in the UK. Edith Hilda Munro was the daughter of John Munro, a Scottish engineer, and Leah Nathan. She grew up and lived in Hackney. She enlisted in the VADs at the start of the war and worked in a seamen's hospital in London. Towards the end of 1916 she contracted pneumonia after an illness caught in the hospital and died as a result. She was buried privately at Plashet Jewish Cemetery in East Ham. As she died at home she was initially given a standard headstone by her family. It was not until 2016 that Edith was finally recognised as a war casualty as she had been on active service when she died. Her headstone has now been replaced with an official Commonwealth War Graves Commission headstone and a service was held in 2016 to recognise her sacrifice.

Another VAD nurse that paid the price for her service was Emily Hartman, who was born in Sheffield in 1895 and was the eldest of six children. She joined the VADs in April 1918 and served in a Manchester military hospital before being transferred to Bermondsey Military Hospital, London. It was there that she

Emily Hartman.

developed pneumonia after catching the Spanish flu that was now sweeping the globe and she died on 20 October 1918. She is buried at Ecclesfield Jewish Cemetery, Yorkshire.

While reading through the Red Cross records for the period, a few Jewish names stand out while others catch your eye for different reasons. Beatrice Hilda Lever (née Falk) was born in Salford in 1884. She married Arthur Lever (formerly Levy), a major of the Royal Fusiliers from a wealthy Leicester family, in 1900. He became a Liberal MP in 1906 and was made a baronet in 1911 after he lost his seat. After the announcement of war he recommissioned into the Fusiliers and served in France on the Western Front, later transferring to Headquarters Staff, Southern Command as a colonel.

With service and duty such a strong factor in the Lever household it is no surprise that Dame Beatrice Lever, as she now was, also decided to volunteer. Instead of joining a committee like many women of her social standing, she volunteered to be a Red Cross nurse. Tragically, she contracted septic poisoning while nursing the wounded in Hampstead General Hospital and died on 28 May 1917. There is a painting of her hanging in the Royal Free Hospital in Hampstead and she is commemorated in a window in York Minster, despite being a practising Jew. In the pages of the British Jewry Book of Honour there are quite a number of women listed as being VADs.

Military Hospitals

Pneumonia and disease as contracted from ill servicemen or as a result of nursing duties in the hospitals seems to be a regular part of nursing during the war years, with a number of cases recorded. Of course, it was not just British Jewish nurses who were struck down in this way. Dorah 'Bunny' Bernstein was born in South Africa in 1988 and joined the South African Military Nursing Service in September

1914. She served in the south-west African campaign until August 1915 in the hospital at Swakopmund. She then served on the hospital ship *Ebani* for over two years. All of these were dangerous postings where injury was possible. She then spent a short time in East Africa and was transferred to Wynberg Military Hospital in 1917. In August 1917 Bernstein was promoted to sister and travelled to Britain to work at the South African Military Hospital in Richmond. It was in the summer of 1918 that the Spanish flu cases started to arrive, and Bunny caught flu which developed into pneumonia. She died on 6 November 1918. There was a report in *The Jewish Chronicle* on 15 November 1918 about her funeral service:

> The ceremony was attended by the Colonel and Matron of the South African Military Hospital, Richmond to which the deceased belonged – as well as by a large number of nurses of the Hospital and Jewish V.A.D.'s from the Hampstead area. The Rev. Michael Adler, D.S.O., and the Rev. H. Goodman (officiating clergymen to troops, London District), officiated at the ceremony, which was terminated by the customary firing of three volleys and the sounding of the Last Post ...

In South Africa the *Springbok* publication of December 1918 described her as being 'a beautiful character and her loss is indeed a heavy one. Her record was one of loving devotion to her unselfish duty.'

There was also a report in the *Richmond and Twickenham Times* edition of 16 November 1918:

> In Richmond she was a general favourite among the staff and patients alike, and many touching tributes to her sweet disposition and devotion to duty have been expressed both by officers and co-workers.

The high esteem in which she was held was manifested at the funeral on Sunday last. The coffin, wrapped in the Union Jack, was borne from the hospital mortuary by Jewish orderlies of S.A.M.C. through lines of the nursing staff drawn up as a guard of honour, and placed in an ambulance for transport to the Willesden Jewish Cemetery, where the interment took place. On arrival there the cortege was met by a military escort and firing party ...

The hospitals in the UK where these women served were a mixture of established military hospitals and hurriedly prepared new ones. In 1914, at the start of the war, an assessment calculated that there were approximately 50,000 hospital beds available and reached the conclusion that this would be more than sufficient to accommodate the wounded.[2] Like so many other things in this war that was a woeful undercalculation. By the end of 1914 approximately 73,000 injured men had already been brought home. It was obvious that extra hospital capacity was desperately needed. Wealthy people with large houses volunteered to take in wounded and turn part or all of their homes into nursing or convalescent homes. The military hospitals tended to deal with the serious cases whereas the homes were required for those who had been returned home following medical care in the hospitals in France, Belgium and across the war zones but were expected to recover. The wounded in such places could be recovering from anything from light injuries to amputations.

The Jewish community provided funding from private donations for a number of homes or hospitals, including Beech House Hospital and, at the end of the war, Tudor House Hospital on the site of Summit Lodge, Hampstead Heath. There were several Beech House branches established over the course of the war; it operated as a franchise run mainly by Jewish staff for Jewish patients.

One was in The Avenue, Brondesbury, London, one in Manchester and another in Brighton.

Beech House in Brondesbury was staffed by five trained nurses and thirty-seven VADs. The VADs did various types of work, from serving the tea, organising the kitchen staff and keeping the stores to being an assistant in the linen room. There were two male doctors, Lowenthal and Gaster, whose wives were both VADs at the hospital. Of the 1,560 patients admitted to the hospital, only one died.

Tudor House in Hampstead was taken over by the Red Cross in 1918, the house having previously been a convalescent home in memory of Baroness De Hirsch which had closed due to lack of funds. Tudor House's running costs were funded by Mrs Clarissa Bischoffsheim, a philanthropist, and run by Miss Janie Joseph OBE, who along with Rose De Beer was a qualified nursing sister. Many of the women, VAD volunteers, worked in excess of 2,000 or 3,000 hours in 1918.

STAFF OF BEECH HOUSE MILITARY HOSPITAL

Back Row: Miss Regensburg ; Miss Greisbach ; Miss Samuels ; Miss Harris ; Mr. Hyams ; Miss Joseph ; Miss Hirschland ; Miss A. Marks.
Second Row: Miss Rosenthal ; Miss Salom ; Mrs. Colman ; Mrs. Stember ; Miss Henry ; Mrs. Levy ; Mrs. Singer ; Mrs. Simmons ; Miss G. Marks ; Miss Rains.
Third Row: Miss Isaacs ; Miss Janie Joseph ; Mrs. Marsden, R.R.C. ; Mrs. Davidson, M.B.E. ; Mrs. Abrahams, R.R.C.
Fourth Row: Miss L. Lazarus ; Miss H. Lazarus ; Miss M. Lazarus ; Mrs. Barnett ; Miss Borginzner.
Miss J. Joseph became Commandant of Tudor House.

The staff of Beech House Military Hospital.

The British Jewry Book of Honour contains photos of about twenty-four of the women who volunteered throughout the country; many of the women at Tudor House, Hampstead and Beech House, Brondesbury lived in West Hampstead, which was a popular place for the Jewish community at that time, near the Lauderdale Road, Brondesbury and Hampstead synagogues.

According the British Jewry Book of Honour, a number of Jews established small hospitals to assist with the injured. In Lancashire, Mr and Mrs Walter Beer (Mrs Beer received the MBE for her services) established, at their own expense, the Bradstones Auxiliary Hospital at West Derby. Over 600 patients were treated there. In Brighton Mr John Howard set up a convalescent home. Elsewhere Mr David L. Jacobs allowed his holiday home in Broadstairs to be used as a hospital throughout the war.

Esther Annenberg, born in 1984 in Russia, was a nurse at the Military Heart Hospital in Hampstead. She had her picture in *Jewish World* in May 1918 under the heading 'Thirteen Jews in one family serving'. She had moved to England as a young child and lived with her parents in London alongside her eight siblings. Over the course of the war four of her brothers served, as did a brother-in-law and cousins. They spanned the services and the regiments, including mounted regiments, rifles, the Royal Engineers, the Judeans and the Royal Air Force. Esther later married, becoming Esther Paris, and went on to found the first baby clinic in Haifa, Israel.

So many of these women completed their service and then returned to normal lives. It makes finding out their stories and experiences very difficult, for although we have their Red Cross cards there is no indication (for why should there be?) on them about their names following marriage. That is why it is so fortunate when we do come across one whose story we can follow, even if only a little. Elsie Borgzinner of London served as a VAD in Beech House. She married after the war and became Mrs Heymann. Her family have kept her story alive as she went on to serve as a nurse again during the Second World War.

Medical Services on the Front Line

Undoubtedly the most dangerous place to serve in any medical capacity was close to the front line. As the war progressed and a greater understanding of emergency care developed, nurses were moved closer to the front line and into the range of the enemy. One such nurse is Nurse Bernstein, who is reported on in the *Jewish World* edition for 16 February 1916:

Brave Jewish Nurse

The Jewish Red Cross nurse Madame Bernstein has been awarded
the Medal of St George for conspicuous bravery in the field in
rescuing wounded under strong fire.

Unfortunately, that is all the paper reports. Of course, it is not just the nurses who carried out medical work. According to the British Jewry Book of Honour there were 124 Jewish officers in the Royal Army Medical Corps and over 1,300 NCOs and other ranks. Not all of these men were medically trained, but they were all engaged with ensuring the medical systems worked and that treatment could be given when needed.

There were Jewish doctors serving in the military across the British Empire. Asher Leventon was born on 29 May 1870 in Leicester. He went to school and university in Dublin, followed by the Royal College of Physicians and Surgeons in the same city. He joined the British Indian Army in 1895 and was a surgeon lieutenant. The following covers his 1895 commission as reported in *The Jewish Chronicle*:

After a brilliant University Career, Mr Asher Leventon, of Dublin, has obtained a commission in Her Majesty's Indian Medical Service. This distinction marks a new stage in the participation of English Jews in the service of their country. A Jewish Army Doctor is at once a true to two old Jewish traditions, the love of the healing art and the love of his country. Mr Leventon's example is one that will, we hope, by widely imitated. This branch of military profession is lucrative, so that poor men need not be dissuaded from entering it. It carries with it military rank and altogether it opens out an attractive career to our young medical students, whose numbers we gladly see increase year by year in this country. Mr Leventon won, it is true, an exceptionally high place in the competitive examination which resulted in gaining him his commission. But this fact is itself encouraging to others. For it proves that merit is the only qualification necessary for success in this career. The competition is open to all who have the necessary certificates and the best men will get the best posts. Mr Leventon deserves our hearty congratulations.

In 1896 he gained his fellowship as a surgeon and in 1906 his directorate of public health from the Royal College of Physicians. Meanwhile, he was promoted to captain in 1898 and then promoted again to major in 1915. He served throughout the First World War and became a lieutenant colonel, eventually retiring in 1925.

Hyman Lush, born in Poland in 1890, arrived in the UK in 1906 using one of the various spellings of his surname: Lushinsky, Lushinski or Luszynski. He lived with his grandmother at a variety of addresses across East London from Commercial Street to Stoke Newington. Hyman was a dedicated member of the St John Ambulance before the war and therefore volunteered for the Royal Army Medical Corps as soon as war was declared. He served as a medical orderly, initially at Connaught Hospital, Aldershot, where he worked with wounded German prisoners. In his diary, Hyman recorded how he acted as an unofficial interpreter (probably mostly in Yiddish), helping to record the Germans' particulars when they arrived. He was kind to the Germans, chatting and helping them to buy things such as chocolate and cigarettes. Many of them signed his autograph books with friendly messages. Following on from Aldershot, Hyman was sent to Mesopotamia and the North-West Frontier.

Hyman's grandson Dean Lush recorded his story:

Grandpa made many visits to the Jewish community in Basra, Mesopotamia. There he encountered an 'Oriental' Judaism at once strange and familiar. Here are some quotes from his letters home:

16 April 1917: 'I have been down to Basra on pass ... the last day of Passover ... although I am only a Private one of the richest Jews in Basra sent his private landau to take me back to the hospital... [My host and his brother] showed me round the town. Then [we went] to a coffee shop (Jewish) where they all congregate & play [backgammon?] regardless of it being Yomtov (Holy day). I was struck with their disregard of religion.'

23 April 1917: 'Then one thinks here I am thousands & thousands of miles away from home, and yet I can find more than one roof to shelter me and food ... even sleeping accommodation provided free of charge and feel absolutely at home. I have been told the other day by a Christian friend that Jews help one another more than gentiles. I now believe it is true (didn't then) for can a gentile find the same hospitality I doubt it.'

12 December 1917: 'For New Year we got two days leave ...
[and went into Basra and participated in] a quaint custom in vogue
here. Instead of our custom of going to the synagogue after meals
to say Psalms & Mincha, the Jews here congregate in a friend's
(generally better off than his neighbours) house ... In the shady
part of the courtyard a group of men & boys are sitting singing
Psalms. Those of us who could read Hebrew joined in. In a few
minutes time I suddenly noticed that I was the only one reading
the Psalms, and that all the others had stopped and were listening,
evidently curious to hear how a European pronounces the Hebrew.
I read on ... two pages and still the others made no effort to begin
so I told the Persian Jew, as best I could make him understand, that
I am not a Chazzan, would he mind reading now.'

A young man who travelled a long way from home to support
medical services was Joseph Silverman, who was born in London
in 1892. He later moved to Australia and settled there, and
therefore joined the Australian Medical Corps, and it was with
them that he was posted to the 14th Field Ambulance. It was while
working in this role during the Third Battle of Ypres in September
1917 that he was killed while assisting the wounded. He is buried
at Menin Road South Military Cemetery, Belgium.

A number of those in the British Jewry Book of Honour have
awards for the courageous and dangerous work that they did in
the medical services.

5

JEWS AS JEWS IN UNIFORM

In the immediate months following the start of the war there were calls from some Jewish groups for a Jewish regiment or battalion. These calls were quickly dismissed; the British authorities and Anglo-Jewry saw no need for a separate regiment. After all, there were no restrictions to Jews joining the forces; there were already Jewish servicemen, and the war would be over quickly enough. Instead, any concern over Jewish involvement in the war was directed at the issues of specifically Russian or eastern European Jews and how they could be allowed – or compelled – to contribute and serve. In this case it was about harnessing non-British Jewish men who wished to fight for Britain – in particular so that these non-British Jews could fight back against the Ottoman controllers of Palestine.

Ottoman Turkey had entered the war in November 1914 on the side of the Central Powers. Those citizens of Allied countries in Ottoman-controlled areas now needed to escape, or they would be interned. The British authorities were in Egypt, which they had controlled for over a hundred years despite it nominally belonging to the Ottomans. The Ottoman involvement in the war meant the British formally seized Egypt, making it the key location in the region where non-Ottoman supporters could gather. By December 1914 there were approximately 11,000 Jewish refugees in British-held Alexandria, three-quarters of them Russian speakers. Many of the refugees were Zionists who had moved to Palestine to escape Russian anti-Semitism and pursue their ideological dream.

Some of those Russians had served (as conscripts) in the Russian Tsarist forces and now as refugees they didn't want to sit around in Alexandria living off the goodwill of the Egyptian Jewish community.

Ze'ev Jabotinsky and Joseph Trumpeldor were Zionists and they led the campaign for a Jewish unit. Jabotinsky, birth name Vladimir, was born in 1880 into a Jewish Russian family in Odessa. The family were middle class and Vladimir went to Russian schools and mixed in a variety of circles. As a student he travelled aboard and failed to take up his degree, becoming a journalist instead. He had grown attracted to the idea of Zionism, and his interest only increased after the pogroms of 1903. He changed his name to Ze'ev as he learnt Modern Hebrew and organised Jewish self-defence units. He campaigned for Jewish civil rights and was prepared to use physical force to establish Jewish equality.

When the war started, Jabotinsky was working in the Middle East as a correspondent for a Russian newspaper. In his eyes, events around him proved that his campaigning for Jewish self-defence and Zionist causes now needed to reach a greater audience. The plight of the Jewish refugees in Alexandria who had fled from Palestine drove his determination for a Jewish military unit and identity still further, and he saw the British as the ideal audience for his cause.

Joseph Trumpeldor was born in 1880 in the Caucasus to a Jewish family that was described as being more Russian than Jewish. It was this identity which led to him volunteering to serve in the Russian forces in 1902. In 1904 he fought in the Russo-Japanese War, where as a result of a shrapnel wound his arm was amputated. Despite this he continued his military career until he was captured at Port Arthur and became a prisoner of war. While in a prisoner-of-war camp he became involved with Jewish community activities and writings. Following the war, the Russian authorities awarded him the Gold Cross of the Order of St George for gallantry; in 1906 he was also the second Jew to be given a commission into the Russian Army and became the most decorated Jewish Russian soldier. In civilian life he switched from studying dentistry (which he was unable to practice with only one arm) to studying law. He also started to gather young Russian Jews around him to discuss the Zionist cause, and in 1911 he and the group moved to Palestine to work the land. He settled near the Sea of Galilee but was forced to flee in 1914 as the Turkish forces arrived into Palestine, and he refused to take on Turkish citizenship.

Although the two men had not met prior to being in Alexandria, Jabotinsky and Trumpeldor put together a plan for raising a Jewish legion to fight with the British for the liberation of Palestine. The Russian government wanted all those of Russian birth sent back to them for service, while the British saw the advantage of having a Jewish legion of some description. The British government and military had a number of leaders who were sympathetic to the Zionist cause, usually because of their own strong evangelical Christian beliefs. Others simply saw an opportunity to harness a willing and capable group of potential volunteers.

Non-British citizens (or Empire subjects) were not permitted to be part of the British forces carrying arms, so General Maxwell, the British commander in Egypt, suggested that he could form them into a voluntary mule corps. This was rejected by many of the potential volunteers, who felt that they should be able to fight – after all, many had experience. Maxwell also said that he couldn't guarantee that any role they were given would involve going to Palestine to fight the Ottomans. Trumpeldor was willing to accept the offer, seeing it as an opportunity to prove that the Russian Jews could be loyal to the British and of use. He also felt it was certainly preferable to any deal that made the Russian Jews of Palestine return to Russia. He said at a meeting of those interested in joining up to fight that 'we've got to smash the Turk. On which front you begin is a question of tactics; any front leads to Zion.'[1] After more rousing sentiments, he convinced them that they should form up into the Zion Mule Corps.

In Egypt at the time was the Boer War veteran Lieutenant Colonel John Henry Patterson DSO. According to Martin Sugarman in his article 'The Zion Muleteers of Gallipoli', Patterson was well read on 'Jewish military and religious history' and sympathetic to the Zionist cause. He was present with Major-General Alexander Godley to persuade the potential volunteers that a mule corps was just as valuable as those that carried arms. When the volunteers had been convinced, Godley stated that 'today the English people have entered into a covenant with the Jewish people',[2] an idea that would be further developed in that region as the war progressed.

Patterson was appointed commander on 22 March 1915 with the support of Godley. Trumpeldor was made a captain and appointed as second in command. Trumpeldor and Patterson would develop a deep respect for one another, leading to Patterson considering Trumpeldor as one of the bravest men he had ever met. Trumpeldor's presence and leadership of the new unit was of considerable importance to the men; he could rally them into any action, no matter how dangerous. He was undoubtedly an inspiration and his courage was legendary. In his own words he described an incident at the front in Gallipoli after the Zion Mule Corps were deployed:

And this is how I was wounded. At 2:15 p.m. the rifle and shell fire grew more intense ... suddenly one of our men came riding up crying out that a man was wounded ... I rode off to the spot ... and when all this was done mounted my horse to ride back ... when I felt as if someone had given me a hearty blow on the left shoulder. The stars on my epaulette tinkled and I thought the bullet ... had knocked it off. When I arrived at the camp ... they examined my shoulder and found a little hole in my tunic ... I took off my tunic and to everyone's surprise it turned out that the bullet had passed through almost the entire thickness of my shoulder and was sticking out on the other side ... the doctor gripped at the end of the bullet with his pincers and pulled ... but the bullet did not come out. He cut away a little of the flesh and pulled again ... but the bullet would not come out. He cut away some more ... but still it would not come out ... finally the doctor took a good grip of the bullet and began to twist as if he were drawing a cork out of a bottle ... then the bullet came out!![3]

The corps received only three weeks of training (most new troops received nearly three months, but as non-combatants it was felt that they would be effective with only the basics), as they were needed for the Gallipoli campaign. In March 1915 General Sir Ian Hamilton declared himself happy with their development and they were told to prepare for departure to ensure they would be ready for the April attacks in the Dardanelles. With kosher food organised by their commanding officer Lieutenant Colonel Patterson, in which he shared, they celebrated Passover on 30 March 1915. After a blessing by the Chief Rabbi in Alexandria, the new Zion Mule Corps, the first organised Jewish military unit in 2,000 years, set sail for the Dardanelles on 17 April 1915.

Colonel Patterson described in *The Jewish Chronicle* on 10 September 1915 that first day that they arrived at the front:

These brave lads who had never seen shellfire before most competently unloaded the boats and handled the mules whilst shells were bursting in close proximity to them ... nor were they in any way discouraged when they had to plod their way to Seddul Bahr, walking over dead bodies while the bullets flew around them ... for two days and two nights we marched ... thanks to the Zion Mule Corps the 29th Division did not meet with a sad fate, for the Zion Mule Corps were the only Army Service Corps in that part of Gallipoli at that time.

As a service corps in Gallipoli the Zion Mule Corps was essential as all of the supplies, including water, had to be brought in via boat and distributed to the men who had landed on the beach areas. Gallipoli was a difficult battle front as the attack was into a hostile area that had steep cliffs not far from the shore with little access to any fresh food or additional support. The men who landed for the attack were in a vulnerable position, frequently pinned down

The Zion Mule Corps.

by enemy fire and totally reliant on what supplies the service corps could bring to them. The Zion Mule Corps found that they were frequently under heavy fire and had to struggle to remain calm amid the noise and danger as they went about their work.

The challenge of the job was not inconsiderable, and the bravery of the men of the Zion Mule Corps was recognised. Private M. Groushkousky was awarded the Distinguished Conduct Medal in the field and promoted to corporal after an incredible display of courage as a non-combatant. During a Turkish assault near Krithia on 5 May 1915 he held onto his mules and stopped them from stampeding despite the amount of noise and fire around him. Even though he was shot in both arms he managed to deliver the ammunition to the trenches, ensuring that the combatants could carry on with the battle.

Although the men of the Zion Mule Corps were not to be combatants, many of them had trained previously to use rifles (especially as conscripts in the Russian forces) and occasionally that training was called upon. In May 1915 the Zion Mule Corps was tasked with bringing supplies to the Royal Inniskilling Fusiliers. As they approached, the men of the Zion Mule Corps could see that the Irishmen were taking heavy casualties and would not be able to successfully fight the Ottoman forces. ZMC corporal Elie Hildesheim (later known as Leon Gildesgame) instructed the corps to pick up the rifles of the men who had already fallen and to enter into the line to assist the Inniskillings in the attack against the Ottoman soldiers. This intervention saved the Inniskillings from an overwhelming defeat and earned them huge support from the men and the commanders.

The exploits and bravery of the Zion Mule Corps were often reported in the British Jewish press and the non-Jewish national press. They were regularly held up as heroes, especially as so many became ill (malaria and dysentery were rampant) as a result of the conditions out in Gallipoli.

On 1 October 1915 there was a short piece in *The Jewish Chronicle* from Rabbi Barnet I. Cohen. He had been to a military hospital in Sheffield where he had met a young private, Abraham Lippman of the Zion Mule Corps. Lippman was originally from Russia and was working for a Russian company in Palestine when the Ottomans joined the war. Fearing attack, he had fled to Alexandria. As part of the Zion Mule Corps he had been hit by a bullet in July 1915 and was sent to England to recover. Apparently Lippman spoke very enthusiastically about Colonel Patterson and how he had a real love for his men, a sentiment many in the ZMC would report. The rabbi finished his piece by adding that 'Lippman is a general favourite at the local hospital, though he does not speak a word of English'.

Other Jews serving in British regiments met the men of the Zion Mule Corps while out in Gallipoli and they often wrote home expressing how pleased they were to see such a sight. A British Christian chaplain reported on how uplifting it was to talk to men fighting for Britain who had come from the 'Holy Land' to do so.

Patterson was evacuated to London in late December 1915 after becoming ill, and as the Gallipoli campaign came to a tragic end all the troops were evacuated. On 28 December, the order came to disband the Zion Mule Corps. Fifteen men had been killed (fourteen were listed originally but another subsequently died of wounds) and over sixty were injured, with many more ill. The last parade was on 31 December 1915, when Trumpeldor addressed the men in Hebrew: 'We are leaving tonight; our work is done. We have a right to say; well done ... we and the Jewish people need never be ashamed of the Zion Mule Corps!'[4]

For some the disbandment of the Zion Mule Corps was not the end, as many now applied to go to Britain, where their service could continue. One of these was Private Aaron Ben Joseph, who was born in 1878 in Baku, then in south Russia, and spoke Persian and Turkish as well as English. He had served in the Russo-Japanese war as a sharpshooter. He had a carpet business in Jerusalem which was looted when the war started and so he went as a refugee to Alexandria. He volunteered for the Zion Mule Corps and wrote about the experience of being injured and nearly left for dead:

The masses of killed and wounded, dysentery and malaria, the scant food, mostly biscuits. It is summer time and I am lying there, swollen from hunger and lousy, lying among the dead. The Indian troops came to bury us with their shovels. I am weak and am half buried before I manage to say something in Persian. They take me out and give me milk; take me to a hospital ship and then to Lemnos and Alexandria. I get malaria even till now. At Alexandria I get discharge papers and come to England on a ship. In 1916, I enlist again in the RAMC and the Labour Corps and go to Belgium and France. I help the Royal Engineers as I am an expert engineer especially in water. I am discharged because of malaria and neurasthenia.[5]

Another volunteer was Percy Apter, who was born in Jaffa, Palestine in 1897. He fled his home for Alexandria and joined the Zion Mule Corps. After the corps was disbanded he was able to join the Royal Field Artillery. In 1919 he arrived in Britain and settled in Glamorgan, where he married and became a carpenter. His original discharge papers describe him as of 'good character and his work and conduct have always been satisfactory'. Very few people in his community knew the long journey he had made to end up in a quiet street in Wales.

Then there was Dr Meshulam Levontin from Palestine who became the commander of the Zion Mule Corps medical unit. His service did not end with the First World War; during the Second World War he was again part of the British forces, and posted to the Middle East as the British Army's chief malariologist.

In recent years another Jewish unit serving in Gallipoli has also come to light. The National Archives at Kew holds many of the official records from the First World War, including the medal rolls. In the file WO 329/2359, about forty sheets into the unnumbered pages, is a list containing 189 names of a 'Jewish Labour Corps' who fought in Gallipoli. The official documents state that the men on the list are entitled to the British War Medal (Bronze) in accordance with 'War Office letter NW/2/18747 (A.G.4. Medals), 3rd March 1928'. The pages are signed by Lt H. Wetherall. The names all appear to be Sephardi, and using other records it can be deduced that they were Egyptian Jewish volunteers from Alexandria (or thereabouts). As non-British citizens they would not have been allowed to be combatants, but it does seem the British were happy to have them working as a labour corps.

Their names are not listed in the Jewish Book of Honour as being members of the Zion Mule Corps, but because of their origin there appears to be some confusion as to what unit they belonged to. In the 1928 document there is a comment that attempts to explain that the unit was formed in Egypt separately from the Zion Mule Corps but may have been misnamed as the 2nd Battalion of that corps. All the men were enlisted between 15 and 22 April 1915 and served only until 22 and 28 May 1915. It can be assumed that the men came to light in 1928 after an appeal for the medal to which they were entitled. Another letter is evidence of this, as it is between the War Office in London and the Chief Rabbi of

Alexandria and the Zion Mule Corps Commission (Veterans) in Alexandria, discussing the medal issue.

In addition to not being listed as Zion Mule Corps members, these men are also not listed in the roll for other Jewish regiments such as the Judeans, or among other labour corps in the British Jewry Book of Honour. As the men did not serve in the usual regiments or corps and were not resident in the UK, they will have missed *The Jewish Chronicle* and Revd Adler's call to register for the British Jewry Book of Honour in 1922.

According to the research carried out by Martin Sugarman, 'none of the many standard works on Gallipoli mention this corps'. There is also no record of them in the 'General Routine Orders or Army Orders for the Egyptian Expeditionary Force/Mediterranean/Gallipoli'. There is also no mention of the corps in the British Jewish press of the time. However, a file on the embarkation of units from Alexandria on HMV *Trevillard* from 17 to 19 April 1915 does list 148 labourers and two officers, Major S. Hutchins and Lt F. Hodsell, of the Jewish Labour Corps. It seems therefore that Jewish volunteers from other Middle Eastern countries were happy to step into British uniform during the First World War and make a contribution. I must thank Martin Sugarman for helping me to make sure their efforts are finally acknowledged.

Russia or Britain?

Back in Britain there was another issue regarding Jewish service and the military. Immigrant Jews who had arrived in the UK before 1914 did not need to become naturalised in order to live and work in Britain, and some never had. Russian Jews in particular often failed to apply for UK citizenship for themselves or their children; their experiences in Russia had made them distrustful of authority, and with no requisite of citizenship to access any welfare provisions (there was no welfare state), they simply didn't bother. They resided largely in the East End of London, and in the big cities of Manchester, Leeds and Glasgow, where they could live without interaction outside of their known community. Anglo-Jewry did encourage the Russian Jews to get citizenship, just as they encouraged them to learn English, send their children to school and start to assimilate themselves into British society. Some of the immigrant communities were keen to take up the chance to become British and to 'fit in', but others resisted any approaches.

Once the war started there was a question of what the Russian Jews living in the UK should do. Recruitment posters were put up encouraging all Jews to enlist, and the posters were also produced in Yiddish to encourage the recent immigrants as well. As foreign nationals they were unable to join the British forces, so those who had been born in the UK to foreign parents were encouraged to acquire citizenship to do so. That still left the problem of those who were born elsewhere but were now resident in the UK. Having large numbers of men of military age not seemingly engaged with the war effort became a source of embarrassment for Anglo-Jewry, and a number of conversations began about what should be done.

In some areas they got around the problem by simply recruiting those of a foreign nationality and allowing the local authority to take responsibility. This appears to be the case for Private Max Markovitz. In a letter published on 5 January 1916 in *Jewish World*, Max's aunt states that despite being born in Russia and not naturalised he joined up at the outbreak of war and the local authority took responsibility. Sadly, he was killed in action on 12 December 1915 at Hill 60, near Ypres. The piece includes the letter sent by his commanding officer to Max's mother:

... I have lost in him a comrade, and the regiment one of its most efficient signaller; one who had been brought to the notice of the Commanding Officer for bravery on several occasions, and a very dear, popular and cheerful comrade to all the signallers of the regiment and the whole of his late company.

LW Row Captain, Sherwood Foresters

Interestingly the aunt also mentions that Mrs Markowitz and her daughter are the only Jews living in Tideswell, Derbyshire, so perhaps the local authorities simply did not see a problem in supporting one young man who wanted to go off and do his bit.

Once conscription was introduced in 1916, the Jewish community became even more concerned that they must be seen to be doing their part. Posters in *The Jewish Chronicle* and *Jewish World* as well as elsewhere declared that 'THERE MUST BE NO JEWISH SLACKERS', encouraging everyone possible to join up. Discussions with Russia led to the passing of Army Council Instruction 1156 (ACI 1156) by the War Office on 8 June 1916. This instruction confirmed that all friendly aliens would now be permitted join the British forces.

Many of the Russian Jews were still disinclined to enlist. They did not want to fight on the side of Russia, a country that they had fled; some had political objections against the war as a whole, some voiced concerns that they would be subject to anti-Semitism or anti-foreigner prejudice, and others simply felt that the war had nothing to do with them. Ze'ev Jabotinsky saw the situation as an opportunity to campaign once more for a special Jewish legion to be raised to serve in the fighting in the Middle East. In 1914 he had started his campaign for a single fighting Jewish force for the liberation of Palestine, although with little impact. However, the success of the Zion Mule Corps in the Gallipoli campaign gave him

January 12, 1916.   THE JEWISH WORLD.   23

"England has been all she could be to Jews, Jews will be all they can be to England."
—*JEWISH CHRONICLE.*

The Country's Call for Men has been nobly responded to by Jews of all Classes

ARE YOU HOLDING BACK?

On the VICTORY of the ALLIES depends the Cause of Freedom and Toleration which is the Cause of England.

THERE MUST BE NO JEWISH SLACKERS

JEWISH YOUNG MEN! Do your duty to your faith and your Country.
ALL BRITISH JEWS SHOULD

ENLIST NOW

DON'T FORGET!

Ask advice of MAJOR LIONEL DE ROTHSCHILD, M.P., at the Jewish Recruiting Committee.

Chairman: EDMUND SEBAG-MONTEFIORE.   Hon. Sec.: S. STEPHANY, NEW COURT, ST. SWITHIN'S LANE, E.C.

a renewed sense of hope. The corps had received praise from many sources, not just Jewish. In the 28 January 1916 edition of *The Jewish Chronicle* a Revd Dr Ewing of the Grange United Reform Church in Edinburgh, serving as a chaplain to the Egyptian Expeditionary Force, wrote in a letter about how strange it was to ask a man in a British uniform who was working where he was from and for him to answer the Holy City (Jerusalem). He went on to add, 'The Zion Mule Corps has done most excellent transport work since the landing … and very earnest these Sons of Jacob are in their endeavours.'

While Jabotinsky had some support from the Jewish community and non-Jews, including from the UK government, others were concerned that a single Jewish force would only separate Jews from the larger British society rather than help them to integrate. Almost as an acceptance of the perceived prejudice that Russian Jews might feel in the UK forces, a concession was made that overruled a previous Army Act. The Army Act of 1908 restricted the ratio of aliens to British citizens within military units to no greater than 1 to 50. The new Army Council Instruction had a paragraph included that stated:

> In the case of the Russian Jews they may be recruited on product of a certificate from the Jewish War Service Committee, New Court, St Swithins Lane, London EC and if they so desire may be posted in batches to serve together in the same unit.

In July 1916 the Home Secretary Herbert Samuel announced that service in either the British or Russian army would become compulsory. Samuel was Jewish and sympathetic on one level to the concerns of the Russian Jews; however, he was an extremely loyal British subject and wanted to ensure that the Russian Jews served in the military and helped the war effort. The Russian Jews were, therefore, given an October deadline to enlist before their service was compulsory – and accompanying it was the threat of deportation. One of those who came forward following the rule changes was Samuel Belovitz, who was born in Russia in October 1880 and joined up on 7 July 1916. He tragically caught tuberculosis on the Western Front and was sent home to the UK, where he died on 27 April 1917 as a result of 'exposure to TB'. He is buried at Manor Park Jewish Cemetery. Before enlisting he was a brush maker and left behind a wife and daughter, Rose and Hilda.

By 25 October 1916, of the estimated 20,000 Russian Jews eligible for military service only 632 had come forward. The Home Secretary had no choice but to enact the compulsory service law. Special tribunals were set up in London, Manchester and Liverpool to assess those claiming exemption from service. The Jewish community was split along different lines, with many believing that the Russian Jews should simply be forced to serve, while others exhibited some sympathy to their objections. Letters about eligibility appeared weekly in *The Jewish Chronicle* and in *The Jewish News*.

Lucien Wolf, a leader in Anglo-Jewry, editor of *Jewish World* and an ardent integrationist, stated his position in a letter to *The Times* on 24 July 1916:

I am afraid I do not agree that Russian Jews of military age living in this country have any right to object to service in the British army on the grounds of Russian persecution of the Jews. Many non-Jewish British subjects hold the internal policy of the Russian Empire in as much detestation ... but they do not on that account hesitate to serve in the British Army. Nor do I see why there should be so much clamour against deportation. There need be no deportation if the Jew does his obvious duty.

This final push meant that 7,600 Jews applied to return to Russia, although only an estimated 3,500 appear to have been sent. Those who did return became known as the 'Conventionalists' as a result of the convention agreed with Russia.

Of those Jews who travelled back to Russia, many were certainly never heard of again. The Russian Revolution in 1917 made communication with Russia difficult and people simply disappeared through starvation, chaos and violence. The Bolshevik

Revolution led to a Russian withdrawal from the war and that meant that no more Russians living in the UK would be dispatched to Russia to join that army.

The Jewish Legion

Throughout 1916, Jabotinsky worked behind the scenes as well arguing for a Jewish military regiment, using the issue of Russian Jews as his main campaigning tool. In a letter published in *The Times* in July 1916, Jabotinsky argued that Russian Jews were asking for a promise 'that if we fight we shall be helping to assure the freedom of the Jewish race'. Staff on *The Times* had some sympathy for Jabotinsky's argument and wrote a favourable editorial. This was very different to many in the leadership of Anglo-Jewry who still feared the idea of a Jewish legion. Jabotinsky used the success and admiration that the Zion Mule Corps had created to garner support for his idea. He, along with Trumpeldor and 120 other former members of the Zion Mule Corps, joined the 20th Battalion of the London Regiment. His military service did nothing to end his frequent visits to Whitehall and his lobbying through person, letter and articles, of which many were printed in *The Jewish Chronicle* and others in *The Times*.

The traditional leaders of the Jewish establishment were appalled at the idea of a Jewish legion and saw it as divisive, something that would incite anti-Semitism and isolation rather than demonstrate Anglo-Jewry's loyalty to the UK and promote integration. Creating a national status for Jews through Zionism was not a popular idea with the Anglo-Jewish leaders; they did not see a Jewish homeland as necessary as they were British. On the other hand, Jabotinsky and other European Jews who had experienced high levels of anti-Semitism in the countries where they were born believed that a Jewish homeland was the only way to end centuries of discrimination and violence. The dislike that both sides had for each other was really very intense.

The debate about a Jewish regiment raged back and forth. However, as the war progressed, the British authorities and politicians began to see the idea of a Jewish, or at least predominantly Jewish, force as a way to manage some of the new conscripts and solve the problem of the Russian Jews. Towards the end of 1916, even Lucien Wolf began to work with Jabotinsky, not because he had changed his mind on the idea of Zionism or on the Jewish legion, but because he wanted a solution to the Russian Jews' lack of engagement, which he felt would bring shame on the Jewish community if it continued. With their eventual cooperation in mind, it is interesting that in his memoirs Jabotinsky would repeatedly fail to mention Wolf's presence at important and decisive meetings, even with key figures such as Chaim Weizmann, who would later become the first President of Israel.

By late spring 1917, the War Office took the decision that a Jewish force or regiment would be a good idea. They had been particularly convinced that a Jewish corps would appeal to Jews living in countries outside of the British Empire, such as the United States. Lieutenant Colonel John Henry Patterson, the non-Jewish Irish officer who had overseen the Zion Mule Corps, was instructed by the War Office to organise a Jewish regiment and the news was announced in the *London Gazette* on 23 August 1917. To placate those sections of Anglo-Jewry who had been against the idea, the Jewish legion was not to be a new regiment; instead, they were to form the 38th, 39th and 40th Battalions of the Royal Fusiliers, with a 41st and 42nd as reserve unit. The Royal Fusiliers were an existing London-based regiment that already had a strong Jewish presence, therefore the new battalions would be an extension of that.

38TH ROYAL FUSILIERS (JEWISH) MUSKETRY STAFF, PALESTINE, 1918.

The 38th Battalion of the Royal Fusiliers.

The 38th Battalion was drawn predominantly from East London Jewish men or those already serving who requested a transfer. Included in the 38th were many of the Russian Jews who had thus far avoided service – they were now happy to serve, or at least they knew their objections would certainly be ignored. Jabotinsky was made an honorary officer and proudly wore his Fusilier uniform.

The 39th Battalion also drew on men from Britain but it also had a high proportion of men from the USA, Canada and Argentina. Certain American newspapers and Zionist organisations in those countries had reported regularly about the formation of the regiment. In many articles the Jewish legion was advertised as a means by which Jews could be instrumental in creating a Jewish presence in Palestine, an ongoing area of fighting for the Allies during the First World War. The men from empire and Allied countries (the USA had entered into the war on 6 April 1917) were all entitled to join the British forces, and recruitment began for the Jewish battalions. Groups of men from areas with a high Jewish presence, such as New York, set sail willingly to join their co-religionists to free the Holy Land and perhaps help to establish a Jewish homeland.

The 40th Battalion was drawn from the men of Palestine, some of whom had served with the Zion Mule Corps; others were new refugees from the 1916 and 1917 purges by the Ottoman forces in Palestine. Some 200 volunteers were Jews captured in Ottoman forces who had been conscripted unwillingly to fight. For many of the men in the 40th Battalion the war was personal; Ottoman forces had attacked Jewish areas across Palestine, burning properties and killing civilians.

Collectively the 5,000 men of these battalions were to be known as the Jewish Legion, but most people knew them as the Judeans. According to historian Martin Sugarman other names were also adopted: 'The *Guardian* newspaper alluded to the term "The New Maccabeans". To the Jewish community the nicknames "Royal Jewsiliers" and "King's own Schneiders" (or 'tailors,' as so many came from that then Jewish dominated profession)'[6] all became popular.

A Jewish force appealed to many who had not wanted to participate previously; the sculptor Jacob Epstein and the artist Bernard Meninsky, members of the Whitechapel Boys, both joined the 38th Battalion. Interestingly, according to letters from February and March 1918, Isaac Rosenberg, the painter and poet, wrote for a transfer from the King's Own Royal Regiment to the 38th Battalion twice.[7] He never received a response to his request and there are no records of letters in the collection at the Parkes Library. Jabotinsky suspected that there was someone at the War Office who still disapproved of the new Jewish Legion and either blocked or ignored requests to transfer. The lack of any evidence of a Rosenberg request seems to corroborate that idea.

Some serving Jewish soldiers did not fancy the new Jewish legion. Philip Lewis was born in 1896 in London. On enlisting in 1916 he joined the London Irish Rifles. Philip was the only Jew in his battalion, but he got on so well with his comrades that he declined the opportunity to transfer to the Jewish battalions of the Royal Fusiliers even when he was out in the Middle East fighting in the same campaign as the Judeans. Philip was comfortable in his unit among his non-Jewish colleagues even while expressing his Jewish identity, including during his time with them in Jerusalem:

When they arrived to Jerusalem, all the Jews came out happy and he was sure he'd get an invite to a Shabbat dinner but no one was interested. Eventually he and his friend received one invite and attended but when they returned to the barracks they were punished as they hadn't been given any leave and were confined to the barracks.[8]

Lewis was not unique as a young British Jew who was comfortable in a non-Jewish crowd. Nonetheless, the new units were a solution for the many who were unsure of how they would be treated in a non-Jewish environment or for those who had experienced anti-Semitism and prejudice. For some the new battalions were an assurance by the British authorities that Jewish soldiers were to be respected, and for some it was another motivator to fight in a war about which they didn't care and that seemed to be returning more casualties than successes.

There were comments in some quarters including the German press that the Jewish Legion was just a gimmick, a token force. Others thought they would never actually be sent to the Middle

East. To show the detractors that they were wrong, and to potentially boost recruitment, the Lord Mayor of London, Sir Horace Brooks Marshall, ensured that these soldiers were given the recognition that they deserved. At the end of January 1918, half of the 38th Battalion were told that they were to return to London from their training camp on 1 February. After spending the night at the Tower of London, the regimental headquarters for the Royal Fusiliers, they formed up ready for inspection on the morning of 2 February. They then marched as a parade through the streets of the City of London, supported by the band of the Coldstream Guards.

At the front of the column they carried the Union flag and the Zionist flag (very similar to the current flag of the state of Israel). They were led by their commander, Col John Patterson DSO, on horseback with Lt Jabotinsky not far behind. To demonstrate that the men were not just a gimmick, the mayor allowed them to march with fixed bayonets – a privilege only granted to a full fighting force. The men were greeted at the Mansion House by the mayor, who received their salute from the balcony with his wife and the city sheriffs all in attendance. Later the mayor said, 'You can tell the Jewish Regiment and their friends that I consider it was a magnificent muster. I am proud of them and wish them God speed and good luck in the service of their King and Country.'[9]

Along the route thousands of Londoners of many ages and social backgrounds turned out to watch the parade. The Jewish East End, in particular, had never seen anything like it, especially as the Guards Band played the *Hatikvah*, the Zionist anthem (which is today the national anthem of Israel). It was not just Jews who turned out to watch the parade; thousands of non-Jews turned out for the spectacle and were just as happy to cheer and wave flags.

Around midday the parade drew to a close once they reached the dignitaries to whom they were to be presented: the mayor and mayoress of Stepney (Dr Jerome Reidy and his wife), Lieutenant General Sir Francis Lloyd, Sir Adolph Tuck, Mrs Hertz (wife of Chief Rabbi Joseph Hertz), Mr James D. Kiley (Liberal MP for Whitechapel), Chaim Weizmann (President of the English Zionist Federation, and later first President of Israel), Mr Myer (Michael) J. Landa (Secretary of the Regiment Committee), Mr H. H. Gordon and W. C. Johnson, members of the LCC (London County Council) for Whitechapel, and many members of the Stepney Borough Council.

Lieutenant General Sir Frances Lloyd, commander of the London District, carried out the formal military inspection. After praising Jewish efforts across the military during the war, he stated that 'you will prove worthy followers of the ancient Jewish warriors... for the glory of the Jewish nation'.[10] After a kosher lunch and a blessing by the Chief Rabbi, who told them of their duty and their responsibilities to their faith and their country, they marched once more – this time to Waterloo station. They departed the same day to Southampton, ready to depart for the Middle East.

Jabotinsky later recorded in his book that 'tens of thousands lined the streets ... blue and white flags over every shop door ... old Jews with fluttering beards murmuring the *Shehecheyanu*'. The *Daily Mail*, the *Daily Express* and the *Daily Sketch* were all present and all reported favourably about the smart young men going off to war. There were journalists there who maintained an anti-Semitic tone and that criticised the soldiers' appearance and their accents, such as those that worked for the *Pall Mall Gazette*, but they were in the minority.

The Jewish press were exuberant in their praise for the Judeans and the parade. The opinion piece in *The Jewish Chronicle* on 8 February 1918 carried the following:

He must be a dull and unimaginative Jew who, without a glow of emotion and pride could have witnessed London's welcome to the Judeans as they marched through the streets of the metropolis ... trampling down in their progress foolish fears and fictions ... in a short while a band of Jews – 'foreigners' and East End aliens be it noted – from the workshop and factory, have been turned into a body of smart troops – looking each one of them every inch a soldier ... The Judeans are a living refutation of many a silly legend that have clung to the name of Jew and the cheers of the London populace ... testified that the whole edifice of calumny and ignorance – the work of centuries – had toppled to the dust.

Meanwhile, *Jewish World* used its article on 6 February 1916 to argue for an appreciation of what the Jew in uniform marching in his own regiment might mean for a whole community:

Never before has London beheld the proud sight presented to it on Monday last, when some hundreds of the Judeans, as the Regiment of Jewish soldiers has come to be fondly known, marched through the City prior to taking their departure from England ... This splendid body of troops would have done credit to any section of the British Army, either on the score of physique, of smart soldierly bearing or of intelligence. Yet they were drawn almost entirely from 'foreign Jews'; they were made up of the oft despised aliens; in private life they were just tailors or cigar-makers, or some of the crafts that are plied in the East End of London ... it was a stirring spectacle to see these men executing in excellent style a difficult turning movement in order to wheel round to the Mansion House ... It was heartening to hear their lusty singing of the *Hatikvah*, alternately to their fine rendering of the National Anthem (British). And every worthy emotion that can stir Jews must have been aroused when these brave lads, with swinging gait, marched to their station to their journey, to the Land of Jewish Hope, at their head as their Regimental 'mascot' – a Sepher Torah! In the annals of London Jewry no event more pregnant with strains of thought more redolent of the best aspirations of our people is recorded, than this march of the Judeans. In the annals of this great country, no event has happened reflecting more than this the true glory and true magnificence of Britain, nor are more typical of its real might.

The leading members of the Jewish community who saw the admiration and respect which the Regiment evoked from all sorts and conditions of men and women on the line of route, the deep impression it made upon the authorities, must have thought of their crassness in opposing the formation of a Jewish Regiment at the beginning of the war ... even though these soldiers are not the best of Anglo-Jewry, made up for the most part of Russian born Jews, brought up and nurtured in conditions that do not tend to physical prowess ... it is difficult to think of what might have been had a Jewish Regiment been given to the government, as was proposed, for the great struggle. The march was the best, the most effective, the most crushing answer to any anti-Semitic gibe or any anti-Jewish screed.[11]

The men reached the Middle East and were sent up into Palestine. They saw active service across the region, fighting in the Jordan Valley and at the Battle of Megiddo. By fighting with General Allenby's forces, many of the Jewish soldiers felt that they had made a real difference to the fate of the Jewish people. Stationed in the desert, conditions meant that the soldiers suffered as much from disease as they did from fighting. The experience of a man named Jacob Schneiderson is typical of the types of men who joined, even if he did have a slightly unusual experience, here recounted by his son:

My father was born in Warsaw, Poland in 1898 and named Jacob Schneiderson. In his very early years his family moved to England and they lived initially in Brick Lane in the East End of London.

Dad's first and only job as an employee was as a barber working for my grandfather Phillip Belchak. Phillip's family moved from Lodz in Poland at the end of the 1890s and lived in Cable Street. Phillip opened a hairdressing salon in Wilson Street, which is just behind Liverpool Street station, and my dad worked there. Dad married Phillip's daughter Florence (Fanny) in March 1925 at Poet's Road Synagogue, Dalston, and I was born in Maida Vale in February 1926.

Dad only told me one thing about the First World War. He was in Palestine in 1918 and was told to deliver a message from his regiment to another place, and when he returned his regiment had gone. He said it took him two months travelling up and down and across the country before he found his regiment. He never told me anything else but I have a photo of him in his Royal Fusiliers uniform and also his 1920 army discharge certificate.[12]

Some were requested to join the Judeans because of their existing success as servicemen. Philip Jacobs was born in London in 1895. By 1914 he lived in Golders Green, North London. He chose to enlist at Rothschild's Bank, St Swithin's Lane on 1 February 1916. He was therefore posted to the 3rd Territorial Battalion of the Bucks Regiment of the Oxford & Bucks Light Infantry.

In March 1917 he was commissioned as 2nd Lieutenant to the 3/19th London Regiment and was posted to the Ypres Salient in Flanders. He recalls being asked to change regiments to the Judeans:

I received an earnest message from the late Chief Rabbi, Dr Hertz to consider a transfer to the Jewish Regt. I obtained special leave to see Lt. Col. Patterson and my uncle Major William Schonfeld.

T.D.I. on the 24.1.1918 I was posted to the 42nd Battalion Royal Fusiliers. In the meantime I had been promoted to full Lieutenant. I was promoted A/Captain on the 12th June 1919 to 21/10/1919 when I proceeded home for demobilisation. During the 2nd World War I was recalled under the Officer's Emergency Reserve on the 7th May 1940 and granted the rank of Paymaster. I was demobilised on the 18th September 1946.

Philip went on to be vice chairman of the Monash branch of the British Legion.[13]

Others such as Charles 'Charley' Horne found that the Jewish Legion was somewhere that they could enlist and hide away disabilities. Charley was taken ill with diphtheria at the age of seven. The illness damaged the nerves in his middle ear, and consequently he was profoundly deaf for the rest of his life. He could hear some noise but could not properly identify sounds. He could lipread perfectly, and so he passed his medical and joined the 38th Battalion of the Royal Fusiliers.

It was not just British Jews from the East End who now felt that they had found their 'military fit'. Herbert Samuel MP, the Home Secretary, responsible for the changes to try and get Russian Jews to serve, had a son named Edwin Herbert Samuel. Edwin had been educated at Westminster and Oxford before he received his commission into the Royal Artillery in early 1917. He was transferred to the Egyptian Expeditionary Force before transferring into the Judeans and serving with them.

During the war the men of the Judeans wore a sewn fabric badge indicating their identity, along with the metal cap badge of the Royal Fusiliers. They were eventually awarded a regimental cap badge in late 1918, containing the menorah (a seven-branched candelabrum used in Jewish worship) and the word 'kadima' (forward/eastward),

Herbert Samuel with future Prime Minister Winston Churchill, often a friend of Anglo-Jewry. (Courtesy of the Library of Congress)

but as this was after the war had finished very few have survived. The battalions were disbanded between 1919 and 1921, with many of the Zionists staying in Palestine while others returned home to London and elsewhere across Britain and America. Some of those in the 40th Battalion who stayed went on to even greater things, with two becoming Prime Minister of Israel and one becoming President of Israel: David Ben-Gurion, Levi Eshkol and Yitzak Ben-Zvi. It is surprising to think that those men started out in British military uniform long before they graced the political stands of the new state of Israel and inspected the troops of the Israeli Defence Force.

In his own recollections Lieutenant Colonel Patterson mused that he had found the men interesting and surprising; among his thoughts on them he expressed the idea that while they all seemed proud of their Jewishness not all of them were Zionists; some simply wanted to serve with other Jews and had no political agenda.

A number of awards were made to the 38th Battalion while under Patterson's command – one Distinguished Service Order, five Military Crosses (three with bars), one Distinguished Conduct Medal, six Military Medals, eight Mentioned in Despatches. He also sadly reported that he had one officer and thirty-one men killed.

The men behind the Jewish Legion are now considered heroes of Zionism. Joseph Trumpeldor returned to Palestine after the war to work on the land. He also helped to organise and lead Jewish defence units on the border in the northern part of Palestine where he lived. In 1920 his defence unit was drawn into an argument at the settlement of Tel Hai between an Arab group and some Jewish settlers over the presence of French soldiers. Fighting broke out and Trumpeldor was fatally wounded defending the settlement. He died as a result of his injuries along with seven other Jews (two of whom had served with him in the Judeans) and five Arabs. He is now a national hero in Israel, with streets and buildings named after him.

Ze'ev Jabotinsky also moved to Palestine following the war. He continued to write and lobby for the creation of a full Jewish state, sometimes working with the British and sometimes against them. He often fell out with other Zionist leaders on a range of issues. Throughout the 1920s and 1930s he travelled extensively for the Zionist cause and was personally involved with trying to rescue Jews from the Nazi territories of Europe. In 1940 he was in New York once again trying to build support for a Jewish army, this time to fight the Nazis. While on this visit he had a heart attack and died. He is remembered as both a Zionist hero and a controversial figure to this day.

6

FAITH AND THE JEWISH CHAPLAINCY

At the start of the war Anglo-Jewry immediately provided its support to the British government. Alongside the communal organisations that took an active role for the British war effort was the majority of the religious leadership of the community. The Chief Rabbi, Joseph Hertz, declared that there was no reason for any Jewish man to not fight, and even further than that he made a number of statements with the message that it was a British Jew's duty to support and fight for their country in a time of war. This view was quite controversial for some, especially as the war continued, with no end in sight. Conscription and the Russian Jewish situation led some religious leaders to question the actions of the British Jewish leadership. However, the Chief Rabbi and the religious leaders of the Spanish and Portuguese community influenced and led the majority of British Jews – and they supported the war. The office of the Chief Rabbi produced Special Orders of Service to be used during the war; sermons were published almost weekly in *The Jewish Chronicle* for use, reflection and inspiration.

When the war started in August 1914 it was only a few weeks until the High Holy Days of Rosh Hashanah (New Year), Yom Kippur and Sukkot – these are three of the key festivals in the Jewish calendar and fall over a four-week period in the autumn (Judaism follows a lunar calendar and the dates for festivals move around in the Julian calendar). For many Jews these are the key

Chief Rabbi Joseph Hertz in 1913. (Courtesy of the Library of Congress)

times (along with Passover, Purim and Chanukah) on which they attend synagogue services. Therefore, in the autumn of 1914, religious leaders were quick to recognise that they would have large audiences and at a time of uncertainty – they would need to have clear messages to share with their congregations. The key religious bodies also sent out prayers for use in the services too, with a special mention for those who were serving in the forces. Rabbi S. J. Rabinowitz of Liverpool included in his service 'a plea for the success of England and her Allies'. A message that, according to *The Jewish Chronicle*, was shared by many of those leading the services as the New Year was celebrated.

Many towns near military camps had small congregations of Jews that now opened up their synagogues for Jewish servicemen training nearby. On 15 September 1914 it was reported in *The Jewish Chronicle* that 'there was a record attendance of Jewish men of the Kitchener's Army at the Services of the New Year held at Aldershot Synagogue'.

Revd A. Plaskow, who led the Aldershot service, said:

In taking up arms against violence and aggression, in order to defend principles of honour and liberty, are you not fighting not only for England's cause but also that of Judaism which always stands for liberty, freedom and honour. You are going into the line of battle not only as Englishmen, but also as Jews. I am sure you will not do anything to bring shame on the flag of Judaism. Remember that Judaism is worth fighting for.

With a high attendance some synagogues joined with other community organisations to use the opportunities of the holidays to spread wider messages for the war. In Leeds it was reported that Mr L. Rosenberg, the local military recruiting officer, was present after the Rosh Hashanah services and would be at the Jewish Institute every evening after the holiday services to receive names for enlisting. In Birmingham the Revd A. Cohen also used the services to let people know that the synagogue at Singers Hill would be 'pleased to receive ... names of all Jews from the Midland towns who have joined any branch of His Majesty's Forces'.

In Gibraltar, British Jews, under the auspices of the Spanish and Portuguese tradition but British nonetheless, opened up their synagogue services to any British military groups stationed there. The Malta synagogue did the same, especially as the Royal Fusiliers were there en route to other destinations. The Royal Fusiliers as a

London regiment had quite a number of Jewish soldiers and were grateful for the support.

Hertz's support of the British authorities was consistent and active. On 11 September 1914 the Chief Rabbi and his aides were reported to be visiting a military hospital in London to meet with the wounded of all faiths; 'the Jewish soldiers were particularly grateful for the visit' according to the newspaper reports. He was a regular visitor at military hospitals throughout the war.

In early October 1914, the United Synagogues issued a special 'Prayer for the time of War to be used by the Hazan during the Service of the Day of Atonement (Yom Kippur)'. The messages were clear from synagogues all over the UK – British Judaism's religious bodies were behind the British government and most importantly they were behind the war; that meant British Jews should be doing whatever was needed of them for war service.

The Jewish civilian religious authorities worked closely with the Jewish military religious authorities, ensuring that there were consistent messages and regular support across the communities. Special prayers were issued for religious holidays and regular services. Jewish military chaplains were in communication with local rabbis to ensure that young men returning injured were supported, and that where men were not to return their families were supported.

The religious authorities also joined in with key religious messages issued by the Anglican authorities. It was agreed that 1 January 1916 would be a dedicated as a national day of prayer to introduce the New Year, across all of the faiths. The Chief Rabbi delivered a rousing sermon:

And then in one day a cataclysm engulfed civilisation ... None could have foretold that civilized mankind would rush back to savagery with such dreadful fervour. No wonder, that for some this world-calamity has put out in their firmament the stars of hope and faith forever; that they find insuperable difficulty in fitting these things into our sense of the overruling Providence of God.[1]

Later in the war, a small booklet of prayers was to be read every Sabbath after the prayer for the king and the royal family.

One of the issues that drew civilian and military Jewish religious leaders together was the discussion over religious observance while serving in the armed forces. Different rabbis – or reverends, as they were often known – then had different interpretations from one another. In Judaism the rule to save or preserve a life is one of the most important rules. For some that meant other religious observance could or should be put to one side.

The interpretations about kosher food and not eating non-kosher food or meat (*treif*) in particular were often contentious. Some believed that they could be relaxed if the alternative was going hungry when staying healthy and fit is essential, such as when you are a soldier. After all, when preservation of life trumps all other rules then eating has to be essential.

There is a story about men of the Zion Mule Corps who were involved with unloading crates containing bacon on the jetty in Egypt and refused to do so until the Grand Rabbi (of Alexandria) granted a dispensation. In addition to the dispensation, he gave them permission to eat the bacon if necessary, that is if these were the only rations arriving. The men immediately applied for the unkosher rations but they were too late; as they had previously rejected them, they had been dispersed to other hungry soldiers. Not letting an opportunity pass, they held on to the dispensation and used it for all future ration allocations.[2] A New Zealand officer later wrote how thereafter it always amused the troops to see the Jews of the Zion Mule Corps returning to their cookhouse with little bags of bacon.[3]

Some of the very orthodox rabbis found the relaxation of the rules or some interpretations outrageous, and there were occasionally demonstrations at synagogues and at religious council meetings.

During the war, many synagogues and their leaders busied themselves with care committees, welfare roles and supporting the families of those who had loved ones at the front or had lost an income due to the conflict. For the men and women in the armed services, their spiritual well-being was now undertaken by the military chaplaincy.

The Military Chaplaincy

It is generally considered that each army enters a battle believing that it has its god or gods on its side. Having religious support is, therefore, considered essential. Men and women who never attend religious services in peacetime are known to go to prayers and services just before battle. Further, on the battlefield itself prayers are sent up and god is cried out for more than any other thought or person – perhaps barring one's mother. It is not surprising that a military chaplaincy is an important part of life in the forces.

The military chaplaincy of Christian reverends had existed long before the First World War. With a war on, a larger army had been called for and it therefore followed that there would be greater religious diversity in the ranks, which necessitated more varied religious leadership and support. Therefore, as the number of Jewish volunteers began to rise, so did the need to minister to their religious needs. Rabbis or Jewish reverends initially became part of the military chaplaincy in the Territorial services. The first Jewish minister to serve as a military chaplain was Francis Lyon Cohen

(1862–1934), minister of the Borough Synagogue, who held this position from 1892 to 1904.

Revd Michael Adler became a commissioned chaplain in the first chaplaincy rank of captain in the Territorial Forces in 1909. He had attended the Territorial Force summer camps on Salisbury Plain, where he had conducted services for Jewish soldiers. Initially the responsibilities were part-time, with the main event being an annual Chanukah military service, which Rabbi Cohen had initiated to bring as many Jewish servicemen together as possible.

Jewish chaplains were not sent to the active theatres of war, unlike Christian chaplains; the authorities did not know how to treat a Jewish chaplain, who would not have the bulk of a regiment following his faith. Jews were dispersed across the regiments and so the military authorities were unsure how to manage all their needs.

ON ACTIVE SERVICE: Rev. MICHAEL ADLER, S.C.F., AND GROUP, ROUEN, MAY 19, 1915.
Back Row: Dvr. S. Schweitzer, A.S.C.; Pte. L. Levy, 2nd Manchester Regt.; Pte. J. Spero, A.S.C.; Sgt. L. Nathan (M.M.), O.V.R.; Pte. J. Hepstone (killed in action), 1st K.O.R. Lancs Regt.; Pte. I. Abrahams, Indian Veterinary Corps; Pte. A. Goldman, 2nd W. Riding Regt.; Rfn. D. Cohen, 12th London Regt.; Pte. A. Carlish, A.S.C.
Second Row: Dvr. J. Hershman, A.S.C.; Pte. S. Lessman, 3rd London Regt.; Pte. F. Spicker, A.S.C.; Pte. R. Friedlander, 7th London Regt.; Pte. M. Needle, A.S.C.; Pte. K. Goodman, R.A.M.C.; Pte. M. Gavson, A.S.C.; Pte. M. Althusen (killed in action), 1st K.O.R. Lancs Regt.; Pte. M. Levy, A.S.C.; L.-Cpl. B. Lyons, 1st West Yorks Regt.
Third Row: Pte. L. Blush, A.S.C.; Pte. J. H. Bernstock, 4th London Regt.; Sergt. J. Harris, A. Cyclist Corps.; Sergt. M. M. Polack, A.S.C.; Rev. Michael Adler, S.C.F.; Capt. M. Joseph, Indian Pay Corps; Pte. B. Salmon, A.S.C.; Pte R. Simmons, R.A.M.C.; Pte. N. Goldstuck, R.A.M.C.
At Foot: Pte. H. Constad, A.S.C.

Revd Michael Adler DSO and an active-service group.

The established feeling was that the Jewish chaplains could be based in the UK and communicate by post with the Jewish soldiers, trying to organise food and special services where they could.

In the first month of the war, Michael Adler wrote a Soldiers' Prayer Book, which Chief Rabbi Hertz (who visited France in June 1915) later enlarged. It was distributed freely to Jewish servicemen. As the war went on the Chief Rabbi's office also made other books freely available to the troops, including *A Book of Jewish Thoughts*, *The Jewish Version of the Book of Psalms*, *A History of the Jews* (by Paul Goodman) and *Prayers for the Trench and Base* (by Captain B. L. Q. Henriques of the Tank Corps). The books became important for seeking solace during difficult times but also as a means of identification at times of injury. There are also stories of Jewish men sharing their prayer books and indeed their prayers with non-Jews when facing battle or recovering from one.

As the months progressed and more and more Jews enlisted and greater appeals went out from the Jewish community for volunteers, Michael Adler decided something more was needed for the Jewish servicemen. With the support of his community, Adler applied to serve on the Western Front as a Jewish chaplain; he was forty-six years of age. The War Office refused.

However, Adler was allowed to apply for pass to go to the Western Front to check that Jewish servicemen were being catered to. In January 1915 he was granted permission to visit the men on the front line and on his return he wrote a report for the War Office. He made his case that currently no one was administering to the Jewish troops and that if their spiritual and physical well-being was to be preserved he needed to be there. Evidently his arguments worked, as soon afterwards he was granted permission to be posted to the Western Front. The British authorities were aware that they were lacking in the accommodations made for

Jewish troops and that if their arguments of being an everyman's army were to be true that had to be addressed.

Interestingly the French army, the army of a republic, already had rabbis serving near the front, as one humorous story from the 16 October 1914 edition of *The Jewish Chronicle* reveals:

> One French army corps has both a Catholic military chaplain and a Jewish rabbi with it. Father Narp and Grand Rabbi Ginsburger were frequently seen together on their common mission of seeking the wounded and caring for the dying, and when they reached the village they found there was only one bed available. Both of them were worn out and lay down fully dressed, to sleep. Father Narp, turning to the Grand rabbi said: 'What a pity there is not a photographer here to take a snapshot of us – The Old Testament and the New sleeping in the same bed.'

Importantly, Revd Adler was also allowed to distinguish himself from the Christian chaplains he worked with by wearing a Magen David (Star of David) as his insignia; he was assisted in making that happen by the chaplain general, the Right Revd Bishop Taylor-Smith CVO, who was supportive of having a Jewish chaplain based on the front line.

According to research by Jonathan Lewis,

> very gradually, more Jewish chaplains were appointed: one in 1915, two in 1916 and larger numbers in 1917 and 1918. By the end of the war there were over twenty Jewish chaplains with British forces. Several were on the Western Front, and two on the Italian Front. Several were in Egypt and the Canal Zone. One was with the Jewish Legion within General Allenby's army which took Jerusalem and the Holy Land from the Ottoman Empire, which

was an ally of the Central Powers. Some served with home forces in Britain, where there were always large numbers of soldiers. There were also ministers who as civilians served in Britain as what were termed officiating clergymen.[4]

The new Jewish chaplains served alongside their Christian counterparts to support those of the Jewish faith wherever they could reach them during the First World War. As the Jewish servicemen were scattered across regiments they couldn't have a rabbi permanently attached to them so the chaplains had to travel great distances to reach all the men.

Due to the fact that the servicemen were spread out among regiments and there were only a small number of Jewish chaplains, Adler created a small service book in English that the Christian chaplains could use for Jewish funerals and prayers. As the war progressed many of the Jewish chaplains found

Revd Michael Adler DSO and Revd V. G. Simmons CF, near Arras.

themselves administering to the Christian troops when needed as well. Adler and his men set up communication systems between the Jewish servicemen, thanks to information supplied by the War Office, and created service notes for festivals so that the servicemen could put services on themselves if there was no Jewish chaplain locally.

In his diaries, 2nd Lieutenant Marcus Segal refers to helping with services and other prayers:

23 May 1917

My dearest parents

Just a few hurried lines to let you know I am feeling very well in this lovely weather and trust you are the same. Yesterday the 22nd inst., Adler came to see me and we are arranging for a Service on the 26th inst., and are going to get as many Yiddisher boys as possible. He was very pleased to see me and took a great interest in me ...

Good-night God bless you,

Your loving son, Marcus

There are plenty of accounts testifying that the army supported Jewish chaplains in getting to their troops, including assisting with transport when it was available for the chaplains and to take soldiers straight from the front line to key festival services, such as Yom Kippur. Of course, that was only possible when there was a lull in the fighting. No service was more important than stopping the enemy or winning the war.

The chaplains wrote regularly to the Jewish press to bring news of the men serving and to provide obituaries. In turn, the press wrote regularly about the activities of the Jewish chaplains and how they travelled this way and that to reach the men wherever they were stationed. Revd Adler barely left the Western Front in three years of war, only returning to the UK to garner more support, arrange for resources to assist with the celebration of Jewish holidays (such as Passover) and to try and get kosher food – at least for the main holidays.

In his recollections in the British Jewry Book of Honour, Adler recounts what it was like to experience shelling and how he carried a Holy Ark and Sefor Torah (religious book for services) around with him in those conditions. He recounts meeting with war artists, including Solomon J. Solomon and Professor Rothernstein, as well as the daily discussions he had with soldiers and officers of all faiths. He became a well-known figure and was often called to meetings or stopped as he travelled around to discuss religious services and questions of faith. He made every effort to reach men to fulfil their religious need and recalled that on some occasions he would find himself meeting with Jewish men and saying prayers in the open, in shelled buildings and on one occasion in a monastery. For a Yom Kippur service in 1915 he recalls that the men walked in 'fully equipped straight from the lines'.[5] He had to take cover from bombardments and frequently shared prayers with Christian chaplains, all of whom he described as being very friendly and warm. He describes how a number of Jewish soldiers reported acts of kindness by Christian chaplains to him. He was, however, keen to point out that he never heard of any proselytising.

In the summer of 1918, Adler's tireless work and constant devotion to duty up and down the battle front (he reported that he was known fondly to many as 'the wandering Jew') got the better of him and, exhausted, he was forced home after becoming ill. It was unfortunate that after so much time at the front he missed the final stages of the war, when the big push against the Germans and their allies finally happened and success began to be within reach.

At the end of the war, Adler's incredible work was recognised when he was awarded the DSO.

Mentioned in Despatches
Distinguished Service Order
Instituted on 6th September 1886 by Queen Victoria, the Distinguished Service Order (D.S.O.) was awarded to Michael, Rev. Adler for meritorious or distinguished service during wartime.

The order was established for rewarding individual instances of meritorious or distinguished service in war. It was a military order, until recently for officers only and normally given for distinguished services during active operations against the enemy.

It is typically awarded to officers ranked Major (or its equivalent) or higher, but the honour has sometimes been awarded to especially valorous junior officers.

The recipient, Michael, Rev. Adler, is known as a Companion of the Distinguished Service Order and is entitled to use the letters D.S.O. after his name.

He was not the only one to be recognised for his devotion to duties. Reverends A. Barnett, M. Gollop and S. Grajewsky were mentioned in despatches, and Revd S. Lipson was mentioned in home despatches.

Adler described his contentment at being the senior Jewish chaplain as follows:

Principal sources of satisfaction in looking back at my varied war experiences are afforded by two considerations, of which the first is that I found ample opportunities to perform useful work, and

Adler with the 17th Regiment.

the second that the reputation of the Jewish soldier on the Western Front stood very high and reflected the fullest credit upon the good name of Anglo-Jewry.[6]

Although Adler then took a step back and a new Jewish chaplain took over the role of Senior Jewish Chaplain to HM Forces, he didn't stop working. Instead, he turned his attention to ensuring that the Jewish service and sacrifice was not forgotten. In this vein he began to put in motion his plan for the British Jewry Book of Honour.

Holding a Festival at the Front

From August 1914 to November 1918 there were four festivals of Pesach, Yom Kippur and Rosh Hashanah, just as there were four Christmases and four Easters – war is not an observer of religious festivals. Pesach, or Passover as it more commonly known in the non-Jewish world, is an important festival of remembrance, reflection and coming together. It is based on the story from Exodus of the Israelites' flight from Egypt with Moses. During the First World War, world Jewry continued to observe the key festivals of the religious calendar on the home front. This meant Seder nights without loved ones who were serving elsewhere or were now never to return. For them the Pesach of those years must have been one of mixed emotions, as well as concerns for future years.

For those serving in the forces, Pesach during the First World War meant trying to fulfil the message of coming together with a new family created from fellow Jewish servicemen and women living far from home – and the occasional non-Jew who fancied a free meal and a bit of solace. The stranger is always welcome at the Seder table: 'You shall not wrong a stranger or oppress him, for you were strangers in the Land of Egypt' (Exodus 22:20). Jewish soldiers often brought their new comrades with them to these events.

Therefore, it became possible to observe Pesach with fellow Jews and with religious support across the world, wherever Jewish troops were serving. It is particularly significant that for the Jewish servicemen and women and their families that lived a hundred years ago, the story and remembrance of exile may have brought them comfort and unity while they were exiled from their immediate family as a result of duty and contribution to their country.

The Men Killed during High Holidays the First World War

Using the records of the British Jewry Book of Honour, it is possible to confirm that twelve Jewish officers and approximately eighty men of other ranks were killed during the four Pesach periods of the First World War. The number is likely to be slightly higher if we assume that not all Jewish men are recorded in the book. In addition to those killed, many more will have been wounded and one can search for their names in the wounded lists of *The Jewish Chronicle*. The list of those killed includes Jewish men from across the UK and the British Empire – Australia, New Zealand, South Africa and Canada.

The men who were killed are buried or remembered on war memorials across the Western Front and the Middle East. The Pesach of 1915 has more officers than other ranks killed, indicating that a number of Jewish men were in the professional British Army or the Territorial Forces prior to the war. It is also proof that it was subalterns or junior officers who would lead their men in any attack, and the Pesach of 1915 was at the same time as the Second Battle of Ypres.

One of those killed in the first Pesach is Major Ernest Alex Myer; he is listed as being killed in action on 3 April 1915. He was a solicitor from London, an expert in apprenticeship law who had served as a Territorial some time before and was immediately put into service when war broke out. He was with the London Regiment (City of London Rifles) when he was killed, aged forty, in the fighting in northern France. He is buried at Guards Commonwealth War Graves Commission Cemetery, Windy Corner, Cuinchy, France and written as his epitaph is 'Perfect in life he was Dulce et decorum est pro patria mori'. He left his wife, Emily, and his parents to mourn him.

In 1916, Isador Steinberg, serving in the Australian Infantry and from Perth in Western Australia, was killed. He was aged twenty when he was reported killed in action on 20 April 1916. He is buried in Rue-du-Bacqureot (13 London) Commonwealth

War Graves Commission Cemetery, Laventie, France, a small cemetery with only 192 burials. He was killed in the everyday fighting along the front line.

The largest year for deaths during Pesach for Jewish men is 1917. On that occasion Pesach coincided with the serious fighting in the northern France area of the Western Front in Arras and around Vimy.

On 10 April 1917 two Jewish men, one a private in the army and one a Mercantile Marine, were killed, but they are without headstones. Mendel Emanuel Levene was the Mercantile Marine; he was killed at sea aged nineteen and is remembered on the Salta Memorial at Sainte Marie Cemetery, Le Havre, France. Private Sydney Bloom of the Middlesex Regiment was killed on the same day with no known grave and is remembered on the Thiepval Memorial to the Missing on the Somme, France.

It seems 10 April 1917 was a bleak day as Emmanuel Schwartz of the Army Cyclist Corps was also killed and is remembered on the Arras Memorial to the Missing.

The final Pesach of the war coincided with the Spring Offensive, the Germans' big push on the Western Front, which led to a period of intense fighting. Private Jack Dion MM was killed on 27 March 1918. He was aged twenty-seven and was with the Northampton Regiment, although he was from East London. According to records he was married to Celia who was living in Cable Street, St George's in the East, London, when he was killed. Dion had received the Military Medal for his bravery in earlier battles. He is remembered on the Pozieres Memorial to the Missing in France.

The High Holidays in the autumn months of Rosh Hashanah and Yom Kippur also had their casualties. There are sixteen killed in action on the dates of Rosh Hashanah and Yom Kippur during the war years that can reliably be proven to be Jewish, including the following:

Second Lieutenant Kenneth Maurice Halgren Solomon. Died 18 September 1915 after sustaining injuries in the fighting at Gallipoli. His parents' address was Town Hall, Sydney, New South Wales, but he fought with the Gloucestershire Regiment. He was evacuated to Britain and died in a military hospital aged twenty-six and is buried in North London.

Second Lieutenant Edward Joseph Leon. Died 7 October 1916. He was in the London Regiment's Post Office Rifles when he died aged twenty-one. His inscription on his headstone simply states that he is 'Dearly Loved son of Joseph A Esther P Leon of London'. He is buried at Warlencourt British Cemetery, France.

Second Lieutenant Martin Alexander Lyone MC. Died 26 September 1917 at the Third Battle of Ypres aged twenty-three. Enlisted with the 27th Canadians as a private on his commission (after recommendation while serving in France) and transferred to Northumberland Fusiliers. He had received his Military Cross from earlier fighting and had been injured earlier in the war. His headstone inscription reads 'In Loving Memory Son of MD Lyone of Winnipeg, Canada'. His death was on Yom Kippur of that year; he was one of ten Jewish men to be killed or die as a result of injuries on that day in 1917.

Private Samuel Harry Rickayzen. Died 7 September 1918. He was attached to the Durham Light Infantry when he was fighting in the 100 Days Offensive, the last hundred days of the war. He was severely injured and taken to No. 8 General hospital near Rouen, where he died. His parents, who were originally from Warsaw, had the words 'Deeply Mourned by his heartbroken parents;

he was the most devoted of children' added to his headstone at Bois-Guillaume Communal Military Cemetery Extension, France.

Private Sam Greyman. Died 8 September 1918. Greyman represents some of the key strands of Anglo-Jewish life at that time. He was born in Russia in 1898 and arrived in the UK as an immigrant. His family settled in Leeds where he grew up. He served with the 38th Battalion of the Royal Fusiliers, the Judeans, and was sent to fight in the Middle East. He died in Egypt (probably at a military hospital) and is buried in the Jerusalem War Cemetery. He was a migrant, a resident, a loyal soldier and a Jewish man buried in the Holy Land.

Immediately after the Armistice, a booklet was issued by the office of the Chief Rabbi containing prayers as a form of thanksgiving to God. Called *Consequent on the Cessation of Hostilities*, it was to be used on the Sabbath, 16 November 1918.

Praise and Thanksgiving to Almighty God
Consequent on the Cessation of hostilities
Memorial Prayer
For those fallen in battle
O God. Who art full of compassion. Who dwellest on high, grant perfect rest beneath the shelter of Thy divine presence, in the exalted places among the wholly and pure who shine as of the brightness of the firmament to all who have bravely laid down their lives for their King and Country. We beseech Thee, Lord of compassion, shelter them for evermore under the cover of Thy wings and let their souls be bound up in the bond of eternal life. The Lord is their inheritance; may they rest in peace. And let us say, amen

The reform movement and the congregation of the Spanish and Portuguese also issued special thanksgiving prayers. The religious leadership of Anglo-Jewry would try to continue providing help for its congregants as much as ever. Synagogues would be important places for support for those affected by the war as well as symbols of normality away from fighting. Of course, some saw their faith destroyed by what they witnessed in the conflict and they would want to break free of religious doctrine, even if they did not wish to break free of being Jewish.

7

THE HOME FRONT

Writing a record of life on the home front is not easy. Even though far more people stayed put in the UK than went off to fight, the records of daily life are scattered and often simplistic. Newspapers and diaries are the main source of information, and unfortunately they don't always survive properly or with much-needed context attached. Daily life for everyone in the UK was affected by the war.

The war introduced a lot of insecurity about the future, with plans often put on hold. Those plans included work contracts and employment, both of which had a lot less protection in legislation then compared to now. Just over a week from the start of the war, *The Jewish Chronicle* ran a story titled 'Effects of the war on the East End – Tailors thrown out of work'. It was quite clear about the impact the conflict was already having at home:

> The effect of the war will largely being felt in the East End: already signs are not wanting of distress. During the week many people in the tailoring industry have been thrown out of employment owing to big contract being cancelled.

For many Jews in Britain the war also meant disruption to the places they had been born, where they might still have family members.

In the same edition of *The Jewish Chronicle*, 14 August 1914, the paper reports of crowds assembling at the offices of the Yiddish newspapers night and day. False reports of Warsaw and other key cities being captured by different forces raised concerns for loved ones elsewhere, and the Jewish authorities feared that there might be panic, but on the whole calm was kept. However, the general unease that the war caused did not help communities that already felt vulnerable.

Everyone was affected by the new sweeping controls brought in by the Defence of the Realm Act (DORA) only four days after the declaration of war on 8 August. The Act was introduced into the Houses of Parliament and passed in the interests of 'securing public safety' and 'in order to control communications, the nation's ports and subject civilians to the rule of military courts'[1] without any debate.

This Act was revised and expanded six times during the war and created an enduring set of social rules and structures, some of which still exist in the twenty-first century. DORA gave the government the power to prosecute anyone whose actions could 'jeopardise the success of the operations of HM Forces or to assist the enemy'. A vague description such as that could be applied to many areas of life, and it was.

A key area of DORA was in the rules on censorship, which affected newspapers, radio and private mail, and in particular targeted any communications between those serving in the forces and their friends or family, or anyone writing to someone outside of the UK. Military censors examined 300,000 private telegrams in 1916 alone.[2]

In the East End of London, one Jewish woman became crucial for helping a community still keep in touch with their loved ones at the front. Rachel Wisotzky was born in Grodno, Belarus, in 1894. The family came to Britain in 1900, settling in the East End of London. Rachel attended school and later, as her father established himself financially, she was taught by a tutor. She was fluent in English and Yiddish, understood and spoke some German and was taught bookkeeping – all quite unusual for a girl from immigrant parents. Her father was naturalised in 1912, ensuring him greater financial security, which led to his increased business successes, they in turn led him to overseas travel. Tragically, while traveling overseas he unfortunately contracted polio in another country. His illness became a real problem and meant that the family suffered both emotionally and financially. Rachel increasingly wanted to use her sharp mind and skills to help and looked around for suitable employment.

When war was declared, appeals for women to replace men in some occupations led to Rachel applying and becoming a Post Office clerk in her local area. It was her way of helping her family and 'doing her bit' for the war effort at the same time. It was in this job that she was able, quite by accident, to play a remarkable and valuable role as an interpreter, helping some of the illiterate or non-English speakers who lived in the area around her. According to her family record:

There were large numbers of Jewish soldiers and sailors away from home. Many of their fathers or uncles had been forcibly conscripted into the Russian army in the 19th century; their first-generation English sons felt honoured to serve in the British forces. The majority of these Jewish servicemen came from London's East End and were proud of the opportunity of fighting for their adopted country; a democracy that offered so much for their future.

It was a long war and the soldiers or sailors would write home frequently. The problem was that British officers had to read all letters home for security and possible censoring. All men were, therefore, required to write their letters home in English. What's the problem? Their parents back in London often could not read. Those who could read frequently did not understand enough English.

In the early 20th century there were three or more postal deliveries every weekday. Parents of frontline troops would arrive at any time of the day; queue in front of Booba's (family name for Rachel) grille at the post office-counter with letters in their hands. Although very busy selling stamps, taking telegrams, paying out allowances (old age pensions had recently been introduced), and a host of other clerical duties, Booba would translate the letters into Yiddish, aloud through the grille, to anxious relatives. For those parents who were able to read, she wrote in Yiddish between the lines of English, so that they could share their letters with other relatives.

Rachel's story provides a small insight into the effect of legislation on communication between families and on the lives of those who might already feel slightly disconnected with the wider society. Her role in the post office is also a reminder of the valuable contribution women played during the war, especially as they were frequently removed from those posts once the men had returned home.

As a result of DORA, property was requisitioned for war use to protect resources that would be essential for the military and to try and maximise wartime production. Under the powers of DORA, British Summer Time was instituted in May 1916. This introduced the time changes in spring and autumn when the clocks are put forward or back. The original purpose was to maximise daylight working hours, particularly in agriculture. Its effect, still with us today, is a standardisation of time across the whole of the UK. There were other rules, too: pubs could no longer have flexible licensing as formal opening times were introduced, and regulations on drugs were introduced to stop recreational use as all cocaine and opium would now be required for medicinal use.

Other rules that may have had a sensible purpose during the war now seem ridiculous and were quickly overturned post-war. These included bans on whistling for London taxis (in case it should be mistaken for an air-raid warning), the purchase of binoculars (in case they were used for spying), ringing church bells (only to be done at the end of the war), and the melting down of gold or silver, which was considered currency fraud.

For the Jewish communities, the majority of the restrictions introduced had the same impact on their lives as it did for anyone else – just another thing to worry about.

Belgian Refugees

Britain and Belgium had shared a strong relationship for a long time, with the two countries having strong trading connections that went back centuries. Germany's attack on a neutral Belgium had been one of the most compelling reasons for the British government to declare war on the Kaiser and his country. The Belgians' appeal to the British for help reached across more than just political and military lines; on 14 August 1914 *The Jewish Chronicle* printed a story about an event that had occurred at the start of the week. Immediately after the German invasion there had been a request for medical support, especially for trained nurses, by the Belgian authorities. The banker Mr Alfred de Rothschild at once arranged for eighteen trained nurses to be sent from England to Belgium. The article reported that the women had been invited to breakfast with 'Mr de Rothschild on the Sunday and afterwards left for Belgium'.

Within weeks of the German attack on Belgium, refugees from that country started to arrive in the UK. The Jewish press ran huge adverts about the plight of the Belgian refugees and formed themselves into committees. Approximately 225,000 to 265,000 Belgian refugees travelled to the UK. British newspapers carried stories of German atrocities against civilians, many of which were based on truth and were not just propaganda (the German leaders were angry that the Belgians had refused their demands to be allowed to pass through Belgium in order to attack France); this resulted in national appeals for the refugees, and on the whole a warm welcome when they arrived. In the UK the British government established the War Refugees Committee to deal with the new arrivals, with temporary camps set up in cities and towns, taking over large sites such as Alexandra Palace in North London. The refugees were then dispersed around the country to spread the responsibility; approximately 2,500 local refugee committees were established.

The exact number of Jewish Belgian refugees is unknown but synagogue and Jewish newspaper records indicate that there were approximately 6,000 to 8,000. There were quite established Jewish communities in cities such as Antwerp and Brussels; however, in some cases the Jewish Belgian refugees were not Belgian at all. They were eastern European Jews who had been resident in Belgium when Germany invaded and feared being picked up as foreigners from countries now at war with Germany. Many of these people were poor and had already fled hardship once, from eastern Europe; now they found themselves destitute and displaced once more.

In September 1914, Dayan Harris M. Lazarus of the Brondesbury Synagogue and London Beth Din (a rabbinical court – the Beth Din carries the law for Jewish religious affairs, such as granting a divorce and settling some disputes) was at a meeting to officially welcome the Belgian refugees to Cricklewood, London. The Jewish community took upon itself the task of housing and feeding this influx of Jews from the Continent, and large numbers of Jews throughout the UK, including in the poorer communities of the East End of London, replied to charitable appeals by opening up their homes to provide refugees with sleeping accommodation as well as by giving money. The Jews Temporary Shelter in Leman Street, London, was used to house many refugees but it could not cope with the throngs arriving daily from Belgium. After a short while a large, disused workhouse of the Westminster Union in Poland Street was made available by the Local Government Board for the refugees. In early November 1914 the Manchester Hotel in Aldersgate Street, which had been vacant for nearly a year, was designated by the Local Government Board specifically for the housing of Jewish families and married couples.

In the opening year of the war there were regular appeals for funds for the refugees, especially as stories of the German atrocities in Belgium increased. Full-page advertisements appeared in *The Jewish Chronicle* and the *Jewish News*, as well as small articles and appeals. Other appeals would continue throughout the entire war as the refugees continued to require care. In the community sections of the newspapers there would be lists of the funds raised for the refugees from communities around the UK. The Jewish groups were often gifted religious scrolls and prayer books as well as food and shelter. Some of the refugees would themselves contribute to the war effort by working in factories and carrying out farm work. Others were entirely dependent on support from regional refugee groups.

After 1918, the majority of the Belgian refugees returned home, encouraged to do so by both the British and Belgian governments. It is estimated that around 10,000 remained, having settled in the

UK and married local people. Within a short period, this group had entirely disappeared from view as they assimilated into their new surroundings.

After the war, people in the UK who had helped the refugees were recognised with the Medal of the National Committee for Assistance and Food Supply (*Medaille du Comite National de Secours et d'Alimentation*) 1914–1918. It was created in four classes: first class, gilt finish with a rosette on the ribbon; second class, gilt finish and no rosette; third class, silver finish; fourth class, bronze. A list of recipients was published in *The Belgian Monitor* (the Belgian equivalent of the *London Gazette*). The medal was known to some as the Haricot Bean Medal because the foodstuff was a regular staple for the refugees.

The Vulnerability of Women

While in some quarters of Anglo-Jewry the war was all about enlistment and service, for others it was keeping the community stable. Lily Montagu, the daughter of the self-made millionaire Samuel Montagu, was a well-known campaigner for women and the poor. She had founded the West Central Jewish Girls' Club in 1893 together with her sister and cousin. When war was declared she wrote to *The Jewish Chronicle* with a plea to Jewish housewives, she wanted them to stop doing their own sewing repairs and needle work and instead to employ Jewish seamstresses. She was concerned – rightly – that the traditional occupation of needlework for many poor Jewish women would be threatened by the instability brought on by the war. Throughout the war years she would speak up for women whose livelihoods were threatened in addition to having their husbands and sons sent off to war.

There was seemingly no shortage of work for men on the home front, but for women with children, finding work that fitted into their schedule was often a challenge. Many ended up doing difficult shift work for the flexibility it offered. They tended to find that the extremely hard work and low pay in garment factories was the only option. *Jewish World* reported in December 1914 how a group of 'Jewish ladies' had come together to open 'Our Babies Home' in Kilburn to help with the babies and young children of the Jewish soldiers. It was a type of crèche to allow the mothers to work or look after other family matters.

Lily Montagu was not wrong about the unsettling effect of the war on some. Alice Stone was born in London in 1893. Before she was twenty years of age she married Louis Hoppen, but approximately thirty-two months later she became a war widow. Her husband had enlisted when their first son was only twenty-six months old and she was three months pregnant with a second son.

Being widowed meant that Alice had to try to raise her two boys on her own, with little family support. She found the financial challenge of this incredibly difficult and eventually, in 1924, she had to put the boys into the Norwood (Jewish) Orphanage. Alice remarried in 1928 and had a daughter, Hannah, in 1930; she always remained in touch with her boys, even if she was unable to provide for them.

Mrs Meyer Speilman of the Union of Jewish Women was often in the press writing about her concerns regarding the problems that women were experiencing as a result of the war. She often focused on the need for there to be greater relief for women who had lost work, not just the working classes but also those from the middle class who could no longer work as governesses on the Continent. She was keen for these women to now turn their hands to nursing. Another area where an appeal for women's work began was in schooling. Many of the male teachers had left their jobs to go to war and now schools were prepared to take women as teachers, even of boys.

On 10 November 1916 *The Jewish Chronicle* reported an appeal from the LCC (London County Council) and Care Committee:

> The Care Committee and the London County Council schools very urgently need the voluntary services of capable young women to serve in connection with schools in which the large majority of children affected by the Care committee's efforts are Jewish.

Schools also took up the cause of the war in the 11 February 1916 edition of *The Jewish Chronicle*; the Poplar Synagogue and Valence Road LCC School are reported to have sent comforts to the Jewish soldiers at Aldershot.

Attacks on the UK

Many people living on the home front also felt a little at risk from the presence of war. On 16 December 1914 the German Navy attacked the British east coast. The coastal towns of Scarborough, Whitby and Hartlepool were bombarded, causing significant damage to buildings. A total of 592 people were injured in the attacks, including 137 who died.

It was not just attacks from the sea that threatened the citizens of Britain. In 1900, a retired German general, Count von Zeppelin, had built his first airship, which became known as a Zeppelin. Zeppelins were introduced as a means of transporting commercial air passengers in luxurious style, something that the new biplanes were completely unable to do. The German military also saw their potential as an addition to their armoury.

In December 1914 the Germans made their first bombing raid against the UK, using a biplane to attack Dover, but the attack dealt little damage as the aircraft could not carry a great deal of explosives. In January 1915, the Germans launched their first aerial attack using Zeppelins; they were able to carry up to 2 tonnes of explosives. The towns of Great Yarmouth and King's Lynn were the first to be hit.

Twenty-eight people were killed on 31 May 1915, when Zeppelin bombers made their first attack on London. Zeppelins had the advantage of being relatively quiet, enabling them to get close to their targets without detection. This was the first of many attacks over the south of England.

Over the next couple of years anti-aircraft guns were installed, barrage balloons put up over cities, and Royal Naval Air Service and Royal Flying Corps aircraft kept in the UK ready to combat the threat. In addition to the horror and fear that Zeppelins caused among the civilian population, they also forced the British military to keep resources at home to defend British citizens from attack while they were in great demand overseas on the front lines.

On 27 September 1916, a young Jewish man in Bognor Regis named Alfred wrote to his grandmother and aunts who were living in London and included his concerns about the Zeppelin raids:

> I have been anxious, for those at home, regarding the Zepps, and hope Booba and Aunts Sarah and Leah are bearing the frights of the Air raids alright, being on your own. One Zepp passed over our way, the other way towards Portsmouth, but I did not hear it.

The letter is now held in the Jewish Museum, London, and offers a valuable insight into just how worried people were about the aerial attacks.

Lieutenant Rex Warneford, a British pilot flying over France on the night of 6/7 June 1915, was the first pilot to bring down a Zeppelin. He was awarded the Victoria Cross (VC) but was killed a few days later. On 2 September 1916, William Leefe-Robinson of the RFC shot down a Zeppelin over Hertfordshire – the massive fire caused by the hydrogen exploding was seen for over 100 miles. Leefe-Robinson was heralded as a hero and was also awarded the Victoria Cross.

For two years the Zeppelins were a serious problem, causing huge amounts of damage and loss of life. By the end of the war, over 1,500 people had been killed in Zeppelin raids. One of the worst took place just before the campaign stopped. In a daytime attack on East London on 13 June 1917, a primary school in Poplar, East London, was hit by a bomb. Eighteen children were killed and a further thirty-seven injured. Local people rushed to help as the teachers tried to save as many children as possible. Hundreds lined the streets for the funerals in the days that followed and a plaque now lists the names of those killed. The children came from a variety of backgrounds and faiths, including Jewish – it was a tragedy that affected all the communities of the East End of London and all age groups.

At the end of June 1917, Zeppelin attacks ceased – their effectiveness now undermined by British air defence. The Germans did not stop trying to attack the British mainland, however, and introduced the new twin-engine Gotha aircraft and the Zeppelin-Staaken R.VI four-engine giant biplanes to bomb London and the south of England. The R.VI required two pilots and was capable of carrying bombs of up to 2 tons. On 7 March 1918 the aircraft flew over London and dropped its bombs on St John's Wood in West London; the target may have been Paddington railway station, which is not far away. Four houses in Warrington Crescent were destroyed, with many more damaged. At least twelve people were killed and a further twenty-three others were seriously injured.

Two of those killed were the Goldring brothers. One of the brothers, Marcus Goldring, was visiting from Australia. A jeweller by trade, he was in the area to see his brother and sort out some business arrangements. His death was announced in the Australian newspapers and he is buried in Willesden Jewish Cemetery – a long way from New South Wales, Australia. He had three sons who served in the Australian Army: Lieutenant Eric G. Goldring, 3rd Australian Infantry Battalion, who was severely wounded during the fighting in Gallipoli but fortunately survived; Bombardier Leslie A. Goldring of the 1st Australian Field Artillery; and Lieutenant Harold (William H.) Goldring, serving with the Signalling Corps of the 1st Infantry Brigade.

It is estimated that there were at least 103 aerial raids on the UK during the war, from airships and aeroplanes. British people were forced to face the fact that, for the first time in centuries, an enemy could attack them in their homes. In *The Jewish Chronicle* and *Jewish News* articles appeared regularly about the attacks, mostly demonstrating the fear that the raids had struck in the wider population. Companies started to advertise home safes so that people could keep their belongings in them, hopefully safe from harm. The advertisements appeared weekly – a reminder of the ever-present threat.

Children and the War

It is often difficult to learn about the conditions and experiences of children during wartime, as they are frequently reduced to victims or 'add-ons' to mothers. There are reports in the newspapers about children helping collect clothes or doing jobs to support soldiers, and there were also articles about the lack of teachers, but rarely is there information on the children as individuals. Unusually, through the research for the *We Were There Too* project, some of what young children were experiencing during the war was uncovered. Discovered in the archives of the Liberal Jewish Synagogue (LJS), St John's Wood, are two books that provide a valuable insight into the imagination and ideas of Jewish children and young people living through this difficult period.

The Liberal Jewish Synagogue was founded in 1911 and its original location was in Hill Street, Park Road. Over the course of the First World War the congregation grew and new premises were sought. An important part of the LJS concept was a religion school that held sessions for all ages, including adults. During 1915 and 1916, children and young people who attended the religion school created pieces of work that were collated into books, two of which have survived and recently been restored. The books include a number of drawings of Zeppelins, indicating that the threat of those machines had certainly reached the children's thoughts.

Quite a few of the children wrote about the German Kaiser, who is presented as some kind of First World War bogeyman who is fully responsible for the whole war and the militarism of the age. The pictures of him are often very well thought out and include the failure of governments to stop him. Many of the pictures are quite dark when you explore them – evidence that, despite their parents' best efforts, the reality of the war really was getting to children. A number of the drawings by girls, such as those by Dorothy and Alice Englebert from London, also depicted their frustration that only boys were allowed to go off to war and that the girls would have to stay at home. Some of the illustrations and writings contain references to the children's disappointment that they are not allowed to go off and 'do their bit' in the fighting – evidence of just how constant the propaganda messaging was, and how effective it was in putting pressure on everyone to contribute.

Rationing

At the start of the war in 1914, the UK produced a lot of its own food and resources, although this was supplemented by imported food and other basic goods. Once the war began, many of the sources of those goods were threatened. The German Navy tried to stop supplies reaching the UK from the British Empire and other regions, although their blockade had limited effect, even despite the presence of the German U-boats and their unrestricted activities. Some established trading partners were no longer friends or allies. Sugarcane came to the UK from the Caribbean but sugar beet, also widely used, was mainly imported from Austria. As Austria-Hungary was aligned with Germany, the result, not surprisingly, was that sugar shortages occurred very early in the war.

As men who traditionally worked in agriculture and rural industries joined the armed forces, women stepped forward to work on the land. However, horses had been requisitioned and sent off to war, meaning that some of the essential heavy work, such as pulling ploughs, had to be done through manpower (or in this case womanpower) alone, resulting in a slower output. Limitations were put on the availability of chemicals so that they could be prioritised for armament production, and this meant that fertilisers were also restricted, which in turn meant that harvests were lower and food prices rose.

Subsequently, the DORA legislation introduced restrictions on bread – one of the staples of many people's diet in the war years. Fines were issued for making white flour instead of wholewheat, and for allowing rats to invade wheat stores.

Government campaigns encouraged people to grow more food, but you had to have a garden to do that, and for many in the cities, including those in the poorer Jewish communities, that was simply not possible. Food shortages occurred and some people began to hoard. Shop owners began to limit the quantities that could be bought to stop unscrupulous individuals and the wealthy taking an unfair share of the goods. Long queues became a regular feature of everyday life.

The government introduced formal rationing at the start of 1918. Everyone was issued with a ration book, including the king and queen. Sugar, butter and margarine, bread and meat were all rationed. Fruit and vegetables were not restricted, but prices limited the amount people could purchase, especially in the urban areas. Some basic food prices were regulated, with fines for anyone who tried to charge more. After the war, some goods remained scarce; butter continued to be rationed until 1920.

The Jewish delis and kosher butchers started to advertise in the papers about what could be purchased with the ration coupons and also promoting kosher foods that were not rationed. Food

A wartime advertisement for meat rations.

was a large part of Jewish life and there were concerns that Jews would particularly lose out with the meat rations, as Jews can only eat certain meats. However, the reality was that everyone suffered from the shortages.

It was not just on the home front that food shortages and food generally were important. Many of the letters that have survived from the front, such as those by Marcus Segal, make references to food, especially food that is sent to them from home. He writes thanking family for Barnett food parcels, and even complaining that having roast chicken sent to him at the front was not a good idea – preferring toffees and soap instead as gifts. Being able to supplement their loved ones' rations seemed extremely important to those back home. E. Barnett and Co's Ltd was a deli company in North London that was very popular for its kosher food. It placed adverts in the Jewish press indicating which of the foods it sold could be sent to the front, so that the men out there could have food that was the same 'As Mother Makes It'.

Internment

For some Jews in the UK the war made them no longer welcome. On 5 August 1914, immediately after the declaration of the First World War, the British government passed the Aliens Restriction Act. The Act changed the status of citizens of Germany and the Austro-Hungarian Empire who were living in or visiting the UK so that they were now designated enemy aliens, marking them as potential spies. For some, unless they had police permission, the Act resulted in restriction of movement; for others it was far more serious.

Enemy alien men of fighting age were interned for the whole duration of the war in special camps for civilian detainees. Camps were created at sites across the UK, including Alexandra Palace in North London (which also housed Belgian refugees at the start of the war), Lofthouse Park in Wakefield (near Leeds) and Castle Green in York. As the war progressed, prisoners of war (POWs) were also put into the camps so that, eventually, the civilian detainees were concentrated into just three camps – in London, the Isle of Man and Lofthouse Park. Over 32,000 civilian men were interned for some or all of the war.

All the camps were inspected regularly and offered good facilities. While privacy was restricted as the men slept in large dormitories, space was provided for exercise, clubs were allowed, and the men organised their own activities and committees. Nevertheless, many of the interned wrote letters of complaint to the British Home Office and to the embassies of their countries, complaining of their imprisonment.

The Jewish Chronicle often printed letters about the internment camps and what the local British Jewish communities were doing to support some of the interned with their dietary needs. The Leeds Jewish community, for instance, helped to provide kosher food and religious support for the Lofthouse Park internees during the key religious holidays. To the British authorities, there was no distinction between Jewish or non-Jewish enemy aliens; it was nationality that mattered.

War conditions often encourage suspicion and opportunity for groups to resume long-held slights. In Leeds there had not always been smooth relations between the Jewish and non-Jewish communities. In June 1917 this broke out into anti-Jewish riots. According to a report in *The Jewish Chronicle* on 8 June 1917, the 'Jewish Quarter was wrecked and looted', with an 'organised attack on the Sunday night' and 'outrages still carrying on Monday'. It also reported fifteen casualties, including 'Driver Rosenbloom of the RFA (one of four brothers on active service) who is home on sick leave'. He was injured 'rescuing a Jewish woman from being attacked'. Part of the outrage of the Leeds Jewish community lay with the police, who are reported to have done nothing to stop the rioters, claiming they did not have enough men to intervene. The police only responded late on the Monday when more police arrived. The article about the riot was in the columns next to the war casualty lists – emphasising the contradiction of service and prejudice. News of the riot failed to make it into most of the mainstream national press.

Entertainment

It was not all doom and gloom on the home front; those in the entertainment industry were busy keeping spirits high.

Sir Abraham Walter de Frece, born on 7 October 1870 and known as Walter, was one of four sons of Henry (Harry) de Frece, of the Gaiety Music Hall in Camden Street, Liverpool. A well-known and wealthy agent in theatre management, Henry de Frece wanted to keep his sons out of the entertainment business and therefore sent them to good schools. Nonetheless, Walter and his elder brother Jack started to manage parts of the business as soon as they finished school; they were shortly followed by their younger brothers.

Although the family was Jewish, the de Freces were not observant and in 1890 Walter married the non-Jewish Tilley Ball, known on stage as Vesta Tilley. Vesta Tilley was a well-known male impersonator and a rising star of the stage; she could attract huge audiences. With Tilly at his side, Walter became heavily involved with theatre management and ownership, running a number of theatres across the UK. According to reports, Walter and Tilley organised quite a number of recruitment activities and war concerts during the war years:

Vesta Tilley was very popular during the First World War, when they ran a military recruitment drive, as did a number of other music hall stars. In the guise of characters like 'Tommy in the Trench' and 'Jack Tar Home from Sea', Tilley performed songs like 'The Army of Today's All Right' and 'Jolly Good Luck to the Girl who Loves a Soldier'. This is how she got the nickname 'Britain's best recruiting sergeant' – young men were sometimes asked to join the army on stage during her show.

She was prepared to be a little controversial. Famously, for example, she sang a song, 'I've Got a Bit of a Blighty One', about a soldier who was delighted to have been wounded because it allowed him to go back to Britain and get away from extremely deadly battlefields.

'When I think about my dugout / Where I dare not stick my mug out / I'm glad I've got a bit of a blighty one!'

Tilley performed in hospitals and sold war bonds.[3]

As part of their campaigning, Walter became an honorary colonel in the Manchester Regiment. He also carried out a number of war duties behind the scenes, such as encouraging famous friends to support government campaigns and activities. After the war they both retired from the theatre and he became a Conservative MP.

Other Jewish entertainers also supported the war effort. Jack Terrisfield was half of a successful vaudeville act, Terris and Romaine, which performed in music halls throughout the country and beyond. According to the records of his family:

During the First World War years they performed in more than 500 performances for wounded soldiers.

Trained in Brighton, Jack first appeared in Con Conrads Minstrels, at one point part of an act as 'Jews in kilts'. Teaming up with a talented pianist, Martin Romaine, they formed a partnership calling themselves Terris and Romaine and became increasingly popular, appearing at one time on the Bill with Sarah Bernhardt. They also provided entertainment for wounded soldiers from 1914 until 1918. His mother had kept press and newspaper cuttings throughout Jack's career. According to the playbills the pair went from performing in a Minstrel group to becoming head-line acts.

Jack, as well as having had rheumatic fever as a child, also caught Malaria when he toured in South Africa; Jack was therefore unable to serve in the armed forces. Martin Romaine on the other hand was conscripted and was killed in France on 9 April 1917; when he went abroad Jack found another musician to replace him, but kept the name of the act. During a season in Ireland Jack fell ill with flu and died on 29 June 1918. He is buried in Cork cemetery.[4]

Overall, however, life on the home front was difficult. Everyone knew someone who was either serving, had served or was engaged in war work. Shortages and danger made life tense and challenging. For some young women it provided opportunities for employment that were not available before the war and showed them some freedom and opportunities for the future. For others the war just meant hardship and loss.

The Arts

Prior to the war and during that period overall there was a scene emerging of young Jewish artists and writers. One group was known as the Whitechapel group and was made up of young men (and one young woman) who were largely of immigrant families and based in the East End of London. There were many influences on this group – their background, wealth or lack thereof, Jewish identity, etc., but also the changing art movements of the time, especially the move towards modernism, and significantly the impact the First World War had on that whole generation. They often expressed an antipathy to the war which could be put down to youthful artistic sensibilities but is just as likely to be based on their own political distaste for war and their immigrant and 'outsider' experiences, as well as the devastating effect the reality of fighting can have on any individual.

The Whitechapel Gallery was founded in 1901 in East London to bring art to the poor of the area; it was next door to the library, which was also there to bring enlightenment to the locals. Both these buildings played a significant role in helping to shape a creative yearning among some of the recent migrants to that part of London. A third place of considerable importance was the Slade School of Art where Mark Gertler, Clare Winsten, Isaac Rosenberg, David Bomberg, Bernard Meninsky and others all went before the war years. Assisting the young Jewish men and women to build on their creative ideas were organisations such as the Jewish Education Aid Society, which had been founded by Jewish philanthropists in the nineteenth century to support and develop the talents and future careers of gifted poor (often immigrant) Jews and wealthy benefactors. This combination of art schools, wealthy sponsors and broad learning allowed those with creative talents to become artists, while it was the experience of conflict that often darkened that art.

David Bomberg was born in Birmingham but his Polish family moved to London where he was part of the large poor Jewish immigrant community in London's East End. Through the support of the Jewish Education Aid Society he was able to attend the Slade School of Art, where he was one of the more adventurous artists of his generation. He was expelled from the Slade in 1913 for his confrontational approach to art and his refusal to conform to one style. In 1914, Bomberg and Jacob Epstein curated a specific section Jewish in the Whitechapel Art Gallery's exhibition 'Twentieth Century Art: A Review of Modern Movements' in order to showcase their work and those of their friends and peers. This exhibition was one of the defining moments of twentieth-century British Jewish art, and came at a major turning point in the century.

Bomberg enlisted in the British Army in 1915 and served as a sapper with the Royal Engineers. Like so many others, he found the war deeply harrowing. In 1916 he shot himself in the foot; no one know if this was accidental or deliberate, but it allowed him some time away from the front, although once he was healed he was recalled to active service. In 1918 Bomberg was commissioned by the Canadian War Memorials Fund to produce a series of paintings to commemorate the war. His first submission of *Sappers at Work*, a modernist depiction of the sappers who dug the tunnels under Hill 60, part of the Battle of Messines (1917), was rejected by the Canadians. The second version was accepted after he had softened the characters, but the initial rejection affected him, making a man already suffering from war fatigue vulnerable.

His art often recognised the horror and the difficulties that the new technologies such as mining brought to warfare. During his lifetime he struggled to make a living from his work, and only after his death was his creativity and influence really appreciated.

In 1891, Mark Gertler was born in a slum lodging house in Spitalfields in London. His parents were Eastern European Jewish immigrants. He was the first and youngest of the 'Whitechapel Boys' to go to the Slade School of Art. Along with Bomberg, Gertler made an impact on British art scene just before and during the First World War. When the First World War broke out Gertler held pacifist views, but in 1916, when a law was passed that all young men must enter the army, he tried to join up. He was turned down partly because of his parents' nationality, which made them enemy aliens, but also due to his own poor health – he suffered from tuberculosis, so the recruiting sergeant rejected him.

Gertler's painting *The Merry-Go-Round* (1916) is of soldiers and sailors trapped on a roundabout and is considered a brilliant piece of anti-war art. His tuberculosis affected his health after the war while his artistic temperament often complicated his relationships. He was another whose work failed to bring him the success he would have liked during his lifetime, and in 1939, like so many of that generation of artists, he committed suicide.

Jacob Epstein was born in America in 1880, the son of Russian-Polish immigrants; he chose to move to London when he was in his twenties. Epstein became a British citizen in 1911, and was by that time a reasonably well-known sculptor; one of his early promoters was the highly influential Walter Sickert, part of the Camden Group of artists. Epstein's new British citizenship meant he was able to enlist, which he did in 1917 after the formation of

Jacob Epstein in 1900. (Courtesy of the Library of Congress)

the 38th Battalion of the Royal Fusiliers, though he was absent without leave when his regiment was deployed and suffered a nervous breakdown. He was allowed to leave the military without ever having left Britain. After the war he continued to work as a sculptor and became one of the most important sculptors of the twentieth century. He is one of the few artists of the Whitechapel Group to receive fame and some fortune during their lifetime.

Bernard Meninsky was born in Ukraine in 1891, and his Jewish parents brought him to England when he was only six weeks old. He grew up in Liverpool, travelled a bit and then in 1912 entered the Slade School of Fine Art in London. In 1917 he enlisted in the 40th Battalion of the Royal Fusiliers and served in Palestine as part of the Middle East campaign. It was not until March 1918 that he became a British citizen, but in April of that year he suffered some form of mental breakdown and was discharged from the Salisbury Road Military Hospital in Plymouth as 'physically unfit on account of neurasthenia' and invalided out of the army. Sickert recommended Meninsky as an artist to the Ministry of Information to 'paint important pictures representing typical London scenes during and after the arrival of a leave train from the front at Victoria Station'. The resulting works can be seen in the Imperial War Collection. Although Meninsky continued life as an artist and was held in high regard by many, he never fully recovered from his war experience, and his mental health was forever affected. He committed suicide in 1950.

Another of the Whitechapel Boys actually came from Leeds. Joseph Kramer attended art classes in Leeds and was sponsored by the Jewish Educational Aid Society and the vice chancellor of Leeds University to move to London and attend the Slade School of Art. It was there that he became friends with the rest of the Whitechapel artists. During the First World War he became a regimental librarian rather than being put on active service. In 1919 he produced a painting titled *A Day of Atonement* which has been described as a 'seminal Anglo-Jewish piece'. Although he was popular and a good artist, he returned to Leeds and never sought great fame, partly due to an alcohol problem. He died in 1962.

Alfred A. Wolmark was born in Poland and was six when his family moved to England. He lived in Devon until he was seventeen years old when his father opened a tailor's shop in the East End of London. Not growing up in the East End provided him with a different outlook to some of his contemporaries, and some of that can be seen in his landscape pictures. He was originally named Aaron but anglicised his name to Alfred while a student, fearing anti-Semitism might hold back his career – Aaron is what the middle 'A' of his name stands for. Despite his fear of prejudice, throughout his career he painted Jewish religious scenes and was very open about his Jewish background.

Wolmark didn't attend the Slade School of Art and instead went to the Royal Academy School of Painting, although living in East London meant that he quickly became part of the Jewish artists' circle of that time. During the war years he was declared medically unfit for military service but his illustrations to support the writer Israel Zangwill's work demonstrate an attitude of revulsion to war and its terrible cost.

Clare Winsten was born Clara Birnberg in Romania in 1892 before arriving in Britain in 1902. She also lived in the East End of London and was the only female artist in the Whitechapel group. She often had a difficult relationship with some of others, which was frequently due to her – rightly – feeling discriminated against by those around her due to her gender. She was involved with a number of campaigns for women's rights and was a member of the Women's Freedom League. She married Stephen Weinstein during the war and they were both passionate campaigners for conscientious objectors. Her husband was imprisoned for his refusal to enlist. After the war they moved away from Jewish beliefs and anglicised their name to Winsten.

Of course, the Whitechapel Boys were not the only Jewish artists of the period. There was the well-respected and well-known William Rothenstein, who was aged forty-two when war broke out and therefore too old to serve. Born in Bradford, he studied there until attending the Slade School of Art in 1888, after which he lived in London and mixed with the Camden group of artists and contemporary writers such as H. G. Wells. He painted a number of Jewish scenes but overall produced a wide body of work embracing many different themes. By 1914, Rothenstein was such an established artist, printmaker and draughtsman that he was approached to produce work for the Ministry of Information as part of its output during the war years. He also nurtured artists such as Mark Gertler and the acclaimed war artist Paul Nash. Rothenstein continued his official role as a war artist during the Second World War, providing many images used in Britain's propaganda war of the time. Both of Rothenstein's brothers changed their names during the First World War to Rutherston to escape any German associations.

Solomon J. Solomon was born in London in 1860 and studied at the Royal Academy and École des Beaux-Arts. In 1886 he became one of the founders of the New English Art Club. He joined the Artists' Rifles, a home defence unit, in 1914 as a private and took an active interest in camouflage. He approached senior military officials with his ideas and in December 1915 was allowed to visit the front lines to examine French camouflage techniques. His ideas were popular and it was agreed that a new unit should be established so that he could begin production of camouflage for the British out on the front lines. On General Haig's instruction

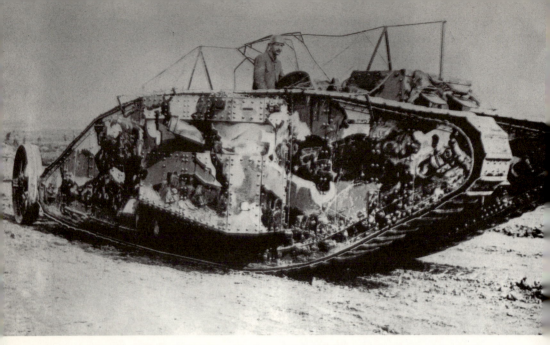

Tank showing Solomon J. Solomon's camo scheme. (Courtesy of the Library of Congress)

Solomon was given the temporary appointment of lieutenant colonel. In 1916 he set up a camouflage school in Hyde Park that was later taken over by the army. His work mainly focused on the use of disguising techniques for netting, spy trees and camouflage for tanks and Royal Navy vessels. Many of the approaches he used can still be found today.

Writing and Poetry

Joseph Leftwich wrote, 'We were the slum children, the problem youth, the beneficiaries of the Board of Guardians and the soup kitchen, and some of us (like Rosenberg and [David] Bomberg) of the Jewish Educational Aid Society.' He was also the person to coin the term the 'Whitechapel Group' for his social circle of Jewish immigrants who made their mark on the arts world. He was born Joseph Lefkowitz in the Netherlands in 1892, and his family moved to the UK while he was a child. He he grew up in East London with Yiddish as his first language. He was friends with the young artists and other aspiring writers of that area and was a regular at the Whitechapel library. Like all the others he dreamed of being something other than another tailor. His talent was writing, and in particular he started to translate Jewish writings on Yiddish into English.

Shortly after the war started Leftwich wrote, 'If we win, and crush the Huns, in twenty years we must fight their sons' in a piece called *War*, which turned out to be tragically prophetic. He was a conscientious objector during the war and was in regular correspondence with Isaac Rosenberg during those years. His lack of war service further pushed him into the writing world and he is now mainly remembered as a translator of Yiddish works into English, but he was a fully published writer in his own right. For him the First World War was a sign of things to come.

Poetry was a far more common way to communicate and express ideas 100 years ago than it is today. Today it is often seen as highbrow, but a century ago poetry was something often published in newspapers and magazines, just as blogs appear regularly online now. Of course, that did not mean that poetry could necessarily help you earn a living. Being able to make a living from writing poetry was something entirely dependent on sponsors as much as talent. One of those who struggled with the dilemma of wanting to be a poet or artist while also making a living was Isaac Rosenberg.

Isaac Rosenberg was born in Bristol on 25 November 1890. His parents were eastern European immigrants who worked hard to make ends meet. In 1897 the family moved to the East End of London, and the boy went to East End council schools. By the time he was fourteen, Rosenberg had already declared his desire to be an artist and his talent was noticeable; however, financial circumstances meant that he was forced to leave school and become an apprentice engraver, a job that he hated. He attended night school and applied for funding to try and go to art school and leave his job.

Isaac Rosenberg.

Rosenberg was offered a place at the Slade School of Fine Art in 1911, and after a lot of letter writing the Jewish Education Aid Society and private benefactors sponsored him, enabling him to take up the place. He was already part of the Whitechapel Group and was close friends with a number of them. However, Rosenberg found it hard to fit in at the Slade, which was not helped by his being in a particularly gifted year.

In addition to painting, Rosenberg also wrote poetry and he often went back and forth between the two disciplines, unsure of where his future lay. When war was declared Rosenberg was in Cape Town, South Africa, where he had moved for the climate and to live with his sister and her husband. He spent his time there as a portrait painter and sometime art lecturer, but he did not achieve the success he had hoped as the war turned most people's attentions away from cultural refinements. In South Africa he continued to write poetry and had some of his poems published in South African magazines.

Rosenberg missed London and was not making a success of things in South Africa, so he returned to Britain in February 1915. He then published a collection of poems, *Youth*, but only ten copies of the book sold. Disappointed and broke, Rosenberg decided that his only option was to enlist. He had never shown any great desire to join the military or even shown any sense that he supported it, but enlistment meant a regular income that he could use to help support his mother. In October 1915 Rosenberg joined the Bantams, a special battalion for men too short to be accepted into other regiments. According to his biographer Jean Moorcroft Wilson in her book *Isaac Rosenberg: The Making of a Great War Poet*, Rosenberg hated most of his military training and was convinced that everyone around him was anti-Semitic.

It was easier for him to write than to paint while he was serving, both at home in the UK and in the trenches, so that is where his attention went. In June 1916 Rosenberg arrived in France with the 11th King's Own Lancaster's. He wrote to friends and family regularly so there is a clear picture of Rosenberg's experiences throughout his time in service. Many of the Whitechapel Group were in touch with each other, checking in on each other's fortunes and misfortunes. Life in the trenches was hard, and Rosenberg wrote home about the rats, the lice and the mud – these topics also featured in his poetry. According to Moorcroft Wilson, Rosenberg's commanding officers regularly thought of him as a 'completely hopeless soldier'; he was uninterested in conforming to military practice or discipline – it was not that he was disobedient, just that he couldn't quite stop being carried away in his thoughts, thinking about his poetry. He was also regularly picked up on his appearance, which was generally dishevelled, and his inability to follow drills.

At one point Rosenberg was put under the command of Captain Frank Waley, a Jewish officer, in the hope that he would fit in a bit more or at least not think that everyone around him was getting at him due to his being Jewish. Waley came from a long line of military men and was just as keen to pass Rosenberg on as his previous officer. Regular transfers to different battalions and pioneer units meant that Rosenberg was kept away from some of the more serious fighting during most of his time at the front until early 1918. Any minute he had free was used to write, and it was at these times that he wrote some of his most important poems, such as 'Dead Man's Dump' and 'In the Trenches', all of which he sent home (see Appendix). As well as his observations on war, Rosenberg began to write poetry that reflected his sense of Jewish identity and hoped to write a 'battle song 'for the Judeans. He did continue to sketch and there are some rather intense self-portraits from that time of him in uniform, but it was his poetry that really stood out.

In March 1918 the Germans launched a major attack – the Spring Offensive – along the Western Front. The aim was to try and defeat the British and French forces before American reinforcements reached the Allied lines. The German attack was brutal and many of the troops out at the front were caught up in the attack. Tragically, Rosenberg was killed by a German raiding party on 1 April 1918 in an area not far from the town of Arras in northern France. His body was never recovered and unusually his headstone in the Bailleul Road East Military Cemetery in France stands over an empty grave. Rosenberg's friends and family arranged for some of his poems to be published in 1922 as *The Collected Works*. His war poetry was different to that of the other emerging war poets; his voice was considered fresh, and after the war he was considered by many of contemporaries as the best of the First World War poets.

Rosenberg is the only non-officer and the only Jewish poet to be included on the Poets of the First World War memorial in Westminster Abbey's Poets' Corner. His poems often refer to the image of the poppy and its beauty amongst the horror of war.

A contemporary of Rosenberg was Siegfried Sassoon. Strictly speaking Sassoon was not Jewish as he had a Jewish father but Christian mother (in Judaism the Jewish line is carried through the mother). He was christened as a child and raised entirely as a practising Christian. His parents' separation and divorce when he was still a young child, followed by his father's early death, meant that he never had much contact with the Jewish side of the family. Nonetheless, he did experience anti-Semitism as the Sassoon family were a well-known and successful family and he carried their name. In later years he often claimed to always feel comfortable in Jewish circles.

Sassoon's upbringing could not have been more different to Rosenberg's. He went to good private schools and already had some success with his poetry prior to the First World War. Sassoon was in the Sussex Yeomanry when the war started, but a riding accident made him unfit for service once the fighting started. After some time recovering, Sassoon was commissioned into the Royal Welch Fusiliers. He often exhibited incredible bravery as well as recklessness, and in July 1916 he was awarded the Military Cross for his actions during the Battle of the Somme. His citation reads as follows:

2nd Lt. Siegfried Lorraine [*sic*] Sassoon, 3rd (attd. 1st) Bn., R. W. Fus.
For conspicuous gallantry during a raid on the enemy's trenches.
He remained for 1½ hours under rifle and bomb fire collecting and

bringing in our wounded. Owing to his courage and determination all the killed and wounded were brought in.

Sassoon's younger brother was killed in Gallipoli, and as the war went on more and more of his friends were also killed and injured, transforming Sassoon's devotion to the war effort into a hatred for the conflict. In 1917 Sassoon famously wrote a letter that criticised the war and its leadership, an act that could have had him court-martialled; instead Sassoon's influential friends convinced the authorities that he was sick and suffering from a nervous breakdown and had him sent to a psychiatric hospital instead. He later returned to active service before being injured in 1918. Sassoon survived the war and was a well-known and acclaimed author and poet, but despite living into his seventies it is his First World War writings for which he is most famous, a mixture of patriotic zeal and cynical disaffection most evident in *Counter Attack* and *Does It Matter?*

Undoubtedly, the war was a major influence on all of these artists and they have left their print on the Jewish and non-Jewish world.

8

NOT ALLOWED TO FIGHT – DON'T WANT TO FIGHT

Ruhleben Internment Camp

In autumn 1914, following the outbreak of war, citizens from the different Allied countries who were living, travelling or working in Germany were interned. While women and children from the UK were usually allowed to return home, the men were taken to Ruhleben racecourse just outside Berlin in Spandau. The site was to become a camp and approximately 5,000 predominantly (though not exclusively) British citizens were kept there. The men came from a wide range of backgrounds and professions – merchant seamen, fishermen, musicians, composers, medical experts, scientists, university students, travelling salesmen, ex-servicemen

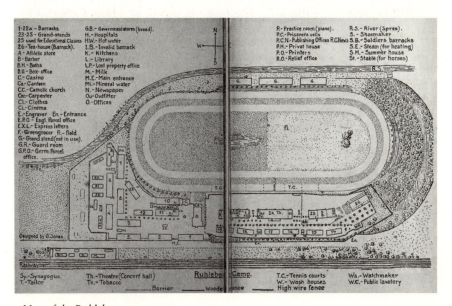

Map of the Ruhleben camp.

and writers. The camp itself was very basic and some of the first to arrive in November 1914 wrote of finding horse dung still in the stables that were to become their living quarters.

The camp was guarded by police rather than the military as the inmates were civilians. Classified as enemy aliens rather than prisoners of war, the men were allowed to organise much of the interior of the camp, apart from the living quarters. In addition to organising the camp for formal roles, such as a management committee, the camp inmates also set up a range of committees for social and sporting activities. There was a regular camp magazine and a yearly Christmas card. The inmates were allowed to correspond to relatives back home and make representations for their release. The range of men inside the camp meant that some were able learn a musical instrument or continue studies with fellow inmates while others were able to set up or continue in their trade. There were a number who worked as tailors, plus a barber and a cobbler. At one point a casino was opened in the camp.

In 1914, a student named James Chadwick was in Germany where he was working with the famous physicist Hans Geiger. On the outbreak of hostilities, Chadwick was interned for the whole of the war. He recorded how cold and cramped the accommodation was in the barracks. Despite this, he converted part of his space into a lab to continue his studies. In 1935 he would receive the Nobel Prize for Physics after discovering the neutron.

In the opening days of the camp, the German authorities offered to provide kosher food for those who identified themselves as Jewish. Approximately 200 of around 300 Jewish men chose to do so and were housed by the German authorities in Hut 6 until 1916, when they were split up into the other barracks. Hut 6 was the smallest and dirtiest of the old stables. It was quickly identified as 'the Ghetto'.

In a book following the war, one of those Jewish internees, J. Davidson Ketchum (*Ruhleben: A prison camp society*, 1967), wrote about the emergence of anti-Semitism in the camp, tying it directly to the separation of the Jews into Hut 6. He notes how Jews were stereotyped in the camp by the other internees and that Hut 6 inmates experienced prejudice, a lot of which was expressed in the camp's magazine articles and shows. While the prejudice was not violent, it was demoralising and divisive. Ketchum also notes that once Hut 6 was closed down as a barrack quarters the anti-Semitism largely disappeared, which he believed was due to the fact that the Jewish inmates were no longer separated off, although he also believed that prejudices subsided due to increased

Sketch of the
Ruhleben camp.

restraint and the protestations of the Jewish inmates and others. The Hut 6 inmates were not afraid to speak out against the treatment they were receiving, and this surely helped. One inmate in particular, Israel Cohen, stood against any prejudice that he heard about and his popularity was enough to deter some of those who would otherwise have continued the taunting.

Israel Cohen was a journalist who had worked for the *Globe* and *Glasgow Herald* newspapers. He was holidaying in Germany when the war broke out. While in Ruhleben he was part of the Debating Society and took an active part in camp life. In July 1915 he and another inmate famously held a mock by-election to provide some tongue-in-cheek political excitement in the camp. Their views, ideas and hustings were all presented in the Ruhleben magazine – and reported in *The Jewish Chronicle*.

The formal adoption of the candidates took place at a crowded meeting on a broiling July evening in the Grand Stand Hall. Each of the candidates sat on the platform, surrounded by his respective supporters. Mr. Boss, wearing an expansive blue tie, gazed through his monocle with an autocratic air upon the serried throng, his supporters having, like himself, adorned their button-holes with blue ribbon. The Suffrage candidate, who is normally shaven, had adopted a monstrous drooping black moustache; and he was encircled by a group of suffragettes whose hats, frocks, and faces were calculated to spoil his chances irredeemably. As it had been rumoured that the Suffragettes were to be arrested on a charge of husband-desertion and might be removed by the police from the platform, they were securely tied to their chairs and to the iron columns supporting the roof. As for myself, I donned a khaki suit for the occasion, with a dazzling red tie, whilst my supporters and I wore red rosettes.[1]

Cohen was released from the camp after nineteen months as part of a prisoner exchange and went on to write *The Ruhleben Prison Camp: A Record of Nineteen Months' Internment*. In his book he provided an insight into life in the camp, in particular Jewish life in the camp, which he described as being a 'Diaspora of men'. He noted how their Jewishness brought them together but also provided them with a regular source of disagreement:

Barrack VI was a miniature Jewish diaspora, for its population was made up of the natives of various climes and the speakers of different tongues. We were all, of course, British subjects, but only the minority were natives of England. The bulk had their birthplace in Russia, Germany, Austria, Hungary, or Rumania; they had acquired naturalisation in England, Canada, South Africa, or Australia; and they had either settled in Germany or been caught there by the war on a holiday or business trip. Some had actually been born in Germany and never seen England, but had derived their British citizenship from a father born or naturalised in British territory; and a few, though born in England, had been brought as infants to the land of the Kaiser, where they had remained ever since, and thus had only a Platonic allegiance to Britain. This diversity of origin formed a frequent theme of discussion and an unfailing source of recrimination, the medium of utterance being English, German, Russian, or Yiddish, or a mutilated medley of them all. '*Du Berditchever Englander!*' the German-born Anglo-Jew would taunt his neighbour for leaving his horse-box sweepings in front of his box. '*Galizianischer Gazlon!*' (Galician robber) the pale-faced Pole would cry out if hustled at the stable tap during the morning's ablutions by a fellow-prisoner born on the other side of the Russian frontier. Each section considered itself as good as, if not better than the rest, and the quarrels that arose through this peculiar instinctive antipathy sometimes developed into a tornado of mutual abuse, but hardly ever into fisticuffs.

Before long two separate congregations came into being, owing to the dissatisfaction of one with the Chazan (precentor) of the other, and then we used to hear two rival strains of sacred melody rising unto the rafters, one from the central passage and the other from the dissident horse-box, and each trying to outdo the other. When the Feast of Chanukah came the candles were lit in the central passage and the whole stable resounded with the joyous song of Maoz Tsur; but the Feast of Purim found us gathered together in the Grand Stand Hall to listen to the ancient story of the defeated machinations of Haman. It was not until the advent of the first Passover that the Ruhleben Jewish Community became properly organized and acquired possession of a synagogue.

The celebration of Passover in captivity — surely the most incongruous of celebrations — was assisted by the Jewish Soup Kitchen in Berlin, which provided us, at ten marks a head, with

Life in Ruhleben, 1918.

eight pounds of Matzo (unleavened bread), and with a package containing two half-bottles of Palestinian wine, two hard-boiled eggs, a little bottle of charoses (nut paste) and another of mar or bitter herbs), as well as with a small packet of salt and a paper-covered Haggadah. We were also able to buy various Passover groceries, such as cocoa, sugar, condensed milk, and cakes, which were supplied by a Jewish firm in Berlin (though at rather high prices), and we furthermore invested in a new set of eating utensils. These various articles were sold in a wooden shed, which was specially erected against the walls of our barrack: it first of all did service as a canteen and was afterwards converted into a synagogue. The special permission of the Commandant had to be obtained for our consumption of wine, which was ordinarily forbidden, and several of the Marannos availed themselves of the privilege. Most of the men held the Seder in their horse-boxes, though a large group combined for a joint service at one end of the passage, which looked quite festive with an array of candles along a narrow table and resounded with the joyous strains of the sacred ritual.[2]

Despite the comedy and cultural exchanges that Cohen writes about he also made it clear that the internment was something the men endured rather than enjoyed. He writes of some men's attempts at suicide and of others falling into depression and insanity. In the preface of the book, published in 1917, he makes a statement that

the British and German Governments have at length agreed to exchange all civilian prisoners above the age of forty-five, but after this agreement is carried out there will still be three thousand British civilian prisoners of war at Ruhleben – all men who have been denied any of the glories or compensations of war, and who will have to resume the battle of life with crippled constitutions. No visitor to Ruhleben, whether official or private individual, whether neutral or Allied, however profound his sympathy, however acute his observation, however shrewd and penetrating his sagacity, and however long his visit, can appreciate even a tithe of the cumulative effect of the physical, mental, and moral sufferings of the men who have been interned there for the last two years and more. Friends of their fellow-Englishmen should spare no efforts, in the interests of humanity and patriotism, to secure the release as early as possible of the remaining captives in the Ruhleben Prison Camp.

ISRAEL COHEN

London,

On the Second Anniversary of my Internment,

November 6, 1916.[3]

Cohen was keen to make clear that the men in the camp were prevented from joining the war – and that they were not avoiding their duty. In letters in *The Jewish Chronicle* after his release he also made this point on behalf of all the men interned, Jews and non-Jews.

Another inmate of Hut 6 who threw himself into activity to avoid boredom and a feeling of uselessness was Charles Adler (F. C. Adler) who was a conductor and musician. He organised an orchestra in the camp as there were many distinguished musicians there (many had been in Germany for a music festival when the war had started and they had not been able to get home). Prior to the war he had toured extensively around Germany and in South America. He put on his first concert in the camp in December 1914. As a resident of Hut 6 he became a victim to some of the insidious anti-Semitic remarks that appeared in the Ruhleben magazine and in some of the subsequent music hall shows. However, the author of those remarks was rebuked in the magazine and at events. Adler went on to produce many of the classical concerts in the camp, which appear to have been very much appreciated by the majority of those there.

An article in the *Manchester Guardian* of 31 March 1915 (p. 3) has the following comments on Adler, written by Walter Butterworth:

> Mr. F. C. Adler, a young conductor to whom is due in great measure the success of these concerts, is a man of unusual energy, capacity and enthusiasm. He has had a wide experience as conductor, especially in opera, successively in Mexico, Switzerland, Bavaria and Prussia. He was born in London and was interned at Ruhleben when the general order was issued on November 6th.

After the war Adler continued to conduct in Germany before moving to the USA in 1933, where he became a pioneer of classical music recordings.

The postal service that operated in the camp allowed all the inmates to write home and to receive parcels, although they were censored. Many wrote about the cold and damp conditions, the limited food and access to clothing as well as day-to-day life there. In July 1916 a letter appeared in *The Jewish Chronicle* appealing for food and clothing parcels for the inmates of the Ruhleben camp. A 'Committee for the Relief of the Interned British Jews in Germany' raised money and goods for the men, who otherwise received limited food from the German authorities as the war progressed. There were reports of vegetables and fats being absent and of men developing sores and other illnesses due to malnutrition. Barnett's, a well-known food shop and kosher deli, was persuaded by the committee to send out food to the camp – how much of it got past the German guards and to the inmates is uncertain.

The conditions in the camp affected both the mental and physical health of many of the inmates. Sigimund (Sidney) Jacobs, of Bethnal Green, who worked in the family leather business, was holidaying in Germany when the war started. His incarceration affected his health for the rest of his life and contributed to his early death at the age of thirty-seven.

At the end of the war the camp was closed down, with the majority of inmates returning to their pre-war occupations. While the German authorities did not treat the inmates particularly badly, the overall experience of being interned during a war along with the poor conditions in the camp led many to not speak of what they had lived through following their release. For some there was a deep sense of shame at not being allowed to fight when friends and relatives were doing so.

While this group of British Jews – and British men generally – were not allowed to contribute to the war effort, there were others who chose incarceration over combat.

Conscientious Objectors

Britain had prided itself on its professional forces. While other countries relied on national service or conscription, Britain had a volunteer military – men who wanted to be there. However, the demands of the First World War meant more and more men would be required. Kitchener's appeal for volunteers had gone exceedingly well – the work of recruiting offices, including the Jewish Recruitment Committee, had provided millions of men – but it was still not enough. As 1915 came to a close, the British government recognised that to bring in sufficient numbers it would need to introduce conscription. For most of the Jewish press the discussion about conscription was mixed into the discussion about the Russian Jews, but it wasn't just this group that had been reluctant to fight; there were others who had chosen not to enlist.

Men from many different walks of life had objected to war service from the start. Some had not wanted to leave their families, but many held firm beliefs that set them in opposition to the war. Political opposition was an issue for some who believed that it was a war between capitalists. Others were pacifists and refused to fight or carry arms of any kind. The only reason accepted for non-service under British law – vague though it was on the subject – was religious opposition.[4]

Jewish objection on religious grounds was problematic as the Chief Rabbi, Joseph Hertz, had deemed that there was no justification in religious law for not fighting. Some Jewish religious scholars disagreed with this verdict. Letters raged between synagogues, especially those which argued that Jewish men of the Cohanim (the religious priestly sect who are not supposed to come into contact with a dead body), more commonly known as Cohen, could not serve in battle. In March 1916 there were protests at the Leeds Beth Din about this, and an expression of outrage that the Chief Rabbi should rule that a Cohen could still serve.

For the majority of the Jewish community the attitude towards conscientious objectors was as negative as it was among the wider British population. Herbert Samuel, the Home Secretary, a proud and patriotic British Jew, stated in *The Jewish Chronicle* on 28 January 1916 that 'everything that is Jewish, even the fine Jewish ideal of peace ... points the finger of scorn, derision and contempt at the Jewish CO'.

The only way to avoid service was to attend a military tribunal and present a case. According to the records in Tower Hamlets and the London Metropolitan Archives, the majority of the Jews objecting were either Russian or extremely poor – they did not want to leave their families in case they would not be provided for. A request to not fight due to poverty or the risk of leaving the family without a breadwinner were arguments that failed to carry any weight with the tribunal authorities.

In Liverpool, Revd John Harris, the rabbi of Princes Road Synagogue, testified at a military tribunal on behalf of a Jewish objector who was objecting on religious grounds. Harris was dismissed by his synagogue as a result, as the congregation felt his support of an objector was not in keeping with their support for the war. Harris felt that he had a right to intervene based on his own principles according to a statement reported in *The Jewish Chronicle*:

> For my part I am an avowed pacifist. I believe intensely in the paramount duty of returning good for evil, and in the final and certain victory of love and love alone over hatred and prejudice.

Most conscientious objectors would still be forced to serve, but as non-combatants; they would be given medical roles as orderlies, stretcher bearers and the like. They would still be in a dangerous position, often based at the front, but they would not be required to kill anyone. Alternatively, conscientious objectors might be given labour roles; if this was at the front it could still be dangerous, but for some it was more bearable than being in a labour detachment in the UK. In the UK the objectors might be given labour roles such as road building – these would be difficult physically and mentally, as passers-by knew these men as objectors and would throw things and shout at them.

For political opponents it was yet more difficult; they did not want to find themselves in the army in any role, especially as once they were in uniform they could be court-martialled for disobedience. Those who continuously refused to serve in any way could be put into prison.

John Rodker was one of the Whitechapel Group. He was born in Manchester to immigrant parents but he had grown up in London's East End. He became friends with the likes of Isaac Rosenberg, David Bomberg and Mark Gertler. Rodker was a poet rather than an artist, and a left-wing thinker. He strongly objected to the war on political grounds and he refused to be conscripted. Rodker twice went on the run to avoid being arrested and forced into the army; on one occasion he was hiding with the poet R. C. Trevelyan. His situation was often talked about among the Whitechapel Group in their letters to each other. Rodker was caught and sent to Wormwood Scrubs and Dartmoor Prison.

> I knew about war, and how inconclusive it always had been and most of my childhood I had seen Boer War veterans begging in the streets, and all through my boyhood and adolescence I had been Socialist then Anarchist, and always anti-capitalist and so anti-militarist, and knew it would be, and was, a bloody mess...[5]

Twin brothers Mark and David Goldberg also refused all service at their military tribunal in London. They were both sent to Winchester Prison for two years with hard labour.[6]

Those who would not agree to any service, including as non-combatants, were known as absolutists. Emmanuel Ribeiro was a Jewish communist and an absolutist. During his imprisonment he went on hunger strike and was force-fed over 150 times, a process he described as 'not only inhuman but barbarous torture of the worst kind'.[7]

Whether due to principle or faith, being a conscientious objector during the First World War was not easy – ridicule, hatred, ostracism and physical abuse were all common for those who would not fight. Many continued to experience that treatment for years following the end of the conflict. Others, like Rodker, had friends who understood why they had not wanted to go and wished that they had never had to themselves. It is difficult to tell how many Jewish conscientious objectors there were during the period – verifiable statistics on Jewish men in this group are hard to come by – but there were some, and their stories are important as well.

AWARDS AND BRAVERY

The award system of the British Army and the Royal Navy of the First World War era was not complicated, but there did seem to be a lot of different awards. This is often because the awards are abbreviated, and it is easy to mix them up. Awards were considered an essential way of providing recognition and moral support, and in some cases financial reward. For the Jewish community the awards meant acceptance and equality with their non-Jewish peers. Awards meant that the contribution of individuals and the community was being acknowledged.

According to the British Jewry Book of Honour, awards to Jews were as follows:

Victoria Cross (VC)	5
Order of St Michael and St George	15
Distinguished Service Order (DSO)	49
Military Cross (MC; commissioned officers only)	263
Distinguished Flying Cross (DFC)	11
Order of the British Empire (OBE)	144
Distinguished Conduct Medal (DCM)	85
Military Medal (MM; ranks and NCOs only)	329
Meritorious Service Medal (MSM)	66
mentioned in despatches	336
foreign honours	138
mentioned in home despatches	155

More men and women were recognised with awards in the First World War than in any other conflict. The large number of men in the armed services during the First World War, technological developments, extreme conditions and requirements for men to still fight in very close proximity to one another are key reasons as to why more Victoria Crosses were awarded then than during any other conflict. However, it should also be noted that many of the Victoria Crosses and the other awards were given for bravery while helping others rather than for combat alone.

Undoubtedly the highest of the awards is the Victoria Cross. The Victoria Cross was introduced by Queen Victoria in 1857 during the Crimean War as the highest award for gallantry. Prior to its introduction there was no single award that could be given irrespective of age, class, rank, colour or religion. It can only be given for the 'most conspicuous bravery or some daring or pre-eminent act of valour or self-sacrifice, or extreme devotion to duty in the presence of the enemy'. It has been awarded to only 1,355 recipients as of 2018, 628 of whom served in the First World War. This may seem like a large number to have been awarded, but once that number has been matched against the number of British forces (including the empire, colonial, and dominion troops) that number equates to roughly 100 for every million men.

If you look at all the recipients of the Victoria Cross, it is soon clear that it is an award for all ranks with no discrimination. The Victoria Cross was given to men of many different nations, class, faiths and skin colours – very unusual for an acknowledgement or award in the highly prejudiced era of the early twentieth century. The five Jewish recipients of the Victoria Cross of the First World War demonstrate that diversity as each of them come from very different backgrounds.

Frank Alexander de Pass was born in 1887, to Eliot and Beatrice de Pass of 23 Queen's Gate Terrace, Kensington. The family were wealthy and Frank and his two brothers were educated at the Abbey School in Beckenham and at Rugby School. De Pass wanted to be a soldier from an early age and went straight from school to the Royal Military Academy at Woolwich. He was commissioned into the Royal Horse Artillery in December 1906, after which he transferred to the 34th Prince Albert Victor's Own Poona Horse (a British Indian Army regiment) in 1909.

While de Pass's schooling and background made him ideal officer material, in 1906 the traditional British Army regiments still tended to be tied to old British families, or those with strong local ties; for example, the men of the Bowes-Lyon family

Frank de Pass's grave at Bethune.

(the former Queen Mother's family) nearly always became officers in the Black Watch. It is likely that de Pass applied for a commission in a British Indian regiment as they were less associated with specific families, although this did require additional training as the commission could only be taken up once the officer could speak an Indian language to a passable degree and understand the religious needs and devotions of the men he was to command.

De Pass spoke a number of languages already and learnt more than one of the Indian languages. He was an excellent horseman, a keen polo player, and interested in the world around him. He was ideally suited to be an officer in a British Indian regiment and therefore enjoyed his time in India and with the regiment. In 1913, he was appointed orderly officer to Lieutenant General Sir Percy Lake, Chief of the General Staff in India. He was engaged to be married the following year. Everything about de Pass set him on course for an illustrious career.

On the outbreak of war, in August 1914, Lieutenant Frank de Pass's regiment was stationed at Secunderabad in India. As an element of the professional forces available to Britain at the start of the war, the British Indian forces were immediately formed up to leave India for the Western Front. The 9th Cavalry Brigade of the 2nd Indian Cavalry Division, the Poona Horse, was sent from Bombay to France, landing at Marseille on 13 October 1914. It was the first time that the British Indian forces had been despatched to Europe. The men marched and rode through the city and received a triumphant welcome from the French locals.

All of the men, including the officers, wore turbans, which were part of the official uniforms. In fact, nearly all of the pictures available now of de Pass have him wearing a Turban.

The men were quickly moved up through to northern France to take part in the battles of La Bassée and Armentières that would establish much of the Western Front. De Pass appeared to have enjoyed himself with his proper soldiering. On 24 November 1914 he was involved in a serious action, and for his bravery he was awarded the Victoria Cross. His citation read:

> For conspicuous bravery near Festubert on the 24th November, in entering a German sap and destroying a traverse in the face of the enemy's bombs, and for subsequently rescuing, under heavy fire, a wounded man who was lying exposed in the open. Lieutenant de Pass lost his life on this day in a second attempt to capture the aforementioned sap, which had been re-occupied by the enemy.

As you can see from the citation he was killed in action the following day, on 25 November 1914, not knowing that he would be the first Jewish man to be awarded the Victoria Cross. Frank de Pass was buried at Béthune Town Cemetery in the military section. He is also commemorated on the Bevis Marks Synagogue war

Tanks at Armentières. (Courtesy of the National Archives and Records Administration)

memorial in the City of London and on the war memorial in the chapel at Rugby School. His award was covered in all the Jewish press and he is probably the most famous of the Jewish Victoria Cross awardees. His Victoria Cross is now held at the National Army Museum, London.

In complete contrast to de Pass's background, Issy Smith was born in Alexandria as Israel Shmulovitch (or Smilovitch) sometime between 1886 and 1890 (there are a number of dates given in the records). His nationality at the time was French, after his father had acquired French citizenship despite being born in Russia. It is said that Issy ran away by smuggling himself onto a ship which arrived in Britain around 1898. He spoke no English, but did speak French, German and Turkish. He went to school in East London, where he quickly learnt English (he would later pick up a few

Issy Smith VC.

more languages during his military travels) and then went out to work; at one point he delivered fish and at another time he was a plumber's mate.

In September 1904 he joined the Manchester Regiment, at which point he also fully adopted his anglicised name of Issy Smith. After training he went with his regiment to South Africa and India. He was present at the Delhi Durbar parade in 1911, after which he was one of sixteen non-commissioned officers to be awarded the Delhi Durbar Medal, a clear sign that he had a good service record and was popular among the regiment. Like a lot of soldiers at that time Smith was keen on sport; he was a middleweight boxer in army competitions.

After retiring from the army in 1912, Issy moved to Australia. However, he remained on the army reserves list. When war was declared on Germany, Issy immediately tried to enrol in the Australian armed forces but as a reservist was turned away and instructed to attend a British Army recruitment centre. After finding the correct office he was immediately re-enlisted and sent back to Europe for active service in 1914. Back in the UK he re-joined the Manchester Regiment and was with them in Flanders during the opening battles of 1915, including at Neuve Chapelle. He was on the front line during the Second Battle of Ypres (April–May 1915), which was initiated by a German gas attack. It was during a counter-attack that he demonstrated the bravery that resulted in his Victoria Cross. His citation in the *London Gazette* read:

For most conspicuous bravery on the 26 April. 1915, near Ypres, when he left his Company on his own initiative and went forward towards the enemy's position to assist a severely wounded man, whom he carried a distance of 250 yards into safety, while exposed the whole time to heavy machine-gun and rifle fire.

Subsequently Corporal Smith displayed great gallantry, when the
casualties were very heavy, in voluntarily assisting to bring in many
more wounded men throughout the day, and attending to them
with the greatest of devotion to duty regardless of personal risk.

He was injured during the action and was in a military hospital
in Dublin recuperating when he heard the news of his award. As
a war hero, he toured the UK to boost recruitment – the ordinary
soldier with a Victoria Cross! Crowds generally cheered him
on, although there is one story of his being turned away from a
restaurant while in his uniform and despite wearing his Victoria
Cross, with the reason provided for his rejection being that he
was Jewish. A fellow non-Jewish soldier wrote to *The Jewish
Chronicle* to say how wrong it was for Issy to be treated in such a
way. He was keen to state how much Issy was liked and admired
by his fellow soldiers of all backgrounds, but it is a reminder
that anti-Semitism could always raise its ugly head. Within a few
months Issy returned to active service, now promoted to sergeant,
and went off to serve in Mesopotamia and Palestine.

Surviving the war, Issy married in 1918 and was able to leave
the army in 1919. He regularly attended commemorative events,
including a royal reception at Buckingham Palace. In 1920 he was
one of the servicemen who helped to form the guard of honour for
the interment of the Unknown Warrior in Westminster Abbey. Like
many ex-servicemen, Issy found it difficult to get work after the
war and once pawned his medals for £20. The Jewish Historical
Society found out, and with the support of Chief Rabbi Hertz and
Hertz's wife the medals were retrieved and handed back to Issy.

In the 1920s Issy and his wife left Britain and went to Australia.
A lifelong supporter of veterans' charities, Issy Smith died in

Australia in 1940. He had two children who continued to attend remembrance events in his honour. His medals were later sold at auction for approximately £30,000; they are now with a private collector.

Another of the Victoria Cross recipients had an Australian connection. Leonard Maurice Keysor was born in London on 3 November 1885 and attended school in the UK, after which he moved to Canada. He failed to make his name there, and migrated to Australia in early 1914 as his brother and sister were there. Ready to start a new way of life, Keysor was working as a clerk when war was declared. He joined the Australian Imperial Force (AIF) as a private and was sent to Egypt before taking part in the Gallipoli landings on 25 April 1915. The fighting in Gallipoli was hard and very physical. By June Keysor had been promoted to lance-corporal and become an expert bomber. He was then part of the brutal and bloody Battle of Lone Pine. It was his actions and bravery here that led to his Victoria Cross. His citation read:

> For most conspicuous bravery and devotion to duty at Lone Pine trenches in the Gallipoli Peninsula on 7th August 1915. Keysor was in a trench which was being heavily bombed by the enemy. At great personal risk he picked up two live bombs and threw them back at the enemy. Though wounded he continued throwing bombs, thereby saving a most important portion of the trench. Next day Keysor bombed the enemy out of a position from which temporary mastery of his own trench had been obtained. Although again wounded he declined evacuation, volunteering to throw bombs for another company, which had lost all its bomb-throwers. He continued to bomb the enemy until the situation was relieved.

Allied troops in a captured Ottoman trench at Lone Pine. (Courtesy of the Australian War Memorial)

His Victoria Cross was celebrated in *The Jewish Chronicle* as yet another example of a Jewish man from a normal background who had shown outstanding courage. He continued to serve and in 1916 was sent to the Western Front, where he became a sergeant in November. His bravery and quick intelligence led to his being recommended and then awarded a commission in January 1917. He made a good officer and was poplar with his men in the many action actions that he led them into. Keysor was gassed and injured on more than one occasion during his war service, resulting in him being medically discharged from the army in December 1918 as a lieutenant, after which he returned to Australia. However, he found that he missed Britain and so returned to London and went into the family business of importing clocks. He was on the reserve officers list and tried to return to military service when the Second World War started, but he was turned away for being medically unfit. He died in October 1951, and his medals are at the Australian War Memorial in Canberra.

Jack White was born in Leeds in 1896 as Jacob Weiss. His father was a Russian immigrant and his mother was British. The family moved to Manchester and Jack attended school there. He worked in the family waterproofing (clothes) business when war was declared, and he enlisted as soon as he could. He enlisted in the King's Own Royal Lancashire Regiment and was due to go to

The British HQ at Kut.

France, but tragically his father suddenly died and he was forced to miss the departure date as he was on compassionate leave to attend the funeral. Instead White left with the 6th Battalion and was sent to Gallipoli. He would spend most of his war service in the Middle East. In 1916 his unit was sent to help relieve the Siege of Kut, where many men were killed. It was in Mesopotamia in March 1917 that he carried out an act of bravery that earned him the Victoria Cross.

His citation read:

For most conspicuous bravery and resource.

This signaller during an attempt to cross a river saw the two Pontoons ahead of him come under heavy machine-gun fire, with disastrous results.

When his own Pontoon had reached midstream, with every man except himself either dead or wounded, finding that he was unable to control the Pontoon, Pte. White promptly tied a telephone wire to the Pontoon, jumped overboard, and towed it to the shore, thereby saving an officer's life and bringing to land the rifles and equipment of the other men in the boat, who were either dead or dying.

White was presented with the Victoria Cross by King George V at Buckingham Palace in April 1919. After the war he returned to Manchester and became a cloth cutter in a factory. He worked his way up in the business, eventually owning the company and calling it Jack White. He was a founding member of the Association of Jewish Ex-Servicemen and Women and was very active in his local British Legion branch. He was always committed and supportive of his fellow veterans and was keen to ensure that Jewish service was also recognised.

Jack White VC.

In 1939, when the Second World War started, White tried to join the Home Guard but was told he couldn't as both his parents had not been naturalised citizens – despite the fact that he had been born in the UK, was a veteran and had the Victoria Cross. He joined the Air Raid Precautions (ARP) as a warden instead but was deeply hurt by the rejection. He died in 1949.

Robert Gee was born in Leicester in 1876. His father died just before he was born and his mother died when he was nine years old. The Gees were a poor family, and he and his siblings were placed in the workhouse, where life was difficult. As a young man he tried a couple of apprenticeships but he was unhappy and decided to join the army instead. He became a Royal Fusilier and was sent with the regiment to the Channel Islands and the West Indies. He married in 1902 while still serving. At the start of the war he was a regimental quartermaster sergeant, one of the most senior NCO positions available. But with nearly twenty-two years' service in the army, his skills would be far better used on the front line than in a desk job. Therefore, he was discharged on 20 May 1915 from the army and the very next day he was commissioned straight back into the Royal Fusiliers.

Gee served in Gallipoli and Suez before his regiment took part in the notorious first day of the Battle of the Somme, 1 July 1916, where his bravery in action led to his being awarded the Military Cross. He was injured and sent to the UK on 4 July to recover, and fortunately his injuries were not life-threatening. He recovered from his wounds in time to be sent to Flanders to take part in the fighting at the Third Battle of Ypres in 1917.

His Military Cross citation is as follows:

For conspicuous gallantry in action. He encouraged his men during the attack by fearlessly exposing himself and cheering them on. When wounded he refused to retire, and urged his men on till, after being blown in the air by a shell, he was carried in, half unconscious.

The 86th Battalion War Diary says the following regarding Robert Gee at the Somme:

I sent forward Capt Gee, Staff Captain, to try and get the attack forward. He was wounded almost immediately but refused to come in, sending me two reports as to the situation; finally a 5.9 unexploded shell lifted him over into our lines.

Although he was older than a lot of his fellow soldiers, he also had a lot of experience, all of which seemed to contribute to his leadership and bravery. Following the terrible fighting around Ypres, Gee was with his men at the Battle of Cambrai on 30 November 1917; it was then that he was awarded the Victoria Cross. His citation read:

> For most conspicuous bravery and initiative and determination when an attack by a strong enemy force pierced our line and captured Brigade Headquarters and ammunition dump. Captain Gee finding himself a prisoner, killed one of the enemy with his spiked stick, and succeeded in escaping. He then organised a party of the Brigade Staff, with which he attacked the enemy fiercely, closely followed and supported by two companies of Infantry. By his own personal bravery and prompt action he, aided by his orderlies, cleared the locality. Captain Gee established a defensive flank on the outskirts of the village, then finding that an enemy machine gun was still in action, with a revolver in each hand, and

German troops dismantling an English tank at Cambrai. (Courtesy of the National Archives and Records Administration)

followed by one man, he rushed and captured the gun, killing eight of the crew. At this time he was wounded, but refused to have the wound dressed until he was satisfied the defence was organised.

His remarkable military career continued and by February 1918 Gee had also been mentioned in despatches three times. In April that year Gee was sent back to the UK as his wounds from his many battles were beginning to affect his health. Long-term injuries also made it difficult to decide on a career after the war, but he did feel he had something to say so he chose to enter politics and was duly elected the Conservative MP for East Woolwich in 1921.

By the 1920s Gee had lost interest in politics and was absent for a long time from Parliament. He had decided instead to move to Australia, where he became a farmer, stating that the climate helped with his war injuries. He died in 1960 at the age of eighty-four. The Jewish workhouse boy had become one of the most decorated Jewish servicemen of all time. At his request his medals were presented to the Royal Fusiliers Museum in London, where they remain.

In addition to the five acknowledged Victoria Crosses, Martin Sugarman, the archivist for the Jewish Military Museum, believes that there is a sixth Jewish Victoria Cross. He has done extensive research to uncover the details of Jewish men who served in the World Wars but are lacking a Jewish designation in the official files. In a short piece published recently the following was announced:

The Missing Jewish VC, Captain David Philip Hirsch, MiD, Yorks. Regiment, 23/04/1917 – no known grave – commemorated on the memorial at Arras, Bay 5, son of Harry and Edith of Leeds.

'For most conspicuous bravery and devotion to duty in attack. Having arrived at the first objective, Capt. Hirsch, although already twice wounded, returned over fire-swept slopes to satisfy himself that the defensive flank was being established. Machine gun fire was so intense that it was necessary for him to be continuously up and down the line encouraging his men to dig and hold the position. He continued to encourage his men by standing on the parapet and steadying them in the face of machine gun fire and counter-attack until he was killed. His conduct throughout was a magnificent example of the greatest devotion to duty' (excerpt from the *London Gazette* of 14/06/1917).

Research in an article shows that Hirsch's parents had converted from Judaism but the family were ethnically Jewish by any definition. In 2003 author and AJEX Museum Archivist Martin Sugarman met Hirsch's niece at a talk he gave at the National Army Museum in Chelsea. She admitted to being well over 90 years old. She said that she remembered David when she was a little girl and seeing him on leave in uniform on several occasions. She said all the branches of the family always remained Jewish including the branch of David's father, who had converted for alleged business advantage in a then anti-Jewish atmosphere in the world of commerce. This was relatively common in this period. As such we count David Hirsch as a Jewish VC, making 6 in total awarded in WW1.[1]

The five recognised Jewish Victoria Cross recipients became household names by the end of the First World War, with their faces on cigarette cards and pictures of them in magazines. Within the Jewish community everyone had heard about their bravery. Today they are largely unknown even among the Anglo-Jewish community. Today it might seem amazing that Frank de Pass was a British Jewish man wearing a turban fighting as part of the British Indian forces who went on to receive the Victoria Cross (the first one to be awarded to an officer in an Indian regiment). It is a great example of the ethnic diversity that existed 100 years ago.

Other Awards

Of course, all the men and women who contributed to the war effort are worth remembering, both those with military medals other than the VC and those who were recognised with civilian awards for nursing and welfare. Their stories are interesting insights into the endeavours of those who contributed over 100 years ago.

David Claud Bauer DFC was born in Australia in 1889 and started his schooling there. However, his family moved to London in 1905 and in 1916 he joined the Royal Flying Corps as an officer. He was awarded the DFC on 3 June 1918 for the following service:

> This Officer has commanded No 18 Balloon Section located near the Lille Gate in Ypres throughout the battles of the Second Army in the autumn of 1917. His camp was continually under shell fire from guns of large calibre, and his balloon was hit many times, but nevertheless much important work was done by his section. He showed courage and set a good example to all, and it was largely due to him that work was carried on at all under such conditions.

Like so many men and women during that period, four years of warfare made Bauer susceptible to illness and he contracted pneumonia and died at a casualty clearing station near Bapaume on 3 November 1918. He is buried at Delsaux Farm Military Cemetery. His colonel wrote, 'Had he not died in hospital he would have headed the list of recommendations for further decorations.'

Lieutenant Colonel J. H. Levey DSO started in the regular army as a private soldier in the Scots Guards. He saw active service in South Africa and was a sergeant major at the start of the First World War. He was given a commission to the Gordon Highlanders but before he even reached his battalion he was appointed as the chief instructor to the newly formed Naval Division. Colonel Levey then became a commandant of the Corps School in France, after which he was given command of the 13th Battalion of the Royal Sussex Regiment. In late 1917 he was at the Third Battle of Ypres where his bravery saw him awarded the DSO. He finished the war as a lieutenant colonel, serving as the Deputy Inspector of Training. He became a campaigner for Jewish veterans following the war.

William Mack DCM was born in Edinburgh in 1890 with the surname Kurtzman. He changed his name before joining the army as a volunteer in Glasgow in 1915. At that time he also married Catherine Goldberg. William served with a Scottish regiment, the Seaforth Highlanders, and rose to the rank of sergeant. In 1917, his actions saw him recommended for Distinguished Conduct Medal for gallantry. The citation for this distinction read:

For conspicuous gallantry and devotion to duty. During the mopping up of a village he organised scattered units into bombing groups, and personally led them, helping to capture five offices and 50 other ranks. He was of the utmost assistance to his company.

William Mack.

Before he could be informed of his award he was injured in an accident; he subsequently died from his wounds. Mack was buried at St Pol Communal Cemetery Extension, Pas de Calais. His DCM was awarded posthumously. With no children or grandchildren to remember him or visit his grave, William's story was nearly lost forever; happily, research during the *We Were There Too* project has rescued him from obscurity. His obituary in *The Jewish Chronicle* for 13 July 1917 reads:

> The death, from wounds, has occurred of Sergt. William Mack (Kurtzman) of the Seaforth Highlanders. His widow has received the following letter from a Chaplain attached to the Seaforth Highlanders, 'We are feeling sad about it. To think that Sergt. Mack has been so long with us and has come through many a dangerous battle and then has lost his life twenty miles back from the line by accident is unspeakably sad. I have known Sergt. Mack all the time he has been here. I know how well he did and how precious he was in his department. He was the great helper of every officer under whom he served and they all thought very highly of him.'
>
> The Lieut. Colonel of the Company has sent the following letter:
>
> 'Your husband has now been awarded the Distinguished Conduct Medal for gallantry on the 11th May, a decoration which I know he thoroughly deserved and earned well. I am sorry to say that the award was not made in sufficient time for him to know about it himself. It may please you to know that the award of the DCM is sparingly granted and is only given for specially gallant and meritorious conduct...'

Wolf Lubelski, who later anglicised his name to Walter Lyttleton, is another who may have been lost to history. He was born in Birmingham but was resident in London when the war started and joined up in London. He volunteered for service and served in the 37th Battalion Machine Gun Corps, although he spent a lot of his time as a despatch rider on a motorbike.

He was awarded the Military Cross, which was for 'marked gallantry', on the morning of 6 October 1918, in the course of an attack in Briseux Wood: 'He rushed his section and got his guns into action in the face of heavy machine gun fire from the Germans.'

Wolf Lubelski, later
Walter Lyttleton.

He was demobbed 1919 and returned to London and his work in accountancy. He was popular with his nephews and nieces but he never married. His MC lay in a shoebox after his death and was nearly forgotten about until his great-niece Sarah Gluckstein began to ask questions about him. It is thanks to her that we have Walter's story at all.

Corporal Abraham Joseph Ferner DCM was born in 1896 in London and trained as a tailor before enlisting in 1914 in the Alexandra, Princess of Wales's Own (Yorkshire Regiment). He was involved with a number of battles until he was killed on 21 August 1917 during the Third Battle of Ypres. He was awarded the DCM posthumously. His citation for the DCM, published 26 January 1918, is as follows:

> For conspicuous gallantry and devotion to duty. During the advance, he moved the line in the open under machine gun fire, directing and encouraging his platoon, and later when ordered with his machine gun section to outflank a strong point, he move up his gun, and though all his men were disabled, and he himself was wounded, continued to fire it until it was put out of action. His pluck and coolness were deserving of the highest praise.

His grave epitaph chosen by his brother David was particularly poignant:

Whose death
was followed by
his broken hearted mother's
five weeks later

Captain Albert Baswitz MC (Military Cross) of London was part of the Officer Training Corps at King's College London before leaving to join the Country of London Regiment in 1914. He was killed during the Battle of the Somme on 16 September 1916. He was awarded the MC and remembered by his college in the *King's College Review* for December 1916:

Captain Baswitz met his death gallantly leading his men against the Germans on September 16th last. A brother officer writing of his death says: 'His sheer keenness for the whole thing was wonderfully infectious. On the 16th his chance came – the chance he had been longing for. He was ordered to take his company up and reinforce another battalion which was going to attack. So he died, gallantly leading his men, doing a work that he was always anxious to do.'[2]

One of those who served with him wrote: 'His men, especially the bombers, adored him. There was no more popular officer in the whole division. His example will always be before us.' His colonel, writing to his bereaved parents, wrote: 'He was one of the bravest men I have ever met and one of the best of friends, beloved by the officers and all of his men too.'[3]

Some of the actions that led to receiving awards have a hint of the 'boys' own' adventure about them, such as the actions of Captain A. Aaronson, a Jewish Palestinian officer who received the Distinguished Service Order for organising a spy ring for British Intelligence in the Middle East in the war against the Ottomans.

In some cases, awards came from the governments of other countries. An example of this comes in the 8 September 1914 edition of *The Jewish Chronicle* where it was reported that 'Mr Harry Abrahams of Hawthorn Lodge, Bracknell has been awarded the Croix de Guerre for his services in France, where he has some time been in command of a convoy of motor ambulance cars presented to the French Army by the British Ambulance Committee'.

In the British Jewry Book of Honour there are fifty pages for those who received awards; unfortunately, detailed information is only provided for those awards that came with citations. For those who received awards without citations there is little to no information about what they did. In the list of MBEs there are a number of women, such as Miss D. I. Jacobs for the Foreign Office, but no information is given – what was it they did? How, to use another example, did Mrs R. V. Rubenstein of the WRNS get her MBE?

Of course, all those who committed themselves to the conflict are worthy of recognition, not just those with medals, but the special honours do remind us that there was nothing tokenistic or soft about the Jewish contribution to the First World War – they gave all their efforts, and often their lives.

10

THE BRITISH JEWRY BOOK OF HONOUR

In the introduction to the British Jewry Book of Honour, the question is raised, 'What is the Book of Honour?' This is followed by the answer: 'The British Jewry Book of Honour has been planned as a permanent record of the services of all the fifty thousand Jews who, from all parts of the Empire, served in the Great War; so that, in days to come, all may have before them , in a permanent form, the remembrance of these men and know how to hold them in honour and lasting thankfulness. To do less, is to fail in duty to them.' This paragraph is on the same page as the statement: 'British Jews have vindicated once and for all their right to British citizenship.'

Taking the two together it is clear that book is a proud record, an extended roll of honour and a document of proof that Anglo-Jewry is not a 'bunch of foreigners' but a dedicated and loyal group that is part of British society. Clearly the service and sacrifice of those Jews in the First World War had not put an end to the anti-Semitism still prevalent in British society after 1918, but the British Jewry Book of Honour was part of the fight against it.

In the early stages of the war, *The Jewish Chronicle* stated that it would collect the names of all those who served to create a roll of honour for British Jews. With those lists, the detailed information that the Revd Michael Adler had collected as Senior Jewish Chaplain to HM Forces, the information collected by the other Jewish military chaplains and the information supplied on appeal to Anglo-Jewry, the substance of the British Jewry Book of Honour was created.

It is quite an incredible feat that 50,000 names were collected and collated. The names are usually in alphabetical order within the regiments. Also, in the main, the men are in their correct service and regiments. There is information about medal winners, about the different armed services and some of the key people involved. All this information is bound together in one book of over a thousand pages. All of this was done using paper records long before computerisation. There is an excellent memoir from Revd Adler about his time as Senior Jewish Chaplain, in which he claims that anti-Semitism among the soldiers during the war was negligible. The book was published in 1922, so it had taken less than four years to complete the task. It is not a perfect document – there are mistakes, repetitions and omissions – but for an historical researcher it is a gift of a document. The book includes some indexed photographs of individuals and military units and also photographs of women as nurses, many of which were often supplied by family members, or by Adler and the military chaplains. The pictures are particularly important as a way to identify individuals, as an important act of remembrance and as an historical source. The pictures can be used to match against records of where regiments were and who was in them. So many of the original pictures undoubtedly ended up in boxes and old photograph albums that have subsequently been discarded or forgotten about.

The British Jewry Book of Honour is a statement of what British Jewry wanted to show to the Jewish community and to wider British society, as well as a record of its contribution and service.

It was felt that some of the Jewish community still needed evidence that British Jewry was accepted, that it was an acknowledged element of society. This was of particular importance to the older, more established Jewish leadership that from the start of the First World War had viewed a Jewish military contribution as a means for Anglo-Jewry to be safe and integrated. The recent announcement of the Balfour Declaration, as well as a growing sympathy for Zionism had unsettled some of those who still felt that integration (though not necessarily assimilation) was the key to a Jewish future. To counter the belief that some Jews held that a successful Jewish future could only be achieved with a Jewish state the British Jewry Book of Honour with its names and images would reassure any doubters of a secure Jewish future in Britain.

Included in the book is an acknowledgement of the important role that many of the Jewish agencies which supported the war effort made throughout the war, as is a thank you to the regional organisers across the country. Even in 1920 there were often accusations of a London bias, so the special mention of the cities of Leeds, Manchester Glasgow and Liverpool was very deliberate.

As part of the concept to 'honour' those who served, the book also contains letters of support and acknowledgments from distinguished men of the day, both Jewish and non-Jewish. The comments by all those distinguished men hint, or point out quite clearly, that the book is to be used to counter any accusations current or future that cast doubt on Jews' loyalty or sense of duty to the United Kingdom. The first of the letters is from the Chief Rabbi, Joseph Hertz, who could not be clearer on what he sees as a key purpose of the book. He states:

> We owe it to the brave sons of Israel who so gladly gave their lives that Freedom and Righteousness prevail, to see to it that their names shall not be blotted out nor the memory of the heroic deeds forgotten.

This permanent written record of the part played by Anglo Jewry in the Great War will help lovers of the Truth in their warfare against the malicious slander that the Jew shrinks from the sacrifices demanded of every loyal citizen in the hour of national danger.

The Chief Rabbi is followed by the most senior Jewish officer in HM Forces, Lieutenant General Sir John Monash GCMG KCB GOC Australian Corps. He uses his letter to reaffirm Jewish loyalty:

I owe much also to the many thousands of Jewish soldiers, scattered throughout all his Majesties Armies, who by their valour, their fortitude, and their devoted sacrifice have combined to achieve a story of Jewish service to our country, which will still further enhance the prestige of every British citizens of the Jewish faith, as second to no other in patriotism or in readiness or ability to bear his full share of all the burdens of the State.

The industrialist and politician the Rt Hon. Sir Alfred Mond, Bt, was succinct in his statement:

This is a record of which we have a right to be proud as Jews and as citizens of the British Empire.

Sir Herbert Samuel GBE, the Jewish Home Secretary, who had forced Russian Jewish participation but had also begun to see the value of British Jewish presence in Palestine, was keen to ensure what he believed should be known about Anglo-Jewry.

Jews care for peace and for liberty as much as others; they are not less ready than others to fight, if need be, in their defence. This book furnishes the proof.

Sir Adolph Tuck, Bt, the art publisher, was keen to emphasise sacrifice and duty for access to rights. It is a reminder that the Anglo-Jewry was in a relationship with the state, that to be treated with equality there must be a tacit agreement to participate equally. He stated that:

The great World War has indeed found England happy in all her sons, not the least among whom are those of Jewish blood who have responded to the call for the freedom of the world. As befits the ancient race from which they have sprung.

The sacrifices that they (the Jewish soldiers) have made for civilisation and for freedom show that those who have been accorded equal liberties irrespective of creed, have not been found wanting, at a time when their country had most need of them.

Non-Jewish members of the establishment also wrote letters of support to be published in the British Jewry Book of Honour. Field-Marshal Earl Haig KT, the man who had been in charge of the British Army for much of the war, was asked to contribute a letter. It should be understood that in the years following the end of the war Haig received endless requests for his support. Although he only wrote a short letter for the British Jewry Book of Honour, it was a very strong one that he was happy to have printed. In it he makes very clear the message he wishes to be taken from the Jewish contribution to the war:

The British Jewry Book of Honour is a striking testimony to a fact that every soldier will gladly recognise – namely, the loyalty with which British Jews of every class came forward to fight for the country of their adoption, and for the great human ideals which they shared with the Christian comrades in arms.

The Marquis of Crewe, KG Robert Offley Ashburton Milnes, a distinguished and admired Conservative politician wrote a letter that praises the Jewish contribution and the book itself:

> I am glad to know that the part taken by British Jews in the Great War is to be duly chronicled. Their services have been appreciated and recognised by their fellow-countrymen, and the value of such services rendered by the King's subjects all over the Empire had never admitted any thought of the race or origin of those who gave and risked their lives. But it is natural and legitimate pride that inspires a special record such as this and we may all be proud that the ancient traditions of Jewry have been revived all through the fight waged by the British Empire on behalf of liberty and justice.

The newspaper publisher (not opposed to a bit of anti-Semitic stereotyping in his papers) Viscount Northcliffe still needed to make a sweeping generalisation about Jews among his praise. Nonetheless, a letter from him was evidence of the attention that the book and the community were getting, even from some of the Jewish community's traditional detractors.

> The Jews are a cautious people and not anxious to make war, but in this great conflict they waged it just as vigorously as they did in the wars of the Bible.

The Rt Hon. Winston Churchill MP, Secretary of State for War in 1920, had long professed his regards for Anglo-Jewry and counted a number of prominent Jews among his close friends. He was far more unequivocal in his praise.

Press baron Viscount Northcliffe.

I can truthfully say that this record is a great one, and British Jews can look back with pride on the honourable part they played in winning the Great War.

Only 3,000 copies of the British Jewry Book of Honour were published and nearly 100 years later they have become quite collectable – fragile, too, as the paper used is prone to crumbling. The British Jewry Book of Honour was to set the bar for Jewish remembrance and the recording of Jewish loyalty. Combined with the creation of the Association of Jewish Ex-Servicemen and Women (AJEX), this should have been all that was required to finally remove any anti-Jewish prejudice or accusations of foreignness. Of course, this was not to be the case. If only a book could change centuries of prejudice.

11

EVENTS, IMPACTS AND CONCLUSIONS

Zionism and the Balfour Declaration

Zionism on the ground and among intellectual circles developed in Britain over the course of the First World War. Prior to 1914 it had a limited appeal among the mainly migrant groups and only a limited appeal among established Anglo-Jewry. Those who were interested in it tended to be Jews who had come to the UK from eastern Europe, especially those areas of Russia and Austro-Hungary where there were high levels of anti-Semitism and popular nationalist movements (such as in Polish territories that wanted a free and independent Poland once more), making campaigns for national determination commonplace across society. The Zionist Federation of Great Britain and Ireland, also known as the British Zionist Federation, was formed in 1899. It held meetings and put on talks. The federation was formed to campaign and raise awareness of the arguments for Zionism.

As stated elsewhere, many British Jews from all social classes felt that Zionism was a distraction from integration in the UK, and potentially dangerous if it presented the Jews as following their own national desires rather than conforming to a British national way of life. The mobilisation of the eastern European Jews, the pressures put on the labour movement and a general confidence for many groups across Europe to want to be counted helped to strengthen the emerging Zionist groups in the UK. However, it is worth noting that Zionism, a belief in a separate Jewish homeland or state, was still something of a distant and incomplete concept. Zionism for some was really just a call for a strong Jewish identity, a pride in being openly Jewish without fear of attack, something that could be comfortably combined with being a citizen of another country (a bit like 'Jew Boy' Sam in Kitchener's Army from chapter 4). For others Zionism was fundamentally about creating a homeland for Jews, but there was still disagreement about whether that was a religious ideal or a secular one. In truth, the reality of what a 'Jewish state' might be was still very much open to debate, especially among Zionists themselves.

In some non-Jewish British political and intellectual groups, Zionism in its many forms was beginning to be discussed, and often favourably – most popularly among some of the liberal Christian intellectuals of the day such as David Lloyd George and those who wished to see an end to anti-Semitism and Jewish exclusions. Across the wider non-Jewish British society, Zionism, or any Jewish national or political movement, meant nothing.

Of course a hundred years ago the idea of national determination was still being developed, and for many governments and leaders, empires and imperialism were the norm that needed to be upheld. Recognition of independent small states, unless they were still under the control of the major political players, was not something to be contemplated – and certainly not encouraged, regardless of their motivations.

For those Jewish individuals who had a grand vision for Zionism, including the creation of a proper Jewish state or home, the First World War and the resulting shift of political priorities and relationships presented a number of opportunities.

Ze'ev Jabotinsky, the Russian Zionist journalist, had directed most of his campaigning and lobbying energies at the Jews of central and eastern Europe before 1914. A prolific speaker and writer, Jabotinsky had travelled around Jewish areas to spread the word in the years before the war. In 1914 he saw many of the Jewish communities he had toured around caught up in a war about which they knew very little. They were treated with little respect and often pitted against each other. What is more, he saw three of the imperial powers that were behind Jewish oppression (Austria-Hungary, Russia and the Ottoman Empire) now creating further instability in the Jewish world.

With the entry of the Ottoman Empire into the war on the side of the Central Powers in November 1914, Jabotinsky saw an opportunity to further his Zionist ideas, and it involved working with the British. It was not that Jabotinsky believed in British imperialism over the imperialism of the other European powers, or that he was a passionate believer in British ideals, but what he did see in the British government was a leadership that did not discriminate in the same way as other European powers (indeed, there were Jews in key political positions in the United Kingdom) and which had ambitions in the Middle East.

Jabotinsky was extremely well connected to politicians and other influential people in many countries. In the UK he started to make approaches to people and write articles urging a Jewish regiment, specifically one that could fight in Palestine. His suggestions were initially rejected, especially as British Jews were already heading to the enlistment centres and the Rothschild offices in London. The Ottoman entry into the war resulted in attacks on those Russian Jews who had settled in Ottoman lands such as Palestine, leading to an influx of refugees into British-controlled Egypt.

The outcome of the increased Jewish presence in Egypt and the British need for more troops was the creation of the Zion Mule Corps. Following the disbanding of the Corps in 1916, Jabotinsky threw his efforts once more into lobbying for the creation of a regular combatant Jewish force, this time with the evidence of the success and respect that that the Zion Mule Corps had achieved as a key argument.

However, it was not just Jabotinsky who was campaigning for steps towards a Zionist cause. While he was publicly directing his attentions into a fighting force, in particular one for British-based Russian Jews, behind the scenes other lobbying was being carried out.

Lionel Walter Rothschild was born in London in 1868. He was the eldest son of Nathan 'Natty' Rothschild and was, therefore, destined for the family business of the Rothschild bank. Although he worked at the bank, he was not interested in finance; instead he was passionate about zoology and the natural sciences. As a Rothschild, however, he took his responsibilities very seriously, and in addition to being at the bank he was a governor of the Board of Deputies, the United Synagogue, the Anglo-Jewish Association and the Jews' Free School. He had suffered poor health as a child, and being fifty-six years old at the time of the war was unable to serve in uniform; instead he was active behind the scenes for the war effort and helped to galvanise Jewish support for the war.

Walter's father had been friends with Theodor Herzl, the father of modern Zionism, although he had made it clear that he was not a believer in it for British Jews. It is not known exactly when Walter Rothschild became a Zionist, but by the time he inherited his father's title of Lord Rothschild in 1915 he was certainly active in that area. He did not see this in any way as being in conflict with his British duty or his patriotism, and expressed his view quite clearly on that:

I can truly say that national Zionism has done nothing, and would never do anything, inconsistent with the status of the true British citizen of which I am proud to be one, just as proud as I am of being a Jew.[1]

Therefore, he was happy to use his connections and influence to the Zionist cause. His beliefs were in direct opposition to those of some of his family members, as Chaim Weizmann noted: 'The House of Rothschild, perhaps the most famous family in Jewish exilic history, was divided on the issue of Zionism.'

Chaim Weizmann was another leading Zionist whose influence grew directly as a result of the First World War. Born in Russia in 1874, Weizmann did well at school and his poor parents pushed him forward into higher education. When he had finished high school he left Russia for Germany and Switzerland, as the Jewish

Chaim Weizmann, first President of Israel. (Courtesy of the Israeli Government Press Office)

quotas for university prevented his progress at home. He worked hard and finished with a PhD in Chemistry and taught at Geneva University. Around 1904/05 he took a place at Manchester University and moved to Britain, and it was at this point in his life that Weizmann was elected to the General Zionist Council. In Britain he met regularly with other Zionists, such as the Manchester-based and British-born Harry Sacher.

Once the war started, many professionals and experts were called upon to 'do their bit'. Scientists were in demand as technology was seen as just as important to the war effort as soldiering. Weizmann worked on a way to extract acetone from maize, which was vital for cordite (an explosive used in bullets and other ammunition and military equipment). His developments in that field brought him into close contact with government circles, where he was admired and respected. One of his good friends from 1906 was the Conservative politician and former Prime Minister Arthur James Balfour.

From the opening days of the war the British government had been consolidating its position in the Middle East. Its first priority was Egypt and the Suez Canal, which was to be protected from Ottoman forces at all costs. In addition to Egypt, British forces had been despatched into Mesopotamia (modern-day Iraq) where they tried to secure territories and oil.

Fighting in the Dardanelles had been the priority in the region during 1915, but by 1916 British eyes started to turn with interest towards Palestine. In 1914, Herbert Samuel MP had first voiced the idea of a Zionist presence in Palestine supported by the British, but the Asquith government had dismissed the idea. In 1915, Mark Sykes, a British diplomat, along with his French counterpart Francois Georges-Picot, were secretly investigating the future control of the Middle East. At the same time, the British High Commissioner to Egypt, Lieutenant Colonel Sir Henry McMahon, had been in correspondence with Hussein bin Ali, Sharif of Mecca and a key figure in the Arab leadership, to establish an Arab federation across the Middle East, following an Arab revolt to remove Ottoman presence.

In 1916 the British and French governments signed the Sykes–Picot Agreement, which divided up the whole of the Middle East between the two imperial countries. Britain's territories would include the area of Palestine. Throughout 1916 the Zionists in London had been doing their best to lobby the British authorities; their chances of a success had been greatly boosted by the removal of the Asquith government and the emergence of a Lloyd George coalition government. In Lloyd George in particular the Zionists had a friend; his Christian evangelical commitment provided him with a strong belief that the Jews should be in Palestine to create Israel as in biblical times.

The key year was 1917, when a culmination of factors came together to push the Zionist idea further than ever before. In February 1917, the Zionist leadership in the UK including Lord Rothschild, Chaim Weizmann and Nahum Sokolow (a Polish-Russian Jew then resident in the UK) met with British government officials. The meetings continued, including some with Mark Sykes, their focus to discuss plans for the post-war era. The decision to create a Jewish regiment in 1917 in order to mobilise Russian Jews provided the first state-authorised military combatant force with a specific Jewish identity in over 2,000 years. This was extremely significant; the recognition that this military unit provided for British and international Jewry at the time should not be underestimated. Among its ranks and officers were a number of prominent Zionists who made clear their ambition to liberate Palestine from the Ottomans to create a homeland for the Jews.

Over in Palestine there had been great gains for the troops under British command, and from autumn General Allenby, who was

*Foreign Secretary Arthur Balfour.
(Courtesy of the Library of
Congress)*

in charge of the British forces had won some decisive victories
to begin his journey towards Jerusalem. For the supporters, the
Battle of Beersheba on 31 October 1917, in a place said to have
been created by Abraham, might have seemed like an omen of the
success that was to come.

In fact, in the summer of 1917 the Foreign Secretary, Arthur Balfour,
had invited the Zionist leadership under Lord Rothschild to write
formally to him. Balfour was a Christian Conservative politician who
supported the belief that a Jewish formalised homeland in the Middle
East would be the right thing while also being a very convenient
tool for the British. The idea of supporting the Zionist ideal was
debated among the Cabinet for some weeks. Finally, with a majority
of consent, Balfour wrote to Lord Rothschild on 2 November 1917:

Dear Lord Rothschild
I have much pleasure in conveying to you, on behalf of His
Majesty's Government, the following declaration of sympathy

with Jewish Zionist aspirations which has been submitted to and approved by, the Cabinet.

His Majesty's government view with favour the establishment in Palestine of a national home for the Jewish people, and will use their best endeavours to facilitate the achievement of this object, it being clearly understood that nothing shall be done which may prejudice the civil and religious rights of existing non-Jewish communities in Palestine, or the rights and political status enjoyed by Jews in any other country.

The letter was formally published on 9 November 1917.

Not everyone in the Cabinet agreed with the promise of what is now known as the 'Balfour Declaration', especially Edwin Montagu, the Cabinet Minister for India, who was also Jewish. Montagu is often described as a radical liberal and was very much of the belief that anti-Semitism would only be eradicated if Jews were fully integrated into British life. He expressed the concerns that a Jewish homeland in Palestine, would make Jews foreigners everywhere else. He also objected to what establishing a Jewish majority in that area would do to the Muslims and Christians already living there.

The Balfour Declaration was met with a mixed response in the UK. Many in Anglo-Jewish leadership were not supporters, but they were also happy to see a statement from the British government that was in praise of the Jews.

Under British military protection, Zionist leaders started to visit Palestine with immediate effect, and campaigning for more Jewish recruits to join the Judeans took off in earnest. The British public seemed largely in favour of the declaration, although its importance was not nearly as great as General Allenby's taking of Jerusalem a month later. It was considered by many Jews and non-Jews as yet another political statement to garner support and secure imperialist ambitions ready for a new world order following the end of the war.

The Balfour Declaration's long-term significance could not have been predicted. The world of 1917 did not know of the horrors that would come under Nazism and the Holocaust. The politicians of that time were unaware of how Britain as an empire would fall just like all the others, leaving the Jewish people to create their own distinct Jewish state following another global conflict.

What is clear is that the First World War created changes to the political order that led to governments making decisions with lasting consequences for the Anglo-Jewish world, international Jewry and the Middle East. Those consequences have subsequently led to changes and actions that still affect the world today.

The Association of Jewish Ex-Servicemen and Women

Long before the First World War, the Jewish military chaplaincy established a traditional annual Chanukah service for all Jewish servicemen. It was an opportunity to bring together the disparate groups of men that served across the forces and across many different regiments.

As far as anyone was concerned, the Chanukah service was an important way for serving Jews to meet up with each other. It was a social event as well as a religious one. When the war started, the service stopped being held in the same way as services were held out in the theatres of war or in the training camps and regimental headquarters when they could be. The service resumed following the war, but increasingly the ex-servicemen now wanted to meet at events where they could remember their fallen comrades and that meant services or events that were non-religious as well as those that were Jewish in character.

It is easy to focus on the dead when it comes to war, but in fact roughly five out of six of those who served in the British forces returned home at the end of the First World War. That meant over 5 million men returned to civilian life across the UK and the Empire and Commonwealth; of those 5 million approximately 2 million now had some form of disability as a result of the fighting and the war. The rest may not have been physically incapacitated but they were still likely to bear scars – physical ones that might heal, and mental ones that might never do so.

Unsurprisingly, therefore, ex-service clubs became popular. It was not about going out to have a good time and reminisce, it was often about being among people who understood what you might have gone through, without actually having to talk about it. For many, an ex-service club or association was about continuing the camaraderie or closeness of the regiment. British Legion branches were established in towns and cities all over the country, as were other veterans' associations. Some of them were about meeting with fellow veterans, and when faced with the economic problems that followed the war, many started to be about welfare as well. On 24 January 1920 *The Jewish Chronicle* reported on the Federation of Discharged Soldiers' Jewish Branch having a meeting at the Jewish Trades Union Institute in Leeds.

A few months earlier, in November 1919, the first Armistice event was held on the anniversary. Supposedly a one-off event, millions attended the main parade in Whitehall. It was soon clear that, for the foreseeable future at least, a commemorative event on the anniversary of the Armistice would be held.

At the Armistice events in 1921, a group of men formerly of the Judeans laid a wreath at the Cenotaph. This small but important gesture became very important to the Jewish community, a physical statement that they had made their contribution. By 1925 the ex-servicemen were having an annual dinner, and by January 1926 *The Jewish Chronicle* reported a parade of 250 men of the Judean Battalions and the Menorah Club, founded by Jewish ex-soldiers.

In December 1926, eight years on from the end of the war, the annual Chanukah service was revived at Bayswater Synagogue, but this now included a visit to the Cenotaph. The Jewish ex-servicemen had no concerns about making their presence felt.

In 1929, international events, including deadly riots in Palestine and a rise in anti-Semitism and fascism in parts of Europe, began to raise concerns among Jewish veterans. A meeting was held in the East End of London and those who attended decided to form the Jewish Ex-servicemen's Legion. There were 200 members straight away. News spread around the country and more and more men signed up. It was agreed that in November they would hold a specifically Jewish veterans' event at the Duke's Place Synagogue, East London.

With a growth in membership, including contact with currently serving Jewish servicemen, the Jewish Ex-servicemen's Legion decided to organise its first annual remembrance parade and service on 8 November 1930 at Horse Guards Parade. The legion began to meet regularly and elected its own rabbi, Louis Rabinowitz, as the first honorary chaplain.

In 1933, the British Union of Fascists established an East London office, deliberately near to the Jewish Ex-servicemen's Legion office. The legion responded by recruiting and training young men and veterans as speakers to counter the lies that the BUF was spreading about Jewish disloyalty and cowardice. After all, they were living proof that the Jewish community had participated and contributed in large numbers during the Great War. One of those, a founding member of the legion, was Isaac Aizen, who had

been born in London in 1888. He had spent the war in the Royal
Army Medical Corps attached to the Leicestershire Regiment. As
a resident of the Teesdale Street, Bethnal Green, East London, and
an ex-serviceman, he was prepared to stand up for himself and for
his community. Another key early member was William Schonfield,
who was born on 26 August 1869 in Vaturleigh, Dirschau,
Germany and later became a naturalised British citizen. He lived
in Scotland before the war, attending a university there. According
to *The Jewish Chronicle* on 11 June 1915:

Major William Schonfield has been appointed to command the 3/ 10th
Battalion London Regiment.

Major Schonfield has had a long army career. He was the first
Jew to join the London Scottish, twenty-three years ago, and was
commissioned as Second Lieutenant in the 17th North Middlesex
Rifles, now the 19th Battalion London Regiment, in 1897, advancing
step by step to the rank he now holds. The greater part of his
military service was occupied with Staff work, holding appointments
as Brigade Signalling Officer in several London Brigades, and
subsequently as Field Officer in charge of Brigade Specialists,
earning repeated recommendations from the Brigadiers under whom
he served. Having retired in 1911 with his rank and the privilege
to wear H.M. uniform, he joined the Reserve, and was called up
for service on the outbreak of war as officer in command of the
administrative centre of his present regiment, to the third battalion
of which he has now been appointed chief. The idea of holding the
annual Chanucah parades is due to him, and-.was conceived for the
purpose of attracting the Jewish youth to the Colours.

The Rev. S. Lipson writes (a member of the Military
chaplaincy):—It was a source of particular pleasure to me to learn
of the appointment of my valued friend. Major William Schonfield,

to command the 3rd/19th Battalion London Regiment. Major Schonfield has helped me considerably with his counsel on many occasions when experienced military advice was needed, and to know that I could always turn to him at a moment's notice, when there was a necessity for immediate action and insufficient time to consult my colleague at the front, has been a source of much comfort. Major Schonfield's influence for good over the Jewish young men has been most marked, and his appointment will be hailed with satisfaction by a wide circle of friends.

In 1916 he was elected the Glasgow representative of the Anglo-Jewish Association in London.[2]

Importantly, he was also a committee member of the Care and Comforts Committee, 38th–42nd Royal Fusiliers, the Judeans. He also encouraged his nephew, Lt Philip Jacobs, to apply for transfer to the Royal Jewish Fusiliers in 1918. Following the war Schonfield became in involved with Jewish ex-service organisations and was one of those who organised annual dinners and meetings. He continued to 'do his bit' even during the Second World War, although not as a soldier. He helped to support initiatives for Jewish veterans and supported the Jewish ex-servicemen's associations right up until his death in 1946.

To avoid any confusion with the British Legion (now the Royal British Legion), the organisation became the Association of Jewish Ex-servicemen and Women in 1936. It continues to exist today as an educational body, raising awareness of Jewish service in the military and as a remembrance and welfare organisation.

Conclusions

The First World War undoubtedly affected all of society in the UK. While empires and governments fell on the Continent, in the UK the changes appeared less dramatic but they were just as important; an old way of life was challenged and the repercussions would be felt for decades. Men and women of different social classes mucked along with each other in the new mass force that was the British Army and also in the factories and fields. Women had new employment opportunities and even if those new opportunities were snatched back from them in 1919, the knowledge that women were capable and skilled could not be forgotten, certainly not by the women themselves. These social changes would affect the Jewish community of Britain just as they did everyone else and in some occasions that would a have a specific impact.

Of the 50,000 or more Jewish men who served, approximately 9,000 were casualties. Of that number, in excess of 2,500 were killed, or subsequently died of their injuries. Junior officers were one of the groups in the British Army that had a high casualty rate – that was because they led their men into attacks. As it was the middle-class men who usually received a commission it was the middle classes that suffered most acutely from what Vera Brittain called the 'lost generation'. Across the UK this led to many middle-class women not marrying in the years after the war, as to marry out of their class was unthinkable. Working-class marriage rates did go up following the war, however, as those women required a husband for their social status and security; they were, therefore, prepared to be a lot less fussy.

In the Jewish community there was a dilemma – for a woman to not marry was really quite unacceptable, as so much status was based on family life. With the shortage of Jewish middle-class men, did a Jewish woman from a middle-class family try and find a non-Jewish husband of the same class, or did her family accept a Jewish husband from the working classes, possibly one of the new immigrant families? Colloquial evidence seems to suggest that the latter was the solution for many. Women from the old established families of Anglo-Jewry found themselves with Jewish husbands they would never have considered only five years earlier. This mixing of communities within the Jewish community made a real difference to the social structures and governance of the community for the next few decades.

Of course, not everyone was prepared to be quite so pragmatic, and some groups held on to their prejudices. Jacob 'Jack' Philips was a tailor from East London; he enlisted in 1916 and became a runner in the Royal Army Service Corps before transferring to the Motor Corps. According to his family, 'he never married and was very shy, living with his sister Bessie and her husband Sam. He had originally fallen in love with a girl who was Jewish but descended from German Jewry and her family stopped the marriage, as they (Jack's family) were from Poland.'³ Jack's brother Barrett, who served with the London Regiment, was killed in September 1916 during the Battle of the Somme. He is remembered on the Thiepval Memorial to the Missing.

For many Jewish men the war was an anglicising experience. Many changed their names so that they sounded less 'foreign' or just so that people could pronounce their names more easily. Moses Lichtenstein became Mark Hart, David Wolfsbergen became David Welby and Londoner David Margofsky, tired of his Northamptonshire comrades thinking he was called MacClusky and therefore must be Scottish, changed his name. However, he changed it to Macdonald, and so while the Scottish associations continued people could now spell his name at least!

The First World War witnessed huge technological changes. The British Army had ridden into the conflict on horseback and left using mechanised armoured vehicles such as the tank. Jewish servicemen had served in the new tank regiments and in the new Royal Air Force; those experiences of a mechanised future would stay with them.

David Margofsky, later Macdonald.

The majority of men who had been in the armed forces had served in regular regiments and travelled across the sea to Europe and beyond. Some had found themselves making lifelong friends with non-Jews where previously they had not stepped out of their Jewish neighbourhoods. Likewise, non-Jewish men and women had now mixed with real Jews who were nothing like the stereotypes presented in magazine cartoons. Prejudices and fears on both sides would begin to be challenged and knocked down. The acceptance of being in the British forces created a sense of pride in British Jewish identity for many, as well as a horror of war shared with anyone who went through it. One of the key global powers of the age, Britain, had not only accepted Jews as equals in its armed forces but had even catered to their needs – dietary, spiritual and cultural.

The creation of the Zion Mule Corps and the Judeans had a huge impact on Jewish self-belief and confidence during that period. For the first time in over two thousand years, Jewish men had fought together as Jews in a legitimate force. That fact is lost now on many, overtaken by the creation of the state of Israel and in a time where striving for equality is usually the norm, but at the start of the twentieth century many countries in Europe openly discriminated against Jews, with quotas and regular physical intimidation. This change, led by the British authorities, influenced other events; the Jewish men who had stood in British uniform and 'done their bit' from 1914 to 1918 would no longer accept threats of anti-Semitic violence in the country for which they had risked their lives. By the 1930s those men and their sons and daughters would be successfully standing up to the British Union of Fascist thugs, such as Mosley's Blackshirts, alongside anti-fascist non-Jews in places like Cable Street.

The issuing of the Balfour Declaration in October 1917 and its promise of a Jewish homeland provided Zionism with an imperial sponsor and a legitimacy that took it out of the Jewish fringes and into the political mainstream – even if large sections of Anglo-Jewry were still unconvinced by it. The Jewish community was no longer a minority group but a potentially nationalist one.

The Jewish community, just like wider British society, was reeling from the loss of life created by the war. Memorials were erected in synagogues, cemeteries and businesses to the ordinary men and women who had suffered, just as in the non-Jewish world. In fact, Jews and non-Jews were now on the same memorials across the UK and also all over the world. In the Imperial War Graves Commission (now known as the Commonwealth War Graves Commission) cemeteries wherever the fighting had taken place, there would now be Magen Davids (Stars of David) carved onto the Portland stone headstones among the near-identical headstones bearing crosses.

The First World War, with its horrors, deprivation and loss of life, pulled communities together. It provided them with a common experience. The First World War entwined Jewish individual and communal life together with that of the non-Jewish British world forever; why, then, don't more people know about the Jewish contribution and the bonds that it created? Two answers – 100 years and the Second World War. A lot can happen in 100 years, and that means things get forgotten, overlooked or cease to have relevancy. In this case, a key reason is that the impact of the First World War is superseded by the Second World War. If the Great War had been 'the war to end all wars' then its history would be that of the last key military event; instead the events and experiences of the Great War were quickly over taken by an even more cataclysmic war, one that had far more deadly consequences for world Jewry. By the late twentieth century, all European Jewish events would be seen through the prism of the Holocaust and anything that went before would pale into insignificance.

However, the contribution and dedication shown by Anglo-Jewry in the First World War should still matter for Jews and non-Jews. It provides a legacy of remembrance and shared sacrifice that has bound the different groups together in perpetuity. The stories of the men and women of the First World War can provide an insight into how communities pull together. Remembering the Jewish contribution is to pay due respect and service to the diversity of the UK and to the loyalty of those that make it its home. The men and women of Anglo-Jewry have a proud history of service in the UK's military as well as being loyal citizens in the civilian environment. The First World War contribution deserves to be better known and most importantly never discounted.

Appendix 1

THE POEMS OF ISAAC ROSENBERG

Below are some poems by Isaac Rosenberg highlighting both his Jewish ancestry and his experiences of the war.

DAUGHTERS OF WAR
Space beats the ruddy freedom of their limbs,
Their naked dances with man's spirit naked
By the root side of the tree of life
(The under side of things
And shut from earth's profoundest eyes).

I saw in prophetic gleams
These mighty daughters in their dances
Beckon each soul aghast from its crimson corpse
To mix in their glittering dances:
I heard the mighty daughters' giant sighs
In sleepless passion for the sons of valour
And envy of the days of flesh,
Barring their love with mortal boughs across—
The mortal boughs, the mortal tree of life.
The old bark burnt with iron wars
They blow to a live flame
To char the young green days
And reach the occult soul; they have no softer lure,

No softer lure than the savage ways of death.
We were satisfied of our lords the moon and the sun
To take our wage of sleep and bread and warmth—
These maidens came—these strong everliving Amazons,
And in an easy might their wrists
Of night's sway and noon's sway the sceptres brake,
Clouding the wild, the soft lustres of our eyes.

Clouding the wild lustres, the clinging tender lights;
Driving the darkness into the flame of day
With the Amazonian wind of them
Over our corroding faces
That must be broken—broken for evermore,
So the soul can leap out
Into their huge embraces.
Though there are human faces
Best sculptures of Deity,
And sinews lusted after
By the Archangels tall,
Even these must leap to the love-heat of these maidens
From the flame of terrene days,
Leaving grey ashes to the wind—to the wind.

One (whose great lifted face,
Where wisdom's strength and beauty's strength

And the thewed strength of large beasts
Moved and merged, gloomed and lit)
Was speaking, surely, as the earth-men's earth fell away;
Whose new hearing drank the sound

Where pictures, lutes, and mountains mixed
With the loosed spirit of a thought,
Essenced to language thus—

"My sisters force their males
From the doomed earth, from the doomed glee
And hankering of hearts.
Frail hands gleam up through the human quag-
mire, and lips of ash
Seem to wail, as in sad faded paintings
Far-sunken and strange.
My sisters have their males
Clean of the dust of old days
That clings about those white hands
And yearns in those voices sad:
But these shall not see them,
Or think of them in any days or years;
They are my sisters' lovers in other days and years."

SPRING, 1916

Slow, rigid, is this masquerade
That passes as through a difficult air:
Heavily—heavily passes.
What has she fed on? Who her table laid
Through the three seasons? What forbidden fare
Ruined her as a mortal lass is?

I played with her two years ago,
Who might be now her own sister in stone;
So altered from her May mien,

When round the pink a necklace of warm snow
Laughed to her throat where my mouth's touch had gone.
How is this, ruined Queen?

Who lured her vivid beauty so
To be that strained chill thing that moves
So ghastly midst her young brood
Of pregnant shoots that she for men did grow?
Where are the strong men who made these their loves?
Spring! God pity your mood!

THE DESTRUCTION OF JERUSALEM BY THE BABYLONIAN HORDES

They left their Babylon bare
Of all its tall men,
Of all its proud horses;
They made for Lebanon.

And shadowy sowers went
Before their spears to sow
The fruit whose taste is ash,
For Judah's soul to know.

They who bowed to the Bull god,
Whose wings roofed Babylon,
In endless hosts darkened
The bright-heavened Lebanon.

They washed their grime in pools
Where laughing girls forgot

The wiles they used for Solomon.
Sweet laughter, remembered not!
Sweet laughter charred in the flame
That clutched the cloud and earth,
While Solomon's towers crashed between
To a gird of Babylon's mirth.

BREAK OF DAY IN THE TRENCHES

The darkness crumbles away—
It is the same old druid Time as ever.
Only a live thing leaps my hand—
A queer sardonic rat—
As I pull the parapet's poppy
To stick behind my ear.
Droll rat, they would shoot you if they knew
Your cosmopolitan sympathies
(And God knows what antipathies).
Now you have touched this English hand
You will do the same to a German—
Soon, no doubt, if it be your pleasure
To cross the sleeping green between.
It seems you inwardly grin as you pass
Strong eyes, fine limbs, haughty athletes
Less chanced than you for life,
Bonds to the whims of murder,
Sprawled in the bowels of the earth,
The torn fields of France.

What do you see in our eyes
At the shrieking iron and flame

Hurled through still heavens?
What quaver—what heart aghast?
Poppies whose roots are in man's veins
Drop, and are ever dropping;
But mine in my ear is safe,
Just a little white with the dust.

DEAD MAN'S DUMP

The plunging limbers over the shattered track
Racketed with their rusty freight,
Stuck out like many crowns of thorns,
And the rusty stakes like sceptres old
To stay the flood of brutish men
Upon our brothers dear.

The wheels lurched over sprawled dead
But pained them not, though their bones crunched;
Their shut mouths made no moan.
They lie there huddled, friend and foeman,
Man born of man, and born of woman;
And shells go crying over them
From night till night and now.

Earth has waited for them,
All the time of their growth
Fretting for their decay:

Now she has them at last!
In the strength of their strength
Suspended—stopped and held.
What fierce imaginings their dark souls lit?

Earth! Have they gone into you?
Somewhere they must have gone,
And flung on your hard back
Is their souls' sack,
Emptied of God-ancestralled essences.
Who hurled them out? Who hurled?

None saw their spirits' shadow shake the grass,
Or stood aside for the half used life to pass
Out of those doomed nostrils and the doomed mouth,
When the swift iron burning bee
Drained the wild honey of their youth.

What of us who, flung on the shrieking pyre,
Walk, our usual thoughts untouched,
Our lucky limbs as on ichor fed,
Immortal seeming ever?
Perhaps when the flames beat loud on us,
A fear may choke in our veins
And the startled blood may stop.

The air is loud with death,
The dark air spurts with fire,
The explosions ceaseless are.
Timelessly now, some minutes past,
These dead strode time with vigorous life,
Till the shrapnel called "An end!"
But not to all. In bleeding pangs
Some borne on stretchers dreamed of home,
Dear things, war-blotted from their hearts.

A man's brains splattered on
A stretcher-bearer's face;
His shook shoulders slipped their load,
But when they bent to look again
The drowning soul was sunk too deep
For human tenderness.

They left this dead with the older dead,
Stretched at the cross roads.

Burnt black by strange decay
Their sinister faces lie,
The lid over each eye;
The grass and coloured clay
More motion have than they,
Joined to the great sunk silences.

Here is one not long dead.
His dark hearing caught our far wheels,
And the choked soul stretched weak hands
To reach the living word the far wheels said;
The blood-dazed intelligence beating for light,
Crying through the suspense of the far torturing wheels
Swift for the end to break
Or the wheels to break,
Cried as the tide of the world broke over his sight,
"Will they come? Will they ever come?"
Even as the mixed hoofs of the mules,
The quivering-bellied mules,
And the rushing wheels all mixed
With his tortured upturned sight.

So we crashed round the bend,
We heard his weak scream,
We heard his very last sound,
And our wheels grazed his dead face.

THE JEW

Moses, from whose loins I sprung,
Lit by a lamp in his blood
Ten immutable rules, a moon
For mutable lampless men.

The blonde, the bronze, the ruddy,
With the same heaving blood,
Keep tide to the moon of Moses.
Then why do they sneer at me?

THE DEAD HEROES

Flame out, you glorious skies,
Welcome our brave;
Kiss their exultant eyes;
Give what they gave.

Flash, mailed seraphim,
Your burning spears;
New days to outflame their dim
Heroic years.

Thrills their baptismal tread
The bright proud air;
The embattled plumes outspread
Burn upwards there.

Flame out, flame out, O Song!
Star ring to star;
Strong as our hurt is strong
Our children are.

Their blood is England's heart;
By their dead hands
It is their noble part
That England stands.

England—Time gave them thee;
They gave back this
To win Eternity
And claim God's kiss.

NOTES

Introduction

1. Alfred Dreyfus was a captain in the French army. He was accused of treason in 1894 and convicted and sent to prison. The evidence to convict him was fabricated and many believed it was based on a distrust and dislike of Jews among the French military and politicians. In 1906 Dreyfus was cleared of all charges. He went on to serve in the French military throughout the First World War.

2. The Tredegar Riots of August 1911.

3. The Board of Deputies of British Jews can trace its roots back to 1760, when a group of representatives of the Jewish community presented an address to King George III on his accession to the throne. By the early nineteenth century the board included representatives from across the communal and religious spectrum.

1 The Jewish Community Responds to the Announcement of War

1. Quoted in Cesarani, David, *The Jewish Chronicle and Anglo-Jewry, 1841–1991* (Cambridge University Press, 1994), p. 115.

2. *The Jewish Chronicle*, 7 August 1914.

3. https://www.rothschildarchive.org/exhibitions/rothschilds_and_the_first_world_war/business_during_the_war.

4. *The Jewish Chronicle*, 25 December 1914, p. 13.

5. Harold Pollins, 'Jewish Officers and the First World War', May 2010.

6. Vol. 3 No. 19, p. 160.

2 *Going off to War*

1. https://www.ourmigrationstory.org.uk/oms/germanophobia-and-germans-in-britain-in-the-early-twentieth-century, Professor Panikos Panayi.

2. Levine, A., *The futility of war: Jewish soldiers of World War I* (Seidelman's correspondence can be found on the Jewish Museum and Archives of B.C.'s website.)

3. Dapin, M., *Jewish Anzacs: Jews in the Australian Military* (NewSouth, 2017).

4. Ibid.

5. Ibid.

6. His official citation as recorded in Govor, E., *Russian Anzacs in Australian History*.

3 *We Were There, Too*

1. He was not actually the first Jewish casualty – that was George Forstein, but Forstein served as Foster and his death was not reported in *The Jewish Chronicle* until later.

2. https://www.jewsfww.london/louis-harris-diary-1991.php.

3. https://www.jewsfww.london/alfred-abraham-pampel-721.php.

4. https://www.jewsfww.london/arthur-teacher-1101.php.

5. https://www.jewsfww.london/edward-joseph-wallis-herberts-2015.php.

6. https://www.jewsfww.london/solomon-fine-374.php.

7. https://www.jewsfww.london/henry-bader-1165.php.

4 Nurses, Doctors and Hospitals at Home and Abroad

1. Norman De Mattos Bentwich OBE MC (28 February 1883–88 April 1971) was a British barrister and legal academic. He was the British-appointed attorney-general of Mandatory Palestine and a lifelong Zionist.

2. https://historicengland.org.uk/whats-new/first-world-war-home-front/what-we-already-know/land/hospitals-convalescent-homes/.

5 Jews as Jews in Uniform

1. Schectman, J. B., *Jabotinsky – Rebel and Statesman* (New York, 1956), p. 205. In Trumpeldor's notes (Tel Chai Archives, Israel) headed 'Via Gallipoli to Zion', he wrote in Russian, 'We will wear other people's uniforms and become a force for the people.'

2. Gilner, E., *War and Hope* (New York, 1969), p. 41.

3. Lipovetsky, P., *Joseph Trumpeldor – Life and Works* (Jerusalem, 1953), p. 50.

4. Ibid.

5. Levy, A. B., *East End Story* (London, 1948).

6. *The Manchester Guardian*, 4 February 1918, p. 4; Samuel, E., *A Lifetime In Jerusalem* (London, 1970), p. 43, quoted in Cecil Bloom, p. 238.

7. Wilson, J. M., *Isaac Rosenberg: The Making of a Great War Poet*, pp. 389–90.

8. *We Were There Too* Project (www.jewsfww.london).

9. *Evening News*, 4 February 1918, p. 3.

10. *Daily Express*, 5 February 1918, p. 3.

11. Taken from Sugarman, M., *The Jewish Legion*.

12. Peter Taylor was talking to Philip Walker, September 2010. http://www.jewisheastend.com/Fusiliers2.html.

13. https://www.jewsfww.london/philip-jacobs-1340.php.

6 Faith and the Jewish Chaplaincy

1. https://www.jewsfww.london/sermons-heard-by-london-jews-during-the-great-war-876.php.
2. Waite, Maj. F., *The New Zealanders at Gallipoli* (Auckland, 1921).
3. Liddle, P., *Men of Gallipoli* (London, 1976), p. 156.
4. https://www.jewsfww.london/british-jewish-chaplaincy-in-the-first-world-war-by-jonathan-lewis-523.php.
5. British Jewry Book of Honour, p. 41.
6. British Jewry Book of Honour, p. 58.

7 The Home Front

1. https://www.parliament.uk/about/living-heritage/transformingsociety/parliament-and-the-first-world-war/legislation-and-acts-of-war/defence-of-the-realm-act-1914/.
2. http://www.iwm.org.uk/history/10-surprising-laws-passed-during-the-first-world-war.
3. https://www.jewsfww.london/sir-walter-de-frece-mp-1722.php.
4. Lola Fraser.

8 Not Allowed to Fight – Don't Want to Fight

1. The Ruhleben Prison Camp: A Record of Nineteen Months' Internment (London: Methuen & Co. Ltd, 1917).
2. Ibid.
3. Ibid.
4. While conscientious objection was not specifically defined in the Act of 1916, the government recognised those whose 'objection genuinely rests on religious or moral convictions'.
5. Rodker, J., *Memoirs of Other Fronts* (Putnam, 1932), p. 111.
6. https://www.jewsfww.london/jewish-conscientious-objectors-717.php.

7. http://digestingthemedicalpast.blogspot.co.uk/2014/05/
   in-feeding-queue-force-feeding-and.html.

9 Awards and Bravery

1. Martin Sugarman.
2. King's College Memorial Page. http://www.kingscollections.
   org/warmemorials/kings-college/memorials/baswitz-albert.
3. Ibid.

10 The British Jewry Book of Honour

1. http://www.balfour100.com/biography/lionel-walter-rothschild/.
2. https://www.jewsfww.london/william-schonfield-3018.php.
3. https://www.jewsfww.london/jacob-phillips-1582.php.

INDEX